AFTER MODERNISM

Comparative Urban and Community Research

Series Editor, Michael Peter Smith

AFTER MODERNISM
Global Restructuring and
the Changing Boundaries of City Life

Comparative Urban and Community Research

Volume 4

Edited by

Michael Peter Smith

Transaction Publishers
New Brunswick (U.S.A.) and London (U.K.)

Second printing 1995

Copyright © 1992 by Transaction Publishers, New Brunswick, New Jersey 08903.

This book is printed on acid-free paper that meets the American National Standard for Permanence of Paper for Printed Library Materials.

Library of Congress Catalog Number: 92-11294
ISSN: 0892-5569
ISBN: 1-56000-598-X
Printed in the United States of America

Library of Congress Cataloging-in-Publication Data

After modernism: global restructuring and the changing boundaries of city life/edited by Michael Peter Smith.
    p. cm.—(Comparative urban and community research; v. 4)
    ISBN 1-56000-598-X
    1. Urbanization—Case studies. 2. Urban policy—Case studies. 3. Community development, Urban—Case studies. 4. Alien labor—Social conditions—Case studies. 5. City and town life—Case studies. I. Smith, Michael P. II. Series.
HT361.A37 1992
307.76—dc20   92-11294
                                            CIP

Contents

Comparative Urban and Community Research is an annual review devoted to theoretical, empirical and applied research on the processes of urbanization and community change throughout the world. The format of *Comparative Urban and Community Research* enables the publication of manuscripts that are longer and more richly textured than the articles a quarterly journal can feature.

Editorial correspondence and manuscript submissions should be addressed to *Comparative Urban Community Research,* Department of Applied Behavioral Sciences, University of California, Davis, CA 95616-8523. Submission requirements: (1) papers should be double-spaced; and (2) author's name, affiliation, address and telephone number should appear on a separate sheet.

Michael Peter Smith, Editor
University of California, Davis

Glenna Klepac, Editorial Assistant

Editorial Board

CITIES AFTER MODERNISM

Michael Peter Smith

The literature in urban studies today is replete with competing metaphors which require a bifocal, if not a polyfocal imagination to simultaneously comprehend. The tone of contemporary discourse on the formation of cities is decidedly "possibilist." Cities are increasingly depicted in terms of "becoming,"—as entities originating, changing, instituted, and reinstituted by human practice. This represents a move away from the staged developmental models of urbanization at the core of modernist thinking, in which the "progress" of people and places was measured in terms of their proximity to some "advanced" stage of economic development, be it capitalist or post-capitalist. In urban studies the once controversial and then nearly hegemonic assumption that urban development was inexorably driven by the systemic "needs" of multinational capital has given way to a more social constructionist view in which the diversity of places, the dynamics of politics, the variety of mediating state policies, and the agency of social actors is widely recognized, if at times only ritualistically invoked, in accounts of the social production of cities.

The centering structuralist metaphors of late modernism deployed in urban studies—the "capitalist city," the "post-fordist city," and the "world city," assigned a central role in city formation to the logic of capital accumulation or the agency of industrial, finance, and real estate capital in alliance with elements of the modern state. These constructions of late twentieth-century urbanization have now been challenged by more decentering culturalist metaphors designed to give voice to the agency of social actors heretofore treated as "marginal," but who are materially and symbolically shaping the character of cities after modernism. Thus, increasing attention is now being paid to such self-produced arenas of spatial practice in cities as the "reterritorialized immigrant enclave," the "multicultural community," the "defended city," and the "transnational social space."

Part of the problem of making sense out of this plethora of images of the city is that they are not really mutually exclusive oppositions. Rather, the displacements that have occurred in the past two decades among economy, polity, locality, and culture have immensely complicated the dynamics of urbanization. We are living in a time of great societal upheaval, economic restructuring, and cultural transformation. Global cultural symbols and practices have penetrated to even the remotest hinterlands. At the same time, economic and political instability in what was once unproblematically described as the "periphery" has displaced millions of transnational economic migrants and political refugees. These migrations have reconstituted the social structures of many "core" centers of wealth and power. The literally overnight dissolution of that social construction we once called the "Eastern Bloc," has added to the fragmentation and complexity of the world-at-large, thus increasing our sense of confusion about the character of the wider context in which urbanization processes occur. This contextual confusion has caused some social scientists and cultural analysts to question whether an "out there" actually exists as a contextual reality apart from our cultural representations of it.

Contemporary nation states, at least those with stable borders and political systems, have not been able to decisively shape the flows of internal and transnational investment and migration to and from cities within their boundaries. Yet, they have differentially mediated these flows through politically produced state policies, adding still another dimension of complexity to the picture. Just as some alliances between private developers and regional policy makers have forged taxation and subsidy policies that have produced "Edge Cities" on what was once open space in the U.S., Europe, and elsewhere, so too have other alliances been formed between popular movements and city policy makers to preserve the walking city, extend sanctuary to or exclude political refugees, slow growth, and regulate plant closures. Urban politics may not be the only force accounting for the social construction of cities after modernism, but it certainly accounts for quite a lot. This is because political structures and processes are an unavoidable point of entry through which cultural and ideological representations of reality mediate the social and economic transformation of cities.

Another part of the problem of making sense of late twentieth-century urbanization is the persistence of binary thinking in the social sciences. Global and local social processes are often framed as alternative explanations for urbanization. Moreover, the global and local are often conflated with the general and the particular. Worse still, the "general" is often used as a trope for the "universal." Once these steps are taken we are left with little or no middle ground between "grand narratives" of urbanization whose very universalism renders them ineffectual and "petite narratives" whose very particularity renders them trivial. However, if we recognize that both global and local social processes are embedded in historical time, both are thus capable of historical particularity. The global-local interplay at the time of European colonialism was not the same as the global-local interplay in today's decentered world; the social actors and forces operating globally are different at different historical junctures; and none have been able to construct themselves as "universals" for very long. If we further acknowledge that a social process that is "spatially general" (i.e., found in many places at the same time throughout the globe, like "transnational migration," "edge cities," or "the welfare state") is also "temporally particular," we are able to consider its deployment in a single place or comparatively across space in all of its historicity. Likewise, "local" phenomena need not be viewed in isolation from the wider historical context in which they occur. Indeed, when doing field work in particular locales, it is impossible to view them as such. This is because local actors inexorably deal with an understood national and international context, however fluctuating that may appear at the present time.

When freed from its confusion with the general vs. the particular, the global-local question becomes a matter of which level of analysis is chosen to view the world when considering the global-local interplay. When we focus our lens synoptically, as Ed Soja does in the second half of his essay comparing Amsterdam and Los Angeles, we are likely to discern many similarities among capitalist conurbations in their types of economic activities, residential settlement patterns, and land uses characterizing metropolitan and regional development. As we move increasingly closer to "the ground," using the case study and ethnographic field methods, we are rendered capable of discerning the culture and politics of a specific city, the spatial practices of its residents, the social organization of its households, and even the identities of its subjects. As we listen to representations of the city made in these micro-worlds we unavoidably hear many voices and thence begin to discern what some have termed the politics of difference. Perhaps the chief advantage of combining comparative historical method with ethnography and the case study in urban studies today is that it forces us to consider both the global and the local, to account for generality and specificity, to "see for ourselves" and "hear the voices of others," and thus to develop the integrative and differentiating capacities of our human imaginations.

After Modernism was chosen as the title of this volume precisely because it represents a more open and contingent way of conceptualizing not only cities but the very field of urban studies at the current historical juncture. To call a city "modern" is to invoke the often exaggerated homogenizing and universalizing power of capitalism and the modern state. To call it "postmodern" is to enshrine the " local narrative" as a privileged repository of the discourses out of which the "living city" is produced, as if these discourses were somehow pure entities, devoid of human understandings of the operation of more general social processes, or of the diverse modes of domination impinging on people's lives, or of popular strategies for accommodating to or resisting their sway. To study the city "after modernism" is to recognize that in urban studies today the most interesting questions are those having to do with changing boundaries—the character of the changing boundaries of academic disciplines, cities, regions, states, and cultures; the meaning of the disjunction between political jurisdictions, economic spaces, and sites of cultural meaning in the world; and the causes and consequences of the practices by which people makes sense of and deal with the general and particular, global and local dimensions of their lives.

The contributors to Volume 4 of *Comparative Urban and Community Research* have chosen a variety of approaches to address the complexity of social change in cities after modernism. These reflect different ways to deal with the shifting boundaries of urban life by drawing discernible "local" borders around their chosen focus. The volume begins at the widest level of analysis with a stimulating discursive essay by Ed Soja comparing Los Angeles and Amsterdam. Soja starts with a close reading of everyday life on Amsterdam's Spuistraat. He then contrasts life in this walking city with the socio-spatial organization of contemporary Los Angeles. Soja paints a picture of the "erogenously-zoned" geography of Amsterdam Centrum, which allows him to contrast its spatial arrangements, encouraging playful enjoyment, with the polarized "spectacle" of Los Angeles' heavily policed and rigidly-zoned streets, separating clashing cultures, extreme poverty and wealth, business and commerce. Soja's narrative recognizes the important role of culture and the state in the social production of Amsterdam Centrum's diversity, and implicitly, its charm. He underlines the significance of Amsterdam's Golden Age property taxation system, its city planning processes, its libertarian socialist political culture, and the evolution of its urban social movements, all of which have played important parts in preserving its accessible social gathering places, attractive built environment, pedestrian character, and climate of multicultural tolerance. In the second half of his essay, Soja assumes a more synoptic view. This enables him to discern similarities in the polynucleated decentralization of the two city's wider regional geographies. He thus reinserts the global restructuring of capitalism into the discourse on contemporary urbanization.

The second contribution to this volume, by Roger Keil and Peter Lieser, sheds light on the global-local interplay in urban life by means of a case study of the dynamics of urban politics in the emergent global city of Frankfurt. This study treats urban politics as the most appropriate site for a contextually situated local narrative. Keil and Lieser attribute the rise of Frankfurt as a global city to local political and ideological struggles, mediated by national party electoral strategies. At both the national and the urban level in Germany the social construction of "immigration" has become a central issue of political debate. In Frankfurt the rhetoric of ethnic exclusion has become part of what the authors term a "postmodern discourse of difference" deployed by the ruling CDU party to legitimate the socio-spatial changes that have been produced by that city's local "growth machine," and the social polarizations that have followed from these changes. Frankfurt's discourse on difference masks the disenfranchisement of the immigrant workers who comprise 25% of its population.

The strength of this contribution is that it carefully specifies the different roles of global, national, and local dynamics in the process of "world city" formation. Keil and Lieser's study also serves as a useful counterpoint to those who view the region as a salient unit of analysis for studying urbanization. The assumption that regional development "matters" is implicit in Soja's mapping of similarities between "Greater Amsterdam" and Los Angeles and explicit in the literature on the "Third Italy" critiqued by Marco Cenzatti. Much of that literature, in fact, deploys the "region" as a trope for the "local." In rebutting the notion that the region is an appropriate entity for comparative analysis, Keil and Lieser point out that differences in socio-spatial change *within* German Laender are greater than disparities among them.

Doubts about the fruitfulness of the region as a unit of analysis of urban change are echoed in the next contribution, Richard Tardanico's study of the changing labor market of San José, Costa Rica. Tardanico's article is a political-economic analysis of the role of Costa Rica's social democratic state in mediating the impact of global economic restructuring in San José. He points out that when considered as a region, Central America has displayed striking internal diversity in social, economic, and political characteristics among its component nation states as well as in the the ways in which local conditions are interacting with global economic restructuring processes. These diverse "local" differences account for a wide variety of distributional outcomes among localities as well as different class, gender, and generational variations within localities.

In Tardanico's case study the role of the modern (or modernizing) state looms large. Unlike other countries in Central America, Costa Rica has had a modernizing political elite with social democratic values, which has used state policies to abolish the standing army, nationalize banks, dampen the labor movement, and incorporate the poor as social program clientele. Yet, the global economic crisis has seriously disrupted this modernist arrangement. The social democratic state has been required to introduce fiscal austerity measures as San José's urban households have pursued survival strategies by mobilizing what Tardanico terms "reserve income producers," primarily middle-aged and elderly women. These women have entered informal work structures to offset job and real income losses by other household members and general cuts in the social wage by the State. Nevertheless, Costa Rica's political elites have tempered the negative impact of fiscal austerity by measures such as food assistance, temporary public employment, and selective price controls, which favored the poor. This has enabled them to maintain a delicate political balance.The austerity policies have allowed them to obtain significant aid and debt relief from the U.S., while their social policy initiatives thus far have enabled them to maintain political stability in the face of austerity policies that have produced food riots and other forms of popular protest elsewhere. The "structural adjustment policies" pursued by the Costa Rican political formation have softened the blow of general retrenchment while the reorganization of urban households and the expansion of informal work at the community level have mediated both the economic crisis and the state restructuring. In the face of continuing global economic crisis, the question of the social conditions and responses of displaced workers in other nations and cities where "fordist" political and economic arrangements have come to an end, but where social policies to buffer the ensuing decline in living standards are absent, remains important.

The next contribution to *After Modernism* is an empirical study of the social and ethnic division of the restaurant workforce in New York City. This study, conducted by Sharon Zukin and the students in her seminar at the Graduate Center, City University of New York, shifts our attention from responses by the State and urban households to global economic restructuring to the internal dynamics of the small service firm, in this instance the restaurant, viewed as a localized site of transnational economic and cultural flows. Methodologically, the study seeks to integrate ethnographic research with structural analysis. It relies on data drawn from ethnographies conducted in four restaurants with 35 subjects, including owners and workers, from 17 different countries in North Africa, Asia, the Middle East, the Caribbean, Latin America, Scandinavia, and the U.S.A. The diversity of this ethnic distribution illustrates the extent to which the social structure of New York City has been affected by the accelerated pace and the global scope of transnational migration in the past decade.

This collaborative study compares the segmented employment experiences of new immigrant and arts employees, paralleling the "front" and "back" zones of the restaurants where they work. In the study, the "dual city" metaphor is played out within the micro-territory of the "front" and "back" regions. "Back" workers tend to be relatively interchangeable ethnic newcomers, whose ethnicity may vary depending on time of arrival, but who monopolize the low paid positions in the back region because the jobs there do not generally require English language or specific employment skills. "Front" workers tend to be arts employees who are both capable of and interested in presenting "themselves" along with the menu. The ethnographies in this study give voice to the complex perceptions and inten-

tions of the social actors who are part of New York's emergent globalized restaurant scene.

The second ethnographically based study of new immigrants in this volume, by Allen Heskin, moves us from New York to Los Angeles and from the workplace to the home. Heskin has conducted an extended participant observation study of the processes of decision-making and the evolution of the politics of multiculturalism in five housing co-operatives in Los Angeles owned by a Community Development Corporation. The co-operatives, located in the Route 2 Corridor port-of-entry neighborhood of Los Angeles are "home" to both new immigrants from fourteen different Latin American countries as well as to established residents, including Chicanos, blacks, and Asian-Americans. Heskin characterizes his methodology as that of a "partisan observer" who has had the opportunity to observe racial and ethnic relations over a long period of time while living in one of the co-operatives.

While predisposed toward the goal of "multicultural populism," Heskin identifies several internal divisions based on ideological, class, language, and social background differences which have produced cultural misunderstandings and political conflicts in the co-operative. For example, ideologically, some native born minority group activists in the project regard race and ethnicity as a social base for oppositional group empowerment. This entails the formation of relatively fixed ethnic and racial identities which are ritually reproduced rather than reconstituted by political discourse. Other native born activists favor the construction of a social space facilitative of free communication across cultural boundaries and the reconstruction of personal and ethnic identities as a result of these exchanges. Many new immigrants, in turn, look to the social relations of clientelism to protect the family and household ties which form the most meaningful dimension of their identities. Democratic decision-making processes in the project thus become suffused with identity politics.

Language, class, and cultural barriers among residents further complicate matters. For example, those from urban backgrounds in Cuba differ with those previously from rural Mexico over which form of Spanish to use as a medium of discourse. Cleavages emerge between primary sector and informal workers over when to hold public meetings. Much of the agenda at public meetings is of a highly technical or legal character. Cultural mediation by translators at meetings often produces misunderstandings and delays; these are sometimes exacerbated by the representations and misrepresentations made by conflict-oriented community organizers serving as translators in settings which require consensus building; it eventually becomes evident that effective multicultural mediation requires a very

high level of bilingualism.

Heskin next discusses the adaptive strategies employed by the co-operatives elected leaders to overcome social divisions and build mutual understanding and participatory democratic outcomes in this frequently conflictual multicultural context. Despite the pessimistic tone of much of his study, Heskin notes that over time, Latino participation increased in all of the co-operatives, indigenous leadership emerged, and four of the five co-ops were functioning reasonably well. Perhaps the problems discussed by Heskin are inherent in the situation studied—an attempt to realize an ideal of multicultural community in the context of a policy-making process, in which the play of ethnic, racial, cultural, and class differences must be mediated by formal participatory decision-making structures which necessarily conflate all of these differences, treating all residents as abstract citizens of the self-managed co-operative. When viewed in the wider context of the globalization of Los Angeles, in which dystopic *Blade Runner* images abound, the social relations being forged, against the grain, in the Route 2 Corridor co-operatives, may actually be a sign of hope.

The third ethnographic study in this issue lucidly describes the everyday forms of resistance by the Latino immigrant tenants of an apartment complex in Houston to efforts by the owners and managers of the complex to marginalize and evict them. This ethnography, by Nestor Rodriguez and Jacqueline Hagan, provides an interesting counterpoint to Heskin's study. Both studies deal with interactions between new Latino immigrants and established residents centered around the housing question. In contrast to the difficulties of building multicultural understandings and social cooperation in the self-managed housing co-operatives studied by Heskin, the politics of resistance practiced in the Houston project not only united Latino immigrants from diverse national backgrounds who faced a common threat of residential displacement, it also mobilized support from among established white and native-born minority residents of the apartment complex who identified with the plight of the new immigrants. This suggests that viable coalitions based on resistance to concretely perceived injustices may be easier to form than those, as in Heskin's study, based on efforts to realize an abstract ideal like participatory democracy.

Rodriguez and Hagan's study is an excellent example of human agency driven, urban ethnographic research. It pays close attention to both global and local details. Contextually, over 100,000 undocumented Salvadorans, Guatemalans, Nicaraguans, and Hondurans, fleeing economic and political turmoil in their countries, migrated to metropolitan Houston in the 1980's, a period precisely coinciding with that oil-based city's economic collapse. They were largely absorbed into

Houston's secondary labor market, which continued to expand despite the collapse of the city's overall economy. This theme of the expansion of informal work as a household survival strategy in the face of economic crisis, amplifies upon the changing urban labor market dynamics discussed in Tardanico's Costa Rican study.

In this context, Rodriguez and Hagan chose a participant-observation approach to closely study the evolving interactions between black, white, and Latino established residents of an apartment complex on Houston's west side and a group of new Central American and Mexican migrants who had been attracted to the complex by the lowered rents offered by its owners and managers as the Houston economy collapsed. One of the authors became a tenant in the complex prior to the two-year study. The first part of Rodriguez and Hagan's study describes in detail precisely how the new Latino immigrants used the opportunity provided by the lowered rents to develop household survival strategies—e.g., expense sharing, complex new household formation, teaching newcomers how to negotiate established institutions—which enabled them not only to survive in an inhospitable economic climate but to appropriate neighborhood space for their own use values. As Houston's economy began to rebound, the owners and managers of the complex tried to restructure its occupancy a second time by selectively upgrading units and amenities and raising rents, while downgrading facilities in the building where most new Latino immigrants lived. The most fascinating part of Rodriguez and Hagan's study deals with the various ways that the new immigrants forged and used evolving relations with established residents to frustrate, circumvent, and at times openly resist these efforts to displace them. They show how the apartment complex on Houston's west side became a social space where the new Latino immigrants, both individually, and in coalition with established residents, adapted to and resisted broad social structural changes impeding their everyday lives. By their local social actions the ordinary men and women living in this complex both materially and symbolically modified their conditions of existence.

The extended literature review essay has become a regular feature of *Comparative Urban and Community Research*. The review essay by Marco Cenzatti which ends Volume 4 links the Italian literature on the significance of "local" conditions in the development of the "Third Italy" to the theoretical debates on locality studies, flexible production, and postmodernism in Britain and the United States. The review essay deals with the decline of both neoclassical and Marxist modernization theory in Italy because of their inability to explain the continuing vitality and growth of the Third Italy. In response to the failure of these grand narratives of modernization to explain this regional pattern of development, a new theoretical approach, which Cenzatti terms the "territorial problematic" has emerged. This approach treats the Third Italy's growth as a matter of endogenous regional development. It envisions the region as a "locale" with particular political, social, and economic features accounting for its current economic vitality. Cenzatti finds parallels in this literature to both the stress in British "locality" studies on the particularity of places and to the death of the "grand theory" theme in poststructuralist and postmodernist writing. In the case of Italy the grand narratives of the inevitable movement of organizations to large size and the evolution of capitalism to the monopoly form have been replaced by invocations of the "traces" of the past craft tradition to explain the Third Italy's economic success. Cenzatti cautions against developing an explanatory focus that loses sight of general social dynamics while focusing on local conditions. He argues that a particularistic approach which excludes any analysis of the interplay of particular phenomena with more general social processes can be as totalizing as the universalism of grand theory. By privileging the "local" and eschewing theorization, it may limit vision to an empiricist view composed entirely of case studies.

Despite Cenzatti's concerns, the case studies and ethnographies in *After Modernism* have each found a fruitful way to negotiate these difficulties and shed new light upon the global-local interplay in late twentieth-century urbanization. They have each situated their "local" readings of urban political, economic, and cultural change within a wider framework in which general political-economic and socio-cultural processes operating at local, national, and global scales complexly interact with each other and with the particular social actions of the people living in actually existing cities after modernism. The complexities they reveal suggest that envisioning cities after modernism is a necessarily difficult task, both frustrating and fascinating, but unavoidably complex.

THE STIMULUS OF A LITTLE CONFUSION: A CONTEMPORARY COMPARISON OF AMSTERDAM AND LOS ANGELES

Edward W. Soja

University of California, Los Angeles

The spectacular individuality of Los Angeles and Amsterdam, each an exemplary model in the evolution of world cities over the past four hundred years, magnifies the more generally applicable insights that can be derived from their contemporary comparison. At first sight almost defiantly incomparable, they are nonetheless responding together to the great urban transformations of the late twentieth century, one as a vigorously promulgated paradigm of urban restructuring and change, the other as a quietly protective paragon of enlightened urban continuity. With Los Angeles in the background, I begin with an experiential reading of the urban texture in Amsterdam's Centrum as a means of discovering its stimulating particularity. I then respond to a more encompassing and generalizable Amsterdam, seeking to learn not only from comparisons with Los Angeles but also from the creative tension of combining an appreciation for both uniqueness and generality, for both ideographic and nomothetic modes of urban analysis.

On Spuistraat

All the elements of the general spectacle in this entertaining country at least give one's regular habits of thought the stimulus of a little confusion and make one feel that one is dealing with an original genius.

> (Henry James, experiencing the Netherlands in *Transatlantic Sketches*, Boston, 1875, p. 384)

What, then, is the Dutch culture offered here? An allegiance that was fashioned as the consequence, not the cause, of freedom, and that was defined by common habits rather than legislated by institutions. It was a manner of sharing a peculiar–very pecu-

liar–space at a particular time . . . the product of the encounter
between fresh historical experience and the constraints of geog-
raphy.
(Simon Schama, *The Embarrassment of Riches: An
Interpretation of Dutch Culture in the Golden Age*,
Fontana Press, 1987, xi)

In Amsterdam in 1990, I dwelt for a time on Spuistraat, a border street on the
western flank of the oldest part of the Inner City. Squeezed in between the busy
Nieuwezijds Voorburgwal (literally, on the "new side" of the original settlement
in front of the old city wall) and the Singel (or "girdle," the first protective canal
moat built just beyond the wall), Spuistraat runs roughly North-South starting near
the old port and the teeming Stationsplein, where the Central Railway Station sits
blocking the view of the sea, pumping thousands of visitors daily into the historic
urban core. At half its length, Spuistraat is cut by Raadhuisstraat which is the start
of the main western boulevard axis branching off from the nearby Royal Palace
(once the Town Hall or raadhuis) and by tourist-crammed Dam Square where the
city was born more than 700 years ago in a portentous act of regulatory tolerance
(granting the local settlers toll-free use of the new dam across the Amstel River,
Amstelledamme becoming Amsterdam).

After passing my house, the street ends in what is simply called Spui, or
"sluice," once a control channel connecting the Amstel and the older inner city
canal system with the great bib of concentric canals that ring the outer crescent of
the Inner City, or Centrum. The Spui (pronounced somewhere in between "spay"
and "spy") is now a short broad boulevard lined with bookstores, cafes, a university building, the occasional open air art fair, and the entryways to several popular
tourist attractions, ranging from the banal (Madame Tussaud's) to the enchanting
(the Begijnhof and just beyond the Amsterdam Historical Museum). The "city
museum" offers the most organized introduction to the historical geography of
Amsterdam, with rooms full of splendid imagery bringing to life what you see first
upon entering, an exemplary model that sequentially lights up the city's territorial
expansion from 1275 to the present. Just as effective, however, as a starting point
for an interpretive geography of Amsterdam is the Begijnhof, or Beguine Court.

The Begijnhof is a small window onto the Amsterdam *mentalite*, that bewil-
dering Dutch mix of the familiar and the incomprehensible that so attracted Henry
James in 1874 and later inspired Simon Schama's brilliant interpretation of the
"moralizing geography" of Dutch culture in its 17th century Golden Age, *The
Embarrassment of Riches* (1987). One enters the Begijnhof through an arched oak

door off the Spui, an innocently unmarked opening to an enticing microcosm of civic refuge and peaceful respite in a cosmopolitan Dutch world of ever-so-slightly repressive tolerance. Before you is a neat quadrangle of lawn surrounded by beautifully preserved and reconstructed 17th and 18th century alms-houses, nearly every one fronted with flower-filled gardens. A restored wooden house dates back to the 15th century, one of two survivors of the many fires which burned down the old city before the more substantial Golden Age. The other survivor is located in a different kind of refuge zone along the Zeedijk, today known as the "boulevard of junkies."

There are also two small churches, one dating back to 1392 but built again in 1607 and known since as either English Reformed or Scottish Presbyterian. Here the fleeing English Pilgrim Fathers prayed before setting sail on the Mayflower, comfortable in their temporary Dutch haven. On one of my visits, the church was filled with the concerted voices of the Loyola College choir from New Orleans, singing American spirituals to the passersby. The other church, a clandestine construction in 1665, was originally a refuge for Catholic sisters escaping post-Reformation Calvinist religious purges. One of its stained-glass windows commemorates the epochal "wafer miracle" of 1345, an event that boosted Amsterdam into becoming a major medieval pilgrimage center and began its still continuing and far reaching internationalization.

The Beguine Court was actually founded one year after the miracle as a sanctuary for the Beguines, a Dutch lay sisterhood that sought a convent-like life but with the freedom to leave and marry if they wished, an early marker of the many Dutch experiments with what might be called engagingly flexible inflexibility. Today, the Begijnhof continues to be home to *ongehuwde dames* (unmarried ladies) who pay a nominal rent to live very comfortably around the lawned quadrangle. Despite the flocking tourists, it remains a remarkably peaceful spot, a reflective urban retreat that succeeds in being both open and closed at the same time, just like so many other paradoxical spaces and places in the refugee filled Amsterdam Centrum.

I lived just around the corner in another of these artfully preserved places and spaces, a relatively modest variant of the more than six thousand "monuments" to the Golden Age that are packed into the sustaining Centrum, the largest and most successfully reproduced historic inner city in Europe. With a frontage that seemed no wider than my driveway back home in Los Angeles, the building, like nearly all the others in the Centrum, rose four storeys to a gabled peak embedded with a startling metal hook designed for moving furniture and bulky items by ropes in through the wide windows. I had visions of having to be hauled up and in myself when I first saw the steep stairwell (*trappenhuis*) to the first floor. Golden Age taxation systems encouraged physical narrowness and relatively uniform facades up front, squeezing living space (and expansive creativity in interior design) upward and inward from the tiny street- or canal-side openings. The patient preservation yet modernization of these monuments reflects that "original genius" of the Dutch to make big things of little spaces, to literally produce an enriching and communal urban spatiality through aggressive social intervention and imaginative grass-roots planning, an adaptive feat on a par with the Dutch conquest of the sea.

Simon Schama roots Dutch culture in this moral geography of adaptation, an uncanny skill in working against the prevailing tides and times to create places that reinforce collective self-recognition and identity. "Dutchness," he writes, "was often equated with the transformation, under divine guidance, of catastrophe into good fortune, infirmity into strength, water into dry land, mud into gold." (1987, 25) In Amsterdam, perhaps more so than in any other Dutch city, these earthy efforts to "moralize materialism" moved out from the polderlands to become evocatively urban, not through divine guidance as much as through secularized spatial planning and an extraordinarily committed civic consciousness that persists to the present. The canal house simulates this rootedness, enabling one to experience within it the very essence of a liveable city, the agglomeration of individuals into socially constructed life spaces that open up new possibilities even as they tightly enclose, that are popularly designed to make density beautiful as well as accommodating, that flexibly enculturate and socialize without imprisoning, and that somehow add to one's regular habits of thought that entertaining stimulus of a little confusion.

To live in a canal house is to immediately and precipitously encounter Amsterdam, as my kind hosts from the University of Amsterdam's Center for Metropolitan Research knew well in finding me such strategically located lodgings. The past is omnipresent in its narrow nooks and odd-angled passageways, its flower-potted corners and unscreened windows that both open and close to the views outside. Every day life inside becomes a crowded reminder of at least three centuries of urban history and urban geography being preserved on a scale and contemporary intensity that is unique to Amsterdam. At home, one is invited daily into the creative spatiality of the city's social life and culture, an invitation that is at the same time embracingly tolerant and carefully guarded. Not everyone can become an Amsterdammer, but everyone must at least be given the chance to try.

The prevailing atmosphere is not that of a museum, however, a fixed and dead immortalization of the city's culturally built environment. The history and geography are remarkably alive and filled with the urban entertainment that makes

Amsterdam so familiar and yet so peculiarly incomprehensible, neat and clean and regular but curiously tilted, puzzling, an island of mud not quite entirely turned into gold but transformed enough to make one believe in the creative alchemy of Amsterdam's democratic city-builders. From my vantage point on Spui Straat a moving picture of contemporary life in the vital center of Amsterdam visually unfolded.

The view from my front windows affirmed for me what I continue to believe is the most extraordinary quality of this city, its relatively (the Dutch constitutionally refuse all absolutes) successful achievement of highly regulated urban anarchism, another of the creative paradoxes (along with the aforementioned and closely related "repressive tolerance" and "flexible inflexibility") that two-sided filter through the city's historical geography in ways that defy comparison with almost any other *polis*, past or present. This deep and enduring commitment to libertarian socialist values and participatory spatial democracy is openly apparent throughout the urban built environment and in the social practices of urban planning, law enforcement, popular culture, and daily life. One senses that Amsterdam is not just preserving its own Golden Age but is actively keeping alive the very possibility of a socially just and humanely scaled urbanization. Still far from perfection itself, as the Dutch never cease telling you, Amsterdam is nonetheless packed with conspicuously anomalous achievements. There is little or no boosterism, no effort to proclaim the achievements or to present them as a model for others to follow. Instead, there is again, *pace* Schama, an unadvertised "embarrassment of riches," modestly reproduced as in the past on the "moral ambiguity of good fortune."

There are many ways to illustrate this peculiar urban genius. For now, the view through my Spuistraat window will do for a start. Immediately opposite, in a building very much like mine, each floor is a separate flat and each storey tells a vertical story of subtle and creative city-building processes. It was almost surely a squatter-occupied house in the past and is probably one now, for Spuistraat has long been an active scene of the squatter movement. On the ground floor is an extension of the garage offices next door. There is a small "No Parking" sign on the window but nearly always a car or two is parked in front. Our ground floor, in contrast, is a used book shop, one of the many dozens densely packed in this most literate of Centrums, the place where enlightened scholars from Descartes to Voltaire, Montesquieu, and Rousseau first found the freedom to have their works published and publicized.

One cannot avoid noticing that the automobile is an intruder in the Inner City of Amsterdam. Spuistraat, like so many others, has been designed and redesigned primarily for pedestrians and cyclists. Alongside the busy bike path there is a narrow one-way car lane and some newly indented parking spaces, but this accommodation to the automobile is tension-filled and wittily punctuated. The police are always ready to arrive with those great metal wheel clamps and the spectacle of their attachment usually draws appreciative, occasionally cheering and laughing crowds of onlookers. Traffic is nearly always jammed, yet (most of the time) the Dutch drivers wait patiently, almost meekly, for they know they are guilty of intrusion and wish to avoid the steel jaws of public approbation. I was told that the city planners have accepted the need to construct several large underground parking garages in the gridlocked Centrum, but only with the provision that for every space constructed below ground, one space above is taken away.

On the first floor of the house across the way were the most obviously elegant living quarters, occupied by a woman who had probably squatted there as a student but had by now comfortably entered the job market. She spent a great deal of time in the front room, frequently had guests in for candlelight dinners, and would occasionally wave to us across the street, for we too had our most comfortable living space just by the front windows. On the floor above there was a young couple. They were probably still students and still poor, although the young man may have been working at least part time for he was rarely seen, except in the morning and late at night. The woman was obviously pregnant and spent most of her time at home. Except when the sun was bright and warm, they tended to remain away from the front window and never acknowledged anyone outside, for their orientation was decidedly inward. The small top floor, little more than an attic, still had plastic sheeting covering the roof. A single male student lived there and nearly always ate his lunch leaning out the front window alone. His space made one wonder whether the whole building was still a "squat" for if he was paying a nominal rent, one would have expected the roof to have been fixed, in keeping with the negotiated compromises that have marked what some would call the social absorption of the squatter movement in the 1980s.

This vertical transect through the current status of the squatter movement was matched by an even more dramatic horizontal panorama along the east side of Spuistraat, from Paleisstraat (Palace Street) to the Spui. To the north was an informative sequence of symbolic structures, beginning with a comfortable corner house that was recently rehabilitated with neat squatter rentals (another contradiction in terms?) above; and below, a series of shops also run by the same group of rehabilitated squatter-renters: a well-stocked fruit and vegetable market-grocery selling basic staples at excellent prices, a beer-tasting store stocked with dozens of imported (mainly Belgian) brews and their distinctively matching drinking glasses and mugs, a small bookstore and gift shop specializing in gay and lesbian literature, a used household furnishings shop with dozens of chairs and tables set out on the front sidewalk, and finally a small hand-crafted woman's cloth hat shop.

This remarkably successful example of gentrification by the youthful poor is just a stone's throw away from the Royal Palace on the Dam, the focal point for the most demonstrative peaking of the radical squatter movement that blossomed city-wide in conjunction with the coronation of Queen Beatrix in 1980. A more immediate explanation of origins, however, is found just next door on Spuistraat, where a new office-construction site has replaced former squatter dwellings in an accomplished give and take trade-off with the urban authorities. And just next door to this site, even closer to my window, was still another paradoxical juxtapositioning, one which signalled the continued life of the radical squatter movement in its old "anarchic colors."

A privately owned building had been recently occupied by contemporary squatters and its facade was brightly repainted, graffiti, and festooned with political banners and symbolic bric-a-brac announcing the particular form, function, and focus of the occupation. The absentee owner was caricatured as a fat tourist obviously beached somewhere with sunglasses and tropical drink in hand, while a white-sheet headline banner bridged the road to connect with a similar squat on my side of the street which was also bedecked with startling colors and slogans and blaring with music from an established squatter pub. I was told early in my stay that this was the most provocative squatter settlement in the Centrum and was scheduled to be recaptured by the authorities several days after my arrival. When I left, however, the situation was unchanged, at least on the surface.

The view south on Spuistraat presented another urban trajectory dominated by much more traditional forms of gentrification. Some splendid conversion, using fancy wooden shutters, modernized gables (no hook here), and vaulted interior designs was transforming an old structure for its new inhabitants, who were much more likely to visit the boutiques and gourmet restaurants in the vicinity than the shops up the road. The transition quickened in a little restaurant row that ranged from what was reputed to be the best seafood place in Amsterdam and one of the grandest traditional centers of Dutch cuisine (called the Five Flies and which fed daily busloads of mainly Japanese and German package-tourists), to a variety of smaller cafes, Indonesian restaurants (considered part of Dutch cuisine), and fast-food emporia.

By the time you reach the Spui, the street scene is awash again with activity and variety. A large bookstore shares one corner with an international news-center, spilling over onto the sidewalk with newspapers, magazines, and academic journals from around the world. There are hash coffee shops and beer pubs nearby, as well as an American-style cocktail bar and several representatives of the astonishing variety of specialized Amsterdam cafes. One is the Centrum's best known "white cafe" (just drinks) but it has been losing its yuppie edge to the stand-up, quick service, "old-style" cafe next door which is much better able to quench the growing thirst for nostalgia. Nearly adjacent but stoically distanced is a famous radical cafe, where an older clientele sits and glares at the sipping elites across the way. The dense territorialities here are invisible to the casual visitor and they may be blurring even for the Dutch, as the cosmopolitan mixture of Amsterdam takes over, globalizing the local street scene.

This Spuistraat panorama concentrates the spectrum of forces that have creatively rejuvenated the residential life of the Centrum and preserved its anxiety-inducing *overvloed* (superabundance, literally overflood) of urban riches. At the center of this rejuvenation has been the squatter movement, which has probably etched itself more deeply into the urban built environment of Amsterdam than in any other inner city in the world. To many of its most radical leaders, the movement today seems to be in retreat, deflected if not coopted by an embracing civic tolerance. But it has been this slightly repressive tolerance that has kept open the competitive channels for alternative housing and counter-cultural lifestyles not only for the student population of today but for other age groups as well. It has also shaped, in distinctive ways, the more "acceptable" gentrification process and helped to make it contribute to the diversity of the Centrum rather than to its homogenization, although this struggle is clearly not yet over.

This contemporary residential rejuvenation of Amsterdam requires some historical and geographical explanation. Decentralization in the 1930s began emptying the inner city of offices and manufacturing employment, and post-war suburbanization continued the process in a heightened flow of residential out-migration not just to the polycentered urban fringe but beyond, to such Christallerian new towns as Almere and Lelystad, planned and plotted on the reclaimed polders of isotopic Flevoland. As has happened in every century after the Golden Age, the continued life and liveliness of the Centrum was threatened by exogenous forces of modernization. A turning point, however, was reached in the 1960s, as cities exploded all over the world in often violent announcements that the post-war boom's excesses were no longer tolerable to the underclasses of urban society. A contrapuntal process of urban restructuring was initiated almost everywhere in an effort to control the spreading unrest and to shift economic gears in an attempt to recover the expansionary capitalist momentum. A comparison of the urban restructuring of Amsterdam and Los Angeles over the past twenty-five years becomes appealing at this point, for each has in its own way been paradigmatic.

But I do not wish to leave my Spuistraat vantage point too quickly, for it continues to be revealing.

The contemporary residential renaissance of Amsterdam's Centrum, more effectively than any other place I know, illustrates the power of popular control over the social production of urban space. It has been perhaps the most successful enactment of the anarcho-socialist-environmentalist intentions that inspired the urban social movements of the 1960s to recover their "rights to the city" ("*Le droit a la ville*," as it was termed by Henri Lefebvre in one of his various incitations to urban revolution). More familiar paths of urban restructuring can be found in Amsterdam, but the Centrum's experience verges on the unique. Uncovering this uniqueness is difficult, however, for it has been blanketed by more conventional wisdoms, right and left, that see only either a continuation of destructive decentralization emptying the urban core of its vital economic base (and hence necessitating more drastic forms of postmodern urban renewal); or the defeat and co-optation of the most radical urban social movements (leading too easily to a sense of popular despair over what now is to be done). Both views can be argued with abundant statistics and effective polemics, but when seen from the outside in a more comparative and global perspective on the past twenty-five years of urban restructuring, Amsterdam looks quite different.

In 1965, while Watts was burning in Los Angeles, a small group of Amsterdammers called the Provo (after their published and pamphleted "provocations") sparked an urban uprising of radical expectations and demands that continues to be played out on Spuistraat and elsewhere in the "magic centre" of Amsterdam. Their "White Bikes Plan" (whereby publicly provided bicycles would be available for free use throughout the city) symbolized the growing resistance to automobile traffic in the Centrum that would far outlive the plan itself. Today, the network of bicycle paths and the density of cyclists is probably the highest in any major industrial or even post-industrial city; urban planners routinely publicize their distaste for automobile traffic while flexibly accommodating its inevitability; and the people continue to take free public transport by simply not paying on the subway, tram, or bus. If the free-riders are caught (by characteristically soft enforcers, usually unemployed youth hired as fare checkers), they make up names, for the Dutch are unique in pre-1992 Europe in having no official identification cards. Driving licenses, the universal stamp and regulator of personal identity in America, are superfluous in the Netherlands and certainly not open to easy inspection.

The Provos concentrated their eventful "happenings" in both Dam and Spui squares and managed to win a seat on the City Council, indicative of their arousal of wider public sympathies. Their artful challenges to hierarchy and authority lasted only for a few years, but they set in motion a generational revolution of the "twenty-somethings" (my term for the youthful households comprised mainly of students between the ages of 20 and 30 that today make up nearly a quarter of the Centrum's population) that would dominate the renewal of the Centrum over the next two and a half decades. In no other major world city today are young householders, whether students or young professionals, in such command of the city center.

The initial provocations were creatively reinvoked in 1970, when the "Orange Free State" was declared as an alternative popular government rallying around the last Provo city councillor, a key figure in the Provo movement who was named ambassador to the "old state" and who today sits again on the Amsterdam City Council as representative of perhaps the most radical anarchist-Green party in Europe. More recently, when it came time to assign a council member to oversee the current plans to construct a luxury office and upscale housing development in the old Oosterdok waterfront–Amsterdam's anticipated version of London's Docklands–the same radical anarchist environmentalist became the obvious choice. No better symbol can be found of the continuing impact of the twenty-somethings: compromised to be sure, far from having any absolute power, but nevertheless aging with significant virtue, commitment, and influence.

The final renewal came with the full-scale squatter or *kraken* movement, beginning in 1976. From its famous "No Housing No Coronation" campaign in 1980, the movement did not decline so much as become a generalized radical pressure group protesting against all forms of oppression contained within what might be called the specific geography of capitalism, from the local to the global. Squatters, for example, merged into the woman's movement, the anti-nuclear and peace movements, the protests against apartheid (a particularly sensitive issue for the Dutch) and environmental degradation (keeping Amsterdam one of the world's major centers for radical Green politics), as well as against urban speculation, gentrification, factory closures, tourism, and the siting of the Olympic games in Amsterdam. Its greatest local success and ironically the cause of its apparent decline in intensity was to keep the right to accessible and affordable housing at the top of the urban political agenda by "convincing the local authorities of the urgency of building more housing for young households and of prohibiting the destruction of cheap housing in the central city for economic restructuring, gentrification, or urban renewal."

The population of Amsterdam peaked around 1965 at over 860,000. Twenty years later the total had dropped to a little over 680,000, but the Centrum had already begun to grow again and after 1985 so has the city as a whole. There are many factors that affected this turnaround, but from a comparative perspective none seem more important than that peculiar blend of democratic spatial planning and regenerative social anarchism that has preserved the Inner City as a magical center for youth of all ages, a stimulating possibilities machine that is turned on by active popular participation in the social construction of urban space.

Off Spuistraat

Anybody who grows up in Amsterdam invariably finds himself (sic) in the area of tension between the imprisonment of the ring of canals and the centrifugal escape via the exit roads of the city. In this area of tension one may not even know major parts of the city and still be an Amsterdammer . . .

> From my very first visit to Los Angeles in the early 1970s, I have had the feeling that the major Dutch cities (with Amsterdam in the lead) deny out of sentimental considerations the fact that they are part of a larger whole (an area as large and diffuse as Los Angeles) and as such completely ignore a dimension of an entirely different order from the one which they traditionally know.
>
> (Dutch architect Rem Koolhaas, in *Amsterdam: An Architectural Lesson*, p. 112.)

At first glance, a comparison of Los Angeles and Amsterdam seems as impossible as comparing oranges and potatoes. These two extraordinary cities virtually beg to be described as unique, incomparable, and of course to a great extent they are. But they are also linkable as opposite and apposite extremes of late twentieth century urbanization, informatively positioned antipodes that are almost inversions of one another yet are united in a common and immediate urban experience. First I will annotate the more obvious oppositions.

Los Angeles epitomizes the sprawling, decentered, polymorphic, and centrifugal metropolis, a nebulous galaxy of suburbs in search of a city, a place where history is repeatedly spun off and ephemeralized in aggressively contemporary forms. In contrast, Amsterdam may be the most self-consciously centered and historically centripetal city in Europe, carefully preserving every one of its golden ages (and also those of other enlightened urban spaces) in a repeatedly modernized Centrum that makes other remnant mercantile capitalist "Old Towns" pale by comparison. Both have downtowns of roughly comparable area, but only one of 100 Angelenos live in the City's center, whereas more than 10% of Amsterdammers are Centrum dwellers.

Many residents of the City of Los Angeles have never been downtown and experience it only vicariously, on television and film. Very few now visit it to shop (except for excursions to the garment district's discount stores and the teeming Latino mercados along Broadway); and surprisingly few tourists take in its local attractions, at least in comparison to more peripheral sites. Amsterdam's Centrum receives nearly 8 million tourists a year and is packed daily with many thousands of shoppers. Amsterdammers may not be aware of the rest of the city, but they certainly know where the center can be found.

It has been claimed that nearly three-quarters of the surface space of downtown Los Angeles is devoted to the automobile and to the average Angeleno freedom and freeway are symbolically and often politically intertwined. Here the opposition to Amsterdam's Centrum, second only to floating Venice in auto-prohibition, is almost unparalleled. It is not the car but the bicycle that assumes, for the Amsterdammer, a similarly obsessive symbolic and political role, but it is an obsession filled not with individualistic expression and automaniacal freedom as much as with a collective urban and environmental consciousness and commitment. This makes all the contrasts even more stark.

Amsterdam's center feels like an open public forum, a daily festival of spontaneous political and cultural ideas played at a low key, but all the more effective for its lack of pretense and frenzy. Its often erogenously-zoned geography is attuned to many different age groups and civically dedicated to the playful conquest of boredom and despair in ways that most other cities have forgotten or never thought possible. Downtown Los Angeles, on the other hand, is almost pure spectacle, of business and commerce, of extreme wealth and poverty, of clashing cultures and rigidly contained ethnicities. Boredom is assuaged by overindulgence and the bombardment of artificial stimulation, while despair is controlled and contained by the omnipresence of authority and spatial surveillance, the ultimate in the substitution of police for *polis*. Young householders are virtually non-existent. In their place are the homeless, who are coming close to being half the central city's resident population despite vigorous attempts at gentrification and dispersal.

In compact Amsterdam, the whole urban fabric, from center to periphery, is clearly readable and explicit. From its prime axis of the Damrak and Rokin (built above the former route of the Amstel River), the city unfolds in layers like a halved cross-section of an onion, first in the "old side" and "new side" (with an Old Church and New Church appropriately placed and streets named by their position inside or outside the old city walls), then in the neat crescents of the ringing canals from the inner to the outer Singel girdles, and finally in segments and wedges of inner and outer suburbs, many of which are helpfully named Amsterdam North, East, Southeast, South, and West. This morphological regularity binds Amsterdammers to traditional concepts of urban form and function and encourages its urbanists to be somewhat cautious when confronted with new theories of urban transformation.

In comparison, Los Angeles seems to break every rule of urban readability and regularity, challenging all traditional models of what is urban and what is not. One of America's classic suburbias, the San Fernando Valley, is almost wholly within the jig-sawed boundaries of the monstro-City of Los Angeles, while many inner city barrios and ghettoes float outside on unincorporated county land. There is a City of Industry, a City of Commerce, and even a Universal City, but these are not cities at all. Their combined populations would be outnumbered by the weekday shoppers on the Kalverstraat. Moreover, in an era of what many have called post-industrial urbanization, with cities being emptied of their manufacturing employment, the Los Angeles region has continued its century-long boom in industrial growth in both its core and periphery. It is no surprise, then, that Southern California has become a center for innovative and non-traditional urban theory for there seems little from conventional, established schools of urban analysis that any longer makes sense.

And then there is that most basic of urban functions, housing. One of the most interesting features of the success of the squatter movement in Amsterdam was the absence of a significant housing shortage. Although much of the Centrum is privately owned, the rest of the city is a vast checkerboard of public, or social housing, giving Amsterdam the distinction of having the highest percentage of public housing stock of any major capitalist city, around 80% and still growing I was told. Even what the Dutch planners consider the worst of these projects, such as the huge Bijlmermeer high-rise garden suburb, served effectively to accommodate the thousands of migrants from Surinam and other former colonies during the 1970s in housing that appears embarrassingly substandard primarily to the Dutch.

As noted earlier, the squatter movement was more than just an occupation of abandoned offices, factories, warehouses, and some residences. It was a fight for the rights to the city itself, especially for the young and for the poor. Nowhere has this struggle been more successful than in Amsterdam. Nowhere has it been less successful than in Los Angeles. In the immediate post-war period, Los Angeles was poised to become the largest recipient of public housing investment in the country, with much of this scheduled to be constructed in or around downtown. In no other American city did plans for public housing experience such a resounding defeat by so ferociously anti-socialist campaigners. The explosion of ethnic insurrections in the 1960s and early 1970s cruelly accelerated the commercial renewal of downtown at the expense of its poor residential inhabitants. On the central city's "new side" grew a commercial, financial, governmental, and high cultural fortress, while the "old side," beyond the skyscraper walls, was left to be filled with more residual land uses, from the tiny remnants of El Pueblo de Nuestra Senora de Los Angeles (where the city was born over 200 years ago) to the fulsome Skid Row of cardboard tenements and streetscapes of despair, to the Dickensian sweatshops and discount marts of the expansive Garment District,

The core of my oppositional comparison is thus amply clear. But what of the periphery, or the "larger whole," as Rem Koolhaas called it? Are there comparative dimensions "of an entirely different order" that are missed when we focus on the antipodal centralities of Amsterdam and Los Angeles? For the remainder of this interpretive essay, I will set the two cities in a larger, more generalizable context that focuses on contemporary processes of urban restructuring. Here, the cities follow more similar paths than might initially seem possible. These similarities are not meant to contradict or erase the profound differences that have already been described, but to supplement and expand upon their emphatic and extreme particularity.

My own research and writing on the urban restructuring of Los Angeles has identified a series of intertwined trends that have become increasingly apparent not only in Los Angeles but in most of the world's major urban regions. Each trend takes on different intensities and forms in different cities, reflecting both the normality of geographically uneven development and the social and ecological particularity of place. More important than their individual trajectories, however, is their correlative interconnectedness and the tendency for their collective impact to define an emerging new mode of urbanization, significantly different from the urbanization processes that shaped the industrial capitalist city during the long post-war boom period.

It is appropriate to begin with the *geographical recomposition of urban form*, for this spatial restructuring process deeply affects the way we look at the city and interpret the basic meaning of urbanization. As with the other trends, there is a certain continuity with the past, lending credence to the argument that restructuring is more of an acceleration of existing urban trajectories than a complete break and redirection. The current geographical recomposition, for example, is in large part a continuation on a larger scale of the decentralization and polynucleation of the industrial capitalist city that was begun in the last half of the nineteenth century and became periodically accelerated as more and more population segments and economic sectors left the central city.

There are, however, several features of the recent round of polynucleated decentralization that suggest a more profound qualitative shift. First, the size and scale of cities, or more appropriately of urban regions, has been reaching unprecedented levels. The older notion of "megalopolis" seems increasingly inadequate to describe a Mexico City of thirty million inhabitants or a "Mega-York" of nearly twenty-five, stretching from Connecticut to Pennsylvania. Never before has the focus on the politically-defined "central" city become so insubstantial and misleading. Complicating the older form still further has been the emergence of "Outer Cities," amorphous agglomerations of industrial parks, financial service centers and office buildings, massive new residential developments, giant shopping malls, and spectacular entertainment facilities in what was formerly open farmland or a sprinkling of small dormitory suburbs. Neither city nor suburb, at least in the older senses of the terms of these reconcentrated poles of peripheral urban and (typically "high-tech") industrial growth have stimulated a new descriptive vocabulary. In addition to Outer City there is also Edge City, Technoburb, Technopolis, Postsuburbia, and my own preferred term, Exopolis.

The growth of Outer Cities is part of the recentralization of the still decentralizing urban region, a paradoxical twist that reflects the ability of certain areas within the *regional metropolis* (including not only "greenfield" sites but the inner cities as well) to compete within an increasingly globalized economy. Over the past twenty-five years, the decentralization of manufacturing and related activities from the core of the older industrial capitalist cities broke out from its national containment. Jobs and factories continued to move to suburban sites or non-metropolitan areas within the national economy, but also, much more than ever before, to hitherto non-industrialized regions of the old Third World, creating a new geographical dynamic of growth and decline that not only has been changing the long-established international division of labor but also the spatial division of labor within urban regions.

The geographical recomposition is paradigmatically clear in Greater Los Angeles. Within a radius of 60 miles (100 kilometers) from the booming Central Business District of the misshapen City of Los Angeles there is a radically restructured regional metropolis of nearly 15 million people with an economic output roughly equivalent to that of the Netherlands. At this scale, a comparison with Amsterdam seems totally inappropriate. But if we follow Rem Koolhaas' "centrifugal escape" via the exit roads of the city, a different picture emerges. A 100-kilometer circle from Amsterdam's Centrum cuts through Zeeland, touches the Belgian border near Tilburg, curves past Eindhoven (where Phillips is headquartered) to touch the German border not far from Nijmegen, and then arcs through the heart of Friesland to the North Sea. Most of the nearly 15 million Dutch live within this densely urbanized region and its scale and productivity come remarkably close to matching its Southern California counterpart.

The southwest quadrant of this "Greater Amsterdam" coincides rather neatly with the Randstad, which can, with a little stretching, be seen as a kind of Outer City in itself, but with the defining central core being not an old urban zone but the determinedly preserved rural and agricultural "Green Heart." Around the Green Heart are the largest cities of the Netherlands: Amsterdam (700,000), Rotterdam (575,000), The Hague (445,000), and Utrecht (230,000), each experiencing a selective redistribution of economic activities between central city, suburban fringe, and more freestanding peripheral centers. As a whole, the Randstad contains the world's largest port (Los Angeles-Long Beach is now probably second), Europe's fourth largest international financial center (after London, Zurich, and Frankfurt) and fourth largest international airport (Schiphol, surpassed in traffic only by Frankfurt, Paris, and London).

Like the Greater Los Angeles regional metropolis, Greater Amsterdam has been experiencing a complex decentralization and recentralization over the past twenty-five years. How useful this larger scale regional comparison of geographical recomposition might be to a further understanding of urban restructuring I will leave to others to determine. For present purposes, however, it at least forms a useful antidote to "Centrumitis," the Amsterdammer version of "Manhattanitis," the tendency of urban observers to persist in seeing the contemporary period of restructuring too narrowly due to an excessive focussing on the long-established central city, thereby ignoring a dimension of an entirely different order from the one they traditionally know (quoting Koolhaas, for the last time).

The recomposition of urban form is intricately connected to other sets of restructuring processes. Already alluded to, for example, has been the *increasing internationalization of the regional metropolis*, leading to the formation of a new kind of world city. Amsterdam in its Golden Age was the prototypical model of the world city of mercantile capitalism and it has survived various phases of formation and reformation to remain among the higher ranks of contemporary world cities, whether combined in the Randstad or not. What distinguishes the global cities of today from those of the past is the *scope* of internationalization, in terms of both capital and labor. To the control of world trade (the primary basis of mercantile world cities) and international financial investment by the national state (the foundation of imperial world cities) has been added the financial management of industrial production and producer services, allowing the contemporary world city to function at a global scale across all circuits of capital. First, Second, and Third World economies have become increasingly integrated into a global system of production, exchange, and consumption that is sustained by an information-intensive and "de-territorialized" hierarchy of world cities, topped today by the triumvirate of Tokyo, New York, and London.

Los Angeles and Amsterdam are in the second tier of the restructured world city hierarchy, but the former is growing much more rapidly and some predict it will join the top three by the end of the century. Amsterdam is more stable, maintaining its specialized position in Europe on the basis of its concentration of Japanese and American banks, the large number of foreign listings on its Stock Exchange (second in the world to London), the strong and long-established export-orientation of Dutch companies, and its control over Dutch pension funds, reputed to be 40% of Europe's total. The banking and financial services sector remains a key actor in Amsterdam's Centrum, feeding its upscale gentrification and drawing strength from the information-rich clustering of government offices, university departments, cultural facilities, and specialized activities in advertising and publishing.

A characteristic feature of increasing internationalization everywhere has been an erosion of local control over the planning process, as the powerful exogenous demands of world city formation penetrate deeply into local decision-making. Without a significant tradition of progressive urban planning, Los Angeles has welcomed foreign investment with few constraints. Its downtown "renaissance" was built on foreign capital to such an extent that today almost three-quarters of the prime properties in the Central Business District are foreign-owned or at least partially controlled by overseas firms. The large number of Japanese firms in particular now routinely contribute to local political campaigns and fund-raising cultural activities, and have even made loans to the City government to maintain its pension fund program. The internationalization of Amsterdam has been more controlled, as one would expect, but the continued expansion of the city as a global financial management center is likely to pose a major threat in the very near future to many of the special qualities of the Centrum.

The other side of internationalization has been the attraction of large numbers of foreign workers into almost every segment of the local labor market, but especially at lower wage and skill levels. Los Angeles today has perhaps the largest and most culturally diverse immigrant labor force of any major world city, an enriching resource not only for its corporate entrepreneurs but also for the cultural life of the urban region. Amsterdam too is fast-approaching becoming a "majority minority" city, a true cosmopolis of all the world's populations. With its long tradition of effectively absorbing diverse immigrant groups and its contemporary socialist and socializing governance system, Amsterdam appears to have been more successful than Los Angeles in integrating its immigrant populations, socially and spatially, into the urban fabric. One achievement is certain: they are better housed in Amsterdam, for Los Angeles is currently experiencing one of the worst housing crises in the developed world. As many as 600,000 people, predominantly the Latino working poor, now live in seriously overcrowded conditions in delapidated apartments, backyard shacks, tiny hotel rooms, and on the streets.

Intertwined with the geographical recomposition and internationalization of Los Angeles and Amsterdam has been a pervasive *industrial restructuring* that has come to be described as a trend toward a "Post-Fordist" regime of "flexible accumulation" in cities and regions throughout the world. A complex mix of both deindustrialization (especially the decline of large-scale, vertically integrated, often assembly-line, mass production industries) and reindustrialization (particularly the rise of small and middle-size firms flexibly specializing in craft-based and/or high technologically-facilitated production of diverse goods and services), this restructuring of the organization of production and the labor process has been associated with a repatterned urbanization, a new dynamic of geographically uneven development.

A quick picture of the changing Post-Fordist industrial geography would consist of several characteristic spaces: older industrial areas either in severe decline or partially revived through adaptation of more flexible production and management techniques; new science-based industrial districts or technopoles typically located in metropolitan peripheries; craft-based manufacturing clusters or networks drawing upon both the formal and informal economies; concentrated and communications-rich producer services districts, especially relating to finance and banking but also extending into the entertainment, fashion, and culture industries; and some residual areas, where little has changed. It would be easy to transpose this typology to Greater Los Angeles, for much of the research behind it has been conducted there. Although the Post-Fordist restructuring has not gone nearly as far in Amsterdam, the transposition is also quite revealing.

The Centrum has been almost entirely leached of its older, heavier industries and 25% of its former office stock has been lost, primarily to an impressive array of new subcenters to the southeast, south, and west (e.g., Diemen, Amstelveen, and Sloterdijk) and to the growing airport node at Schiphol (15 kilometers away), where more than 35,000 people are now employed. One might argue, as many Dutch observers do, that this dispersal represents a sign of major decline in the inner city, due in part to a shift from a concentric to a more grid-like pattern of office and industrial development. Just as convincing, however, is a restructuring hypothesis that identifies the Centrum as a flexibly specialized services district organized around international finance and banking, university education, and diverse aspects of the culture and entertainment industries (fashion, especially for the twenty-somethings, television and film, advertising and publishing, soft drugs and sex, and, of course, tourism, with perhaps the most specialized attractions in the world for the young and the poor visitor). Except for the University of Amsterdam, which is being pressured to reduce its space in the Centrum, each of these other specialty areas has started to reconcentrate in recent years in the infor- mation-intensive inner city.

A fourth trend needs to be added, however, before one goes too far in tracing the impact of Post-Fordist industrial restructuring. This is the tendency toward *increasing social and economic polarization* that seems to accompany the new urbanization processes. Recent studies have shown that the economic expansion and restructuring of Los Angeles has dramatically increased poverty levels and hol- lowed out the middle ranks of the labor market, squeezing job growth upward, to a growing executive-professional-managerial "technocracy" (stocked by the largest urban concentrations in the world of scientists, engineers, and mathemati- cians), and downward, in much larger numbers, to an explosive mix of the "working poor" (primarily Latino and other immigrants, and women, giving rise to an increasing "feminization of poverty") and a domestic (white, African- American, and Mexican-American, or Chicano) "urban underclass" surviving on public welfare, part-time employment, and the often illegal opportunities provided by the growing informal, or underground economy. This vertical and sectorial polarization of the division of labor is reflected in an increasing horizontal and spa- tial polarization in the residential geography of Los Angeles. Old and new wealth is increasingly concentrated in protected communities with armed guards, walled boundaries, "neighborhood watches," and explicit signs that announce bluntly: "Trespassers will be shot;" while the old and new poor either crowd into the expanding immigrant enclaves of the Third World City or remain trapped in mur- derous landscapes of despair. In this bifurcating urban geography, all the edges and turf boundaries become potentially violent battle-fronts in the continuing struggle for the rights to the city.

This bleak and foreboding picture of contemporary Los Angeles can be inverted to describe a brighter side to urban restructuring, but such a flip-flopping descrip- tion is too simple and would only dilute the need to recognize and respond politically to the urgent problems facing this still expansive, and still largely unre- sponsive, urban region. Here again, the Amsterdam comparison is both informative and ambiguously encouraging, for it too has been experiencing a process of social and economic polarization over the past two decades, and yet, it has managed to keep the multiplying sources of friction under relatively successful social control. The Dutch "Job Machine," for example, shows a similar hollowing out of the labor market, with the greatest growth occurring in the low-paid services sector. Official unemployment rates have been much higher than in the U.S., but this difference is made meaningless by the contrasts in welfare systems and methods of calculating the rate itself. Overall job growth, as in almost every other OECD member country, has been much lower than in the U.S. and, except for the producer (i.e., mainly financial) services sector, there has been a decline in high-wage employment thus limiting the size of the executive-professional-managerial "bulge." Increasing flexibility in the labor market, however, is clearly evident in the growth of "temporary" and "part-time" employment, with the Netherlands having the largest proportion of part-time workers in the EEC and perhaps the highest rate (more than 50%) in the Western World for women.

Terhorst and van de Ven have examined the particular forms taken in Amsterdam by the widespread expansion of low-wage, often temporary, and/or part-time services jobs. Focussing on the revival of personal services, they gently provide evidence of social and economic polarization in Amsterdam and link this to restructuring processes elsewhere in the world. But again, there is a more human face to this polarization in Amsterdam. Personal services have flourished with expanding immigration, the entry of larger numbers of women into the low-wage workforce, the growth of the informal economy, and the gentrification of the Centrum; but the downside of this process has been ameliorated by, and indeed made to contribute to, the very special nature of the inner city area.

With its exceptional concentration of young, educated, often student households, high official levels of unemployment, still solid social security system, and two distinctive waves of gentrification (one fed by the high-wage financial services sector and the other by multi-job households typically comprised of former students and squatters still committed to maintaining the distinctive quality of life in the Centrum), an unusual synergy has developed around the personal services sector and between various age and income groups. As Terhorst and van de Ven point out, income polarization has been producing a growing complementarity between the higher and lower income groups with respect to the flexible use of time and place, especially in the specialized provision of such personal services as domestic help and babysitting, late-night shopping, entertainment and catering, household maintenance and repair, educational courses and therapies, fitness centers, body-care activities, etc. Such activities in Amsterdam take place primarily in the underground economy and are not captured very well in official statistics. They are also not likely to be a major factor in stimulating rapid recovery from economic stagnation and crisis. But they nonetheless provide a legitimate and socially valuable "survival strategy" for the poor and unemployed that has worked effectively to constrain the extreme effects of social polarization that one finds in Los Angeles or New York City. Moreover, it is a strategy that draws from the peculiar urban genius of Amsterdam, its long tradition of grass roots communalism, its sensitive adaptation to locality, its continuing commitment to libertarian and participatory social and spatial democracy, and its unusual contemporary attention to the needs of the twenty-something generation.

There is, of course, a dark side as well to this revival of personal services in Amsterdam's Centrum and the Dutch analysts are always careful to point it out. But here again, the comparative perspective produces a different picture. Viewed comparatively, the restructuring of the Centrum over the past twenty-five years has produced two reconfigurations of the urban political economy that distinguish Amsterdam from other major urban regions. The first arises from what may be the most successful urban implementation of the anarchist, environmentalist, and "situationist" principles that mobilized the student and other social movements in the 1960s in cities all over the world. That this success is far from complete and continues to be constrained and challenged by both internal and external forces takes nothing away from its distinctive achievement relative to other urban regions. That it can be better understood by rooting it in the deeper historical context of the "moralizing geography" of Dutch culture and its always paradoxical "embarrassment of riches" I have discovered after my stay in Amsterdam and have only begun to explore in this essay, thanks mainly to the magnificent spade-work of Simon Schama.

The second distinctive quality of Amsterdam becomes clearer when conjoined with the first and linked to the current literature on flexible specialization and urban-industrial restructuring. Although it would require much more empirical analysis to demonstrate convincingly, there appears to be taking shape in the Centrum of Amsterdam a new kind of specialized agglomeration that is as reflective of current trends in the world economy as the technopoles of California, the craft-based industrial districts of the "Third Italy," or the concentrated nodes of global financial management and control in Lower Manhattan and the City of London. It is primarily a services agglomeration, although small scale, technologically advanced, design and information intensive industries remain a significant part of the "complex." Producer services, especially in banking and finance, are also very important, for the Centrum remains the focus for a major world city of global capitalism. The most intense and decidedly flexible specialization, however, is locally focussed, extraordinarily innovative, and more advanced in Amsterdam than perhaps anywhere else in the developed world. A large part of its innovativeness lies in the simultaneous preservation and modernization of a unique urban heritage and built environment at a lively human scale–no small achievement in this age of the megacity. That it has not yet become a Disney-fied theme park for tourists is another achievement rooted both in the power of historical traditions of participatory democracy and socially responsible planning and in the contemporary influence of several generations of vigorous twenty-something activism. This has produced a services complex of remarkable diversity and interpersonal sensitivity in which basic needs take precedence over market demands to a degree difficult to find in any other world city center. I have no idea what to call this specialized space, but however it might be categorized, it is worthy of much greater attention, analysis, and appreciation–especially by those interested in comparative urban and community research.

I had originally intended to conclude by addressing *postmodernism and post-modernization* as a fifth restructuring theme and to explore the extent to which this restructuring of the "cultural logic" of contemporary capitalism can be traced into the comparison of Amsterdam and Los Angeles. In my own recent research and writings, I have argued that a neoconservative form of postmodernism, in which "image" replaces reality and the simulated and "spin-doctored" representations assume increasing political and economic power, is significantly reshaping popular ideologies and everyday life all over the world and is fastly becoming the keystone for a new mode of social regulation designed to sustain the development of (and control the resistance to) the new Post-Fordist regimes of "flexible" and "global" capitalist accumulation and the accompanying "new urbanization processes" discussed on the preceding pages. After experiencing Amsterdam, where resistance to the imposition of this neoconservative restructuring seems exceptionally strong, it is tempting just to add another polar opposition to the comparison with Los Angeles where this process is probably more advanced than almost anywhere else on earth. But I will leave the issue open for future research and reflection, and conclude with another example of the "stimulus of a little confusion"–a suggestion that perhaps the entire text of this paper arises from the political challenges posed in its last paragraph.

FRANKFURT: GLOBAL CITY–LOCAL POLITICS

Roger Keil
Toronto, Ontario

Peter Lieser
Technical University, Darmstadt

The internationalization of Frankfurt am Main which has characterized the development of the city since the late 1970s has been conceptualized as a result of economic necessity and global capital needs. However, we argue in this paper that the formation of Frankfurt as a global city has been shaped by local and regional dynamics as well. The case is made for an integration of various levels of theory in order to capture the entire process of Frankfurt's restructuring in its historical and geographical complexity. Frankfurt's 20th-century history is briefly reviewed covering the city's development from fordism to post-fordism. Assuming that each growth period has been accompanied by an era of social conflict, we provide a short history of socio-spacial conflicts in Frankfurt during the post-war era. Particular attention is given to the politics of internationalization during the conservative-urban regime that ruled the city from 1977 to 1989. Its policies are being analyzed as elements of a new form of urban regulation which, so we argue, is both necessitated by and itself shaping the internationization process. Finally, the paper interprets the results of the local elections of 1989, which ended the conservative rule as a consequence of growing social cleavages in the newly formed world city. We argue that a new local mode of regulation is emerging with both the urban society and the political structure, reorganizing and adapting.

World-city theory by definition faces a dilemma: the attempt to develop an abstract theory that must be global in both the geographic and the figurative sense of the world is marred by the evasiveness of obvious variations in the world's current historical geography. This structural shortcoming of the world-city debate can best be eliminated by integrating and combining theories that operate on the global level with approaches that deal with urban restructuring from a point of view of the reorganization of national systems of cities and with theories of sub-national forms of regulation. Further, current processes of urbanization can be properly understood only when the politics and the political economy of place (Logan and Molotch, 1987) are taken into account. The local political process is a key element in "world-city formation" (Friedmann and Wolff, 1982).

To substantiate our theoretical argument, a case study of urbanization processes in Frankfurt am Main will be highlighted. Frankfurt has recently been going through a comprehensive process of internationalization that has established the city as a "world city" (Friedmann and Wolff, 1982) or "global city" (Ross and Trachte, 1983; Smith and Feagin, 1987). The socio-economic and spatial aspects of world-city formation in Frankfurt has been dealt with elsewhere (see Lieser and Keil, 1988; 1989); we argue here that the transition of Frankfurt from a national economic center of West Germany's "economic miracle" (Wirtschaftswunder) and of the "Modell Deutschland"1 to a prospective and real mode of the European and world economies has in part been a product of a specific politics of place that have characterized, helped, modified or hindered the emergence of Frankfurt as a "world city."

Theories of Space, Theories of Place: A Quest for Integration

The world-city debate has generally established a heuristic and analytical framework to deal with the consequences of, rather than the local preconditions for, the formation of nodes of the restructured international economy at specific places. Peripheralization of the core, polarized labor markets (see Sassen-Koob, 1984; 1986), citadel and ghetto (Friedmann and Wolff, 1982), socio-spatial restructuring (Soja, Morales and Wolff, 1983), etc. are concepts that, above all, have implied the notion of externally induced urban restructuring in various cities that appear as victims or beneficiaries in a period of globalization of capital (Ross, 1988). The various strands of theory on world or global cities tend to see local politics as inherently reactive towards changes in the global capitalist system. The thesis that local events are governed and determined mainly by global capital strategies of transnational companies in a manner unheard of before has, indeed, been a major contribution to the conceptualization of current urbanization processes (Hill, 1986). The "global" level of analysis must be the starting ground for any significant venture into research on current restructuring in most of the world's big cities. Yet the tale of global hegemony over localities does not tell the whole story.

Most approaches in the world-city debate have emphasized the dominance of the global over the local. Most outspokenly, this position has been taken by Robert

Ross and Kent Trachte (Trachte and Ross, 1985; Ross and Trachte, 1983; Ross, 1988; 1983). Similarly, Logan and Molotch stress the growing "dependency" of U.S. cities in an age of increased internationalization, an observation that can be made in Europe as well. In particular, the straddling of the "sovereignty levels of all units of government" is emphasized because of the multinational scale of capital's operation (Logan and Molotch, 1987:249-51). One consequence of this "increased mobility of capital and the lower capacity of the State to enforce development conformity among localities" is a new socio-spatial diversity making metropolitan economies seem "uneven" and "distorted" (Logan and Molotch, 1987:258). John Friedmann and Goetz Wolff (1982) view the local space of global capitalism as determined by the logic and politics of the "citadel" that seems to rule over a "ghetto" from which it is antiseptically separated.

Joe Feagin and Michael Peter Smith, in their survey of approaches on the role to community politics in the formation of the global city, have recognized the need for the restructuring of the state on all levels of government as a precondition for current urbanization processes. They maintain that "changing urban development patterns are best understood as the long-term outcome of actions taken by economic and political actors operating within a complex and changing matrix of global and national economic forces. It is historically-specific political-economic processes through which contemporary corporations must work rather than expressing general economic laws of capitalist development" (Feagin and Smith, 1987:17).

While "Leviathan" is being redefined in the period of globalization (Ross, 1983), new instruments of urban management like the notorious public-private partnerships have sprung up in the process of state restructuring. Class compromises and coalitions of a new kind have emerged from economic and political struggles at the local level in response to excessive pressure on places and regions by global economic restructuring. Both of these struggles and their institutional results have taken distinctively local, regional, or national forms due to the historical geography of the places where they occurred.

In a second strand of theory, the change in national regimes of accumulation and modes of regulation has been conceived as the pacesetter for the current restructuring of urban areas. National systems of cities have been analyzed with respect to the modifications they underwent in the wake of crises of the national political economy of the countries where they are located. This approach does not in itself fully grasp the issues at stake in the current period of urban restructuring since it does not transcend the national level. Despite this obvious shortcoming, the reference to the national level in the sense of the discussion of distinctive national paths of development of social formations is an important feature of theorizing and research accomplished in the framework of the regulation school approach. It is also worth noting that while several phase models of urbanization, which have recently been put forward, stress the dawn of a global urban order (Trachte and Ross, 1985; Soja, Morales and Wolff, 1983), the national framework cannot be overcome in a capitalist world. Incorporation of the national experience into our analysis, therefore, seems appropriate (see Hirsch and Roth, 1986:46-8).

In West Germany, debates based on the restructuring of the national political economy have been waged for the most part around the issue of the impact on cities of regional shifts in the national economic geography. Observers noticed a distinctive "South-North grade" of urban development (see Friedrichs, Haeussermann and Siebel, 1986), with such prosperous cities as Munich, Stuttgart and Frankfurt in the equally prosperous South where industrial innovation seemed to mix with the post-fordist knack for political experiments. In the North and the West, there remained urban areas like Bremen, the Ruhr cities or the Saar (facing equally distressed Lorraine) where the disastrous effects of technological decline appeared to be coupled with the inflexibility of traditional Social-Democratic corporatism.

This hypothesis has recently been called into question even by some of its original initiators (see Haeussermann and Siebel, 1987). It was argued instead that it does not make sense to characterize the changes in the spatial structure in the FRG as a south-north division. It is more accurate to talk of a division in the north and the south, for within individual Laender there are greater disparities than between the Laender. In other words, winner and loser regions are to be found distributed throughout the entire FRG (Esser and Hirsch, 1989:427ff).

The same authors detect three types of post-fordist societalization that mix in a specific way at different places: first, the urban region that can compete internationally; second, the "normal" urban region as a site for production, (collective) consumption and housing; and third, the marginalized urban region (ibid). While this model comes closer to describing the reality of current West German urbanization as an integrative part of the "West German variant of the post-fordist strategy of accumulation," it does not fully succeed in grasping the current restructuring of cities like Frankfurt because of its sole focus on the national political economy.

In the third strand of theory, concepts of subnational forms of regulation can make significant contributions to the understanding of the political mechanics of world-city formation. Several processes involved in the formation of such regional or local modes of regulation will be explored in this paper, using the case of Frankfurt. Some of the more meaningful approaches to theorizing local forms of regulation have produced the notion of a "structured coherence" (Harvey, 1985), a regional regulation of flexible production complexes (Storper and Scott, 1988), as well as systems of reproduction (Wolch and Dear, 1988) of "space-specific modes of the subsumption of labor and the organization of class struggles" (Davis, n.d.) and the "political economy of place" (Logan and Molotch, 1987).[2]

Global, national, and local processes need to be seen as inherently intertwined—even if these connections are not always explicit in the empirical world. Thus, a certain degree of integration of the three different but complementary levels of analysis that correspond with these geographically differentiated processes must be achieved for urbanization in the current period to be understood. The integrative method may provide a shield against undue generalizations in the age of "global capitalism:" the national and global frameworks of research define a "theory of space," that will have to be supplemented and concretized by a "theory of place," emerging from the study of various regions and cities. Understanding the local effects of these mechanisms necessitates their conceptual integration with local historical geographies?" As Harvey (1987b:375) has recently cautioned, however, this project must not get lost in the postmodern fetishism of specificness.

The remainder of this paper will highlight such an integrative approach by specifying some of the features of Frankfurt's development into a fordist city, of its crisis and the beginning of its dissolution into a post-fordist, internationalized urban area. The genesis of the world city will be presented with a close look at its place-specific history, which again is viewed against its peculiar national background. The emphasis will be on local modes of regulation, the local political process and local economic specialization. Our sketch will be organized in three parts: the genesis of the fordist city, the crisis of the fordist city, and the emergence of the structured coherence of post-fordist, world-city Frankfurt.

Frankfurt: Fordist City

Frankfurt am Main, a city of roughly 620,000 people and 560,000 jobs, is the center of the fastest-growing and perhaps wealthiest region in the European community, the Rhein-Main Area. Over the past century, the city grew from its position as a regional hub of southwest Germany into the economic center of the Federal Republic and finally into a "world city." Between the 1920s and the 1970s, the city developed into an "exemplary fordist city" (Prigge, 1988b:226; Lieser and Keil, 1989). This development had three distinct phases.

"das Neue Frankfurt." In the 1920s, Frankfurt was the site of an extensive public housing project that created a local "para-fordism."[3] This was achieved primarily through the initiative of the Social-Democratic and liberal urban regime of mayor Ludwig Landmann, which made the city a center of modernist housing production bearing characteristic features of the fordist link of mass production and consumption that was yet to develop as a national regime of accumulation.

"The City of the German Crafts": The Return of the Dark Ages. Between 1933 and 1945, the specific brand of "Gothic Fordism" in Nazi Germany put an end to the reform efforts of the previous decade. The Nazis labelled Frankfurt "the city of the German crafts" and proceeded to redevelop the old town center— Germany's largest medieval core at the time—into a spectacle for national and international tourism, thought of as a competition for romantic Heidelberg (Haverkampf, 1985; Durth, 1988). While Landmannn's regime constituted a modern, self-confident mode of local regulation with qualities reminiscent of current urban management, the Frankfurt of the 1930s and early 1940s seemed to have vanished into a void. Innovative politics and planning were lacking, and even to the centralist planners of Nazi Germany, Frankfurt was pale and nondescript. "Frankfurt am Main: Planning unknown," said Albert Speer, Sr., Hitler's chief planner in Berlin in 1941 (quoted in Durth, 1988). It seems, therefore, that in stark contrast to the activity of the local growth machine in the 1920s, which created a place-specific "para-fordism," it was the lethargy of the re-feudalized regional bourgeoisie in a highly centralized national geography that allowed external trends of fordization—national or international in origin—to take hold over the urban region. Frankfurt's case clearly illustrates the peculiar mix of gothic "blood and soil" romanticism and hyper-modernist barbarism that characterized Nazi Germany.

"The Earth is Uninhabitable like the Moon":Wirtschaftswunderstadt Frankfurt. The third phase of Frankfurt's development into an early bastion of German fordism was the reconstruction of the city's economy and building stock after the disastrous bombardments between 1942 and 1944 had left little more than rubble (Durth, 1988). The result was what local writer Gerhard Zwerenz (1973) called a place "uninhabitable like the moon." While Frankfurt was growing into the financial center of the Federal Republic, it also became synonymous with urban horrors and the cruelty of post-war, socio-economic development in the period of the economic miracle.

Frankfurt-Rhein-Main, moreover, became a leading location early-on for economic activity characteristic of the specific kind of German fordism, the "Modell Deutschland," which was constructed on an export economy. In 1951, 17 percent of the production of Frankfurt's industrial firms went abroad. The figure was 23.5 percent in 1960, and by 1975 had almost reached the 40 percent mark. In 1950, the local Chamber of Commerce claimed jubilantly: "When numerous enterprises export 30 to 40 percent of their production, one may talk about a considerable success" (Schrader, 1950:49). Consolidation of the city's share of production for international markets above the 40 percent mark, however, was reached only when national trends had shown similar dynamics and the world city was in the works locally (Schwanzer, 1987:32).

Local politics and planning were governed by the "growth ethic" typical at the time after World War II (Logan and Molotch, 1987). Nobody questioned the necessity of unrestrained economic expansion, and the activities of local political actors followed rather than preceded the dynamics of growth. The main task of urban development politics was the creation of general conditions for production, "mostly adaptive measures with respect to the growing rate of motorization of the population." City planning at the time was called "adaptive planning" (*Anpassungsplanung*). It was "in no way systematic and comprehensive, but much more reactive, limping behind the real challenges" (Stracke, 1980:30).

Frankfurt: City in Crisis

When the economic crisis of the mid-1970s hit the miraculous post-war boomtown Frankfurt, its socio-spatial arrangement was strongly affected. As on the national level, the "urban crisis" took a definite political form (see Hirsch, 1986:36ff). The established system of local political regulation came under fire: the structured coherence of Frankfurt-Rhein-Main had to be redefined. The growth coalition was shuffled and reorganized. For decades after the war, Frankfurt had been governed by the bipartisanship of the "Roemerkoalition," the coalition or "regime of endurance" of the two largest parties, the Social Democrats (SPD) and the Christian Democrats (CDU). Now, the "planning of growth" was to be substituted by the "planning of order and consolidation" (Arndt, 1974), a concept quite in line with contemporary signs of stagnation in the national and urban economies on the eve of the major crisis of 1974–75. Consolidation did not mean stopping growth altogether but rather channeling development dynamics into what the SPD at the time considered appropriate for the balance of offices and housing. The displacement of the population from inner city neighborhoods and the conversion of housing into office space had become the constitutive issue of the urban discourse, and Social Democratic policy was directed toward control of ensuing conflicts around this issue. This implied a more repressive local state trying to make its stand in a political and planning process, whose actors started to gain autonomy through the activity of urban social movements and who began to represent a threatening challenge to the existing hegemonic policies and institutions of fordist Frankfurt.

The "politics of place" during the 1970s was characterized by an odd combination of extremes: comprehensive planning was sought by the SPD city government while large-scale destruction of such neighborhoods as the Westend was taking place. Citizen participation was introduced into the planning process while political repression against the "housing struggle" (*Haeuserkampf*) turned Frankfurt into a local stronghold of tendencies that Hirsch (1986:112-25) pointed to in his analysis of the German "security state." The city's SPD regime of postwar reconstruction, which for a long time had the support of the CDU, found itself fighting a two-way battle against radical urban social movements in struggles over housing speculation, transit fares as well as cultural issues, and the assault of an increasingly aggressive neoconservative CDU. The 1970s ended with the housing struggle quelled, the conservatives in power, and a large-scale regional conflict over the expansion of the Rhein-Main Airport in the wings. All three areas were indicators for the creation of local preconditions for world-city formation in Frankfurt.

Frankfurt's development into a fordist core city was accompanied by spatial segregation processes, functional separation, expansion of the office economy in the downtown area and surrounding neighborhoods, and a heavy increase in the use of the automobile in urban transportation. This development was supported by the policies and planning of the bipartisan and corporatist growth machine and executed with the aid of a host of "place entrepreneurs" (Logan and Molotch, 1987), most notably a group of real estate speculators who were acting as blockbusters for the conversion of housing into office space. They received financial backing for their operations from banks who remained on the sidelines of the ensuing political conflict (Stracke, 1980:56). Political support could be mustered through the General Plan of the city of 1968, the so-called "Fingerplan," which provided for high-rise strip development of offices along corridors reaching out from downtown into residential neighborhoods like the fingers of a hand (Stracke, 1980:46).

In the late 1960s, neighborhoods began to resist the growth policies of this coalition. A community group in the Westend, the "AG Westend," consisting primarily of political moderates, started to fight the conversion of their neighborhood into a displaced downtown. They represented a classical territorial, petty-bourgeois urban movement that was directed against the politics of the city government yet not against the local state itself (Stracke, 1980). Simultaneously, a radical housing movement—the *Haeuserkampf*—sprang up. Organized mainly by students, but backed by rent strikes of immigrant workers, the *Haeuserkampf* questioned the fundamental arrangement of economic and political power in the urban realm while

Frankfurt was getting ready to expand the logic of its growth to the level of internationalization.

The housing struggle of the early 1970s involved several thousand people who were active in squattings of houses that had become objects of speculation, other forms of direct action, cultural protest, and legal battles with the local state. The episode ended with the elimination of both radical opposition to the continued expansion of the uniformity of the fordist city core into residential neighborhoods and of the Social-Democratic hegemony over the city.

The Wallmann Regime: Frankfurt Goes Post-Fordist

The conservatives' electoral victory of 1977 was a consequence not so much of the plausibility of their opposition program as of the political bankruptcy of the local SPD regime that, under the pressure of popular opposition, was not (yet) able to make the transition from the growth machine policies of the reconstruction period to coining a post-fordist brand of urban management. The conservatives of Walter Wallmann were willing and politically capable of this transition. The change of power in Frankfurt, and other former SPD cities like Munich and Berlin, preceded the *Wende* in Bonn by five years and established a local workshop for the authoritarian populism of the federal CDU under Chancellor Helmut Kohl (see Esser and Hirsch, 1984). They replaced the spirit of stagnation that had characterized the final years of the Arndt-regime by a policy of unrestricted economic development, internationalization, socio-spatial centralization, and boosterism (Scholz, 1989). They were able to co-opt several unfinished SPD projects, such as, the reconstruction of a block of pseudo-medieval buildings opposite the historical city hall, the Roemer, and the rehabilitation of the imperial opera building, which had been badly hit in the war. The CDU combined a postmodern urban management that bent the political and planning processes in the city in favor of international capital with a culturalization of urban development. Prigge has shown that "the political right appropriated the urban by articulating it in opposition to the SPD Moderne culturally. This way they stabilized their current local political hegemony" (Prigge, 1986:110). They did so with the help of the reputed SPD Director of Cultural Affairs Hoffmann and Building Director Haverkampf, who functioned as the liberal showpieces of the Wallmann government. This seemed a necessary strategy of legitimation, indeed, when the city government under Wallmann pushed through severe cutbacks in housing and social services and continued the political repression against political opponents. The new regime could not have succeeded with a full renunciation of the political logic of the past Roemerkoalition, especially since the social and political forces of the city had to be rallied behind a renewed project of unconditional growth.

The specific mix of drastic change in the political form and of continuity in some of the substantial dynamics of urban development (urban growth) in Frankfurt lends credibility to Mayer's (1988:7) observation that there is a peculiar connection between the current and the preceding growth model:

> The reduced distance and global mobility that fordist policy efforts sought to facilitate, now turn out to be material preconditions of flexible accumulation and of competition on the basis of particular place-specific characteristics.

The Wallmann regime guaranteed a continuation of the fordist urban process where needed. It did not, however, perpetuate the post-war model, which, despite the reform rhetoric that characterized the interim Social Democratic regime of Arndt, had become politically unworkable. Instead, the conservative alternative put the built and social environments of the fordist city to work for the emergent world-city economy. In this process, the local mode of regulation changed, and with it urbanization in Frankfurt.

The "Startbahn West": Frankfurt Goes Global

The first large-scale social upheaval the fledgling urban regime had to master was the conflict around the expansion of the Rhein-Main Airport through the construction of a new runway, the Startbahn 18 West. Tens of thousands of people erected a "village of cottages" (Huettendorf), an assemblage of "anarchist architecture," on the projected site of the runway in the forest next to the airport; mass demonstrations with up to 120,000 participants took place. For years after the initial conflict, demonstrators battled the police at the "construction fence" in paramilitaristic fashion, and opponents of the runway waged long legal and institutional political fights demanding a stop to construction. A total of 220,000 signatures were collected calling for a plebiscite, which was declined by the *Land* government of Hesse (Rucht, 1984:195-272).

The Startbahn movement was defeated by the combined forces of the social-liberal *Land* and federal governments, the conservative city government of Frankfurt, and the local growth machine. The latter included not only local place entrepreneurs [those purposeful actors at the local level (Logan and Molotch, 1987), the web of state and private corporations and persons running the airport

(Flughafen AG), and subsidiaries of national-international corporations interested in the potential of the expanded economy of place of the airport] but also the majority of the labor unions who were convinced by the argument that jobs would be created through construction of the runway. All branches of the economy that hoped to gain from the expansion of the airport—banking, commerce and tourism, airlines, manufacturers, etc.—made their support known.

The struggle that preceded the defeat spelled out some of the central conflicts that the formation of an internationalized city entailed (see Friedmann, 1988). These included: 1) the encroachment of superstructural arrangements on the living spaces and ecologies of the urban region; 2) the inclusion of Frankfurt-Rhein-Main into an increasingly internationalized system of production (the airport was supposed to help establish the "expanded workbench" needed for the production of the "world car" in the nearby General Motors plant); 3) the continued militarization of the area [Rhein-Main Air Base whose expansion was feared in the process is the largest American Air Force Base outside the U.S. (Hechler, 1981)];[4] 4) the disfranchisement of the local population in the face of general interests of capital accumulation; and 5) the complete subordination of any development in the region to the demands of these interests.

The Startbahn movement was a frontal attack against the emerging superstructure of the world city. Much of the struggle, however, was waged in the forest outside the city and in the cul-de-sac of the plebiscite on the level of the *Land*. This geographical and functional dislocation of struggle from the seat of decision-making was partly responsible for the fact that the "movement" did not have the strength to turn their presence—in the street and in the ballot boxes—into lasting political power.[5] One participant in the struggle characterized the situation in this way in 1981:

> The core of the conflict around the expansion of the Frankfurt Airport, especially the construction of the Runway 18 West, is a conflict between powerful economic interests, particularly the stake in a possibly unlimited growth of air traffic on the one hand, and the life interests of the people around the airport and, on top of this, the entire Rhein-Main Region, including their well-understood job interests, on the other hand.
> (Alexander Schubart, quoted in Rucht, 1984:198).

Indeed, the alleged necessity of the new runway was "legitimized" by the function of the airport as an international hub, by its significance for the regional economy, and by the promise of job creation for the area. Opponents of the project implicitly and explicitly questioned the emerging logic of the new regime of accumulation that the "Startbahn West" and Wallmann's Frankfurt stood for. They protested the relegation of their environment to a functional node of a restructured global economy. The acceptance of the formation of world-city Frankfurt could not be taken for granted in City Hall or at any other level of the State.[6] Rather, the resistance to the runway became the symbolic fissure that needed to be incorporated into the new structured coherence of Frankfurt-Rhein-Main.

Global City – Local Politics: An Interpretation

An analysis of these three cases contains supportive evidence for the initial hypothesis: the concept of a "political economy of place" has to be interwoven with national and international trends in order to understand the formation of the "world city." Equally, the birth of a new local mode of regulation, as shown in the shift from the "Roemerkoalition" to the Social Democratic regime to the conservative hegemony, brings to life new contradictions and fissures. While radical local/internal (*Westend/Haeuserkampf*) and regional/external (Startbahn West) resistance to the projects of the late fordist and post-fordist world city were quenched, the regional growth machine reorganized itself into the neoconservative Wallmann-regime. Remaining resistance in the city and the region was, to a large degree, incorporated into the political structure of the local and regional state. Co-optation also meant, however, that the emerging structured coherence of world-city Frankfurt was built on the thin ice of latent opposition to any new step the growth machine would take in the future.

One indicator of this opposition and of a substantial uneasiness with the dynamics of growth in the population was the success of the Green Party after 1981 in the city and the regional communities. The Greens entered the Frankfurt City Parliament in 1981 when they received 6.4 percent of the vote. This trend was confirmed in 1985 (eight percent) and 1989 (10.1 percent). In the residential neighborhoods close to downtown, which have had to bear much of the expansionary pressure of the city's office economy (the main issue of the Westend housing struggles of the 1970s), the Green constituency easily passes the 20 percent mark in four out of 43 districts. It numbers more than 15 percent in six districts. In 23 districts (50 percent), the Greens had between ten and fifteen percent of the vote at the latest national election in 1987 (Frankfurter Statistische Berichte 48, 1988:30).[7] In the region, especially in the communities around the Startbahn West, voting patterns were even more favorable for the Greens. In Gross-Gerau County

(Landkreis), where the runway is located, 14.2 percent voted for a Green slate in 1981. In the Startbahn community of Moerfelden-Walldorf, the Greens gained 25.2 percent in the local elections of 1981 and 33.4 percent in the regional election of 1983 (Rucht, 1984:221*ff*).

In addition, Pfotenhauer (1988) has pointed out that the city government did not respond to resistance against the local state's planning and development policies of the early 1970s. The lines of conflict remained clearly separated, like Katznelson's (1981) "city trenches." The political divisions that characterized the final phase of fordist urbanization could not be synthesized into a new system of local political regulation. The radical wing of the housing movement had challenged "the system," but the dominant SPD growth machine was not able to identify this phenomenon as a consequence of their own political action (Pfotenhauer, 1988:152). Only after the demise of the *"Haeuserkampf's"* radical assault on what was left of the fordist growth machine did the city's planning process open up to more democratic procedures. Citizen participation was established, community college classes on planning issues were institutionalized, and zoning agreements such as the Westend zoning plans of 1977 and 1978 established feeble "compromises between business interests and the preservation of housing areas" (Bott, 1988:8). The planning process finally worked like an "early warning system, an instrument for pacification by which potential conflicts could be recognized early and were able to be defused" (Pfotenhauer, 1988:158). Substantial reforms were not achieved because the city was moving into a new phase of urbanization, which demanded a more comprehensive restructuring of the local mode of regulation than the one offered by the SPD.

World-City Frankfurt:
Emerging Forms of Local Regulation after Fordism

After 1977, Frankfurt's evolution into a world-city became the explicit political project of the neoconservatives under Mayor Walter Wallmann. For roughly a decade, they seemed to succeed in providing local political "answers" to the challenges of the emerging global urban center (Prigge, 1988:227). We now trace some of these "answers" with specific reference to their significance for the process of world-city formation. The politics and policies of the conservative regimes of Wallmann and his successor Brueck will be described as one possible "solution" to the demands of the internationalization of the city. The contradictions this regime implied and produced were responsible for its fall in 1989.

Frankfurt's structured coherence in the transition from the fordist to the post-fordist era is being thoroughly redefined by a set of local and regional actors who can be called the city's growth machine. In contrast to the corporatism and machine politics of the Social Democracy of the 1970s, the conservative-led coalition of power organized around the ideology of free enterprise and efficient urban management. The political parties remained major transmission belts and policy laboratories for the growth machine. This contrasts sharply with the insignificance of parties at the local level in many American cities. Privatization of formerly public enterprises and the dissolution of the separation between the private and public sectors in urban areas seemed to be the centerpieces of the conservative regime.[8]

Important parts of the growth machine consist of and use semi-public corporations that form the physical and institutional framework of the emerging world-city superstructure: the fairgrounds, the airport, the railways, planning offices, economic development agencies, etc. The public-private institutional structure has been held together by an old-boy network, including business leaders such as Horstmar Stauber (the manager of the city's fairgrounds, who was promoted to head the reconstruction of the airport), architects and developers (such as A. Speer, Jr., drafter of the city's General Plan, or O.M. Ungers, epitomic builder of postmodern Frankfurt), and politicians. Not incidentally, Wallmann, the ex-mayor and current prime minister of the state of Hesse as well as Brueck his three-year, mayoral successor, were members of the board of directors of both the fairgrounds and the airport.

The growth machine has explicitly articulated its stake in furthering the internationalization of Frankfurt-Rhein-Main. Horstmar Stauber, the most eloquent of Frankfurt's place entrepreneurs, in one of his famed and widely publicized rhetorical highlights, called the "Messeturm" of Jahn/Speyer (that will, for awhile, be the highest building in Europe) "a combat gear in the international competition among cities." The former planning director of the city, Kueppers, made the "continuous development of Frankfurt into an international financial center" his most important task, while Haverkampf, his colleague in the Building Department, saw Frankfurt in a close race with Paris and London to become the leading European link with the emerging Pacific economy. Kroell, former head of the (privatized) municipal Economic Development Corporation, saw Frankfurt-Rhein-Main caught in a competition with such regions as Lombardia, Catalonia, and even such nations as Portugal. Property market reports characterized Frankfurt as the location for first offices of international firms in Germany. Similarly, an official advertising brochure of the city's Office of Economic Development praises "Frankfurt— Preferred by Decision-Makers" as a logical location for foreign firms (for further references see Keil and Lieser, 1989; Lieser and Keil, 1988a; 1988b).

A private Economic Development Corporation (Wirtschaftsfoerderungs GmbH) was founded in 1987 and placed beside Frankfurt's departments for economic affairs (*Dezernat and Referat Wirtschaft*). Following the neoconservative philosophy of the "entrepreneurial city" (Duckworth, McNulty and Simmons, 1987), this private enterprise was established by the city independent of the bureaucratic apparatus and was quasi-independent of political control. It holds a mediating position between (international) capital willing to locate in the city and the increasingly rarer "free spaces" or "used up" residential quarters.

The corporation's proposed "Guidelines" are explicit: "Frankfurt's chances lie in the city's further internationalization" (Leitlinien, 1987). Regardless of the sudden reappearance of Berlin on the map of Central Europe, Frankfurt is likely to be maintained and expanded as the nodal point in the internationalized economy of the nation. Geoeconomic strategies, especially oriented toward the economic miracles of East Asia and *Pazifistan* (Haverkampf, 1985), belong to the repertoire of the world-city, economic development effort as well as planned structural change beyond banking and the chemical industry. The wooing of such growth industries as biotechnology or genetic engineering, micro-electronics as well as the propagation of the introduction of new materials and new production procedures into local industries, are supposed to guarantee that the economy of Frankfurt can expand its international economic links.

In addition, the corporation lends its support to existing sectors in the crafts and in manufacturing. Industrial parks for small businesses (*Gewerbehoefe*), the fur trade or the publishing industry, for example, are meant to dislocate these industries from expensive downtown areas, but they also create for them new spaces where the physical closeness of the enterprises, as well as their electronic sectorial self-organization and the availability of skilled and specialized productive and consumptive services for the economy of the world-city citadel, are guaranteed (Kroell, 1988; Frey, 1988).

The Politics of Selective Exclusion

The attack of the neoliberal conservative city government of Frankfurt on the local post-war Social Democratic mode of regulation made it obvious that the new system of regulation would create smoother conditions for internationalized capital accumulation in and through urban space. The political program of the conservative local government between 1977 and 1989 consisted of a two-pronged strategy of post-fordist citadel formation and diversified postmodern cultural populism. In contrast to the "discourse of integration" of the SPD regime, which tried to balance the contradictory tendencies of mass production and individualized consumption through an egalitarian and indifferent urbanism, the conservative regime's "discourse of difference" presented social differentiations as the natural character of urban society (Prigge, 1988b:228). This shift in urban policy and local regulation, though, hardly produced what Prigge calls a "postmodern diversity of a truly plural, post-industrial democracy" (Prigge, 1988b:228), but rather a rigid, new urban polarization. The "discourse of difference" is biased in favor of the world-city citadel.

Although the economic development policy in Frankfurt does not contain a working program for the construction of low-wage labor markets, their existence is implicitly taken for granted. In this sense, the city sells peripheralization of the local workforce as a benefit of the economic boom. Former Planning Director Kueppers used to emphasize that even Frankfurt's janitors profit from the city's rapid economic rise. As important, Former Mayor Brueck accepted the polarized class society of the world-city as a programmatic feature of development dynamics in Frankfurt: "To us, the banks are the head of the development. They attract everything that has to do with the head. From the software producer to the janitor" (Brueck, 1988). In this sense, the mode of local political regulation represented by the strategic policies of the conservatives has facilitated the locational dynamics of global capital and caused a proactive construction of local structures of global capitalism. The conservative political discourse constructs the formation of the world-city as a tale of selective exclusion.

A case in point, is the way in which the Wallmann and Brueck governments dealt with the internationalized workforce of more than 100,000. While counting on their economic availability as a flexible and cheap workforce, the conservative regime pursued an aggressive strategy of disfranchisement for the foreign population of Frankfurt on a political level. This strategy helped prepare the ground for the vote of 6.6 percent of the city's voting population for a neo-Nazi party in 1989. In line with German voting laws, foreigners—about 25 percent of the city's population—were not allowed to vote in local elections. There were also policies for which the local government was solely responsible. First, the city explicitly denied sanctuary to political refugees in 1980, which meant that even in 1989 they were not allowed in the city as long as their cases are pending. (By 1988, the number of refugees arriving at the Frankfurt airport had reached 15,000. They are funneled into camps in the regional periphery.) Second, Mayor Wallmann unsuccessfully attempted to reach a "total stop" of the influx of foreigners into the city in 1981. He wanted to "send a signal," another example of the kind of "symbolic politics" so typical of the postmodern discourse exercised by the CDU. Third, the city government favored and executed the confinement of fugitives in 1982 to barracks even before this policy became national praxis. Last, the city actively pursued the prevention of immigrant sponsorship, so as not to "increase unemployment" (see Michels, 1989; Keil and Lieser, 1989).

In 1985, the Wallmann mayoral campaign set the tone for the coming years by featuring the slogan, "The problem of the foreigners lies in your hand." Those neighborhoods in which up to 90 percent of the population are foreigners were not even allowed to speak at community councils. The attempts of several progressive councils to establish political organs for foreigners were unsuccessful. The inherent racism of Frankfurt's policy of selective exclusion was worsened by demands of the conservative city government in 1989 to reject foreign political refugees when German immigrants from Eastern countries are taken in (Michels, 1989). Finally, the recent campaign of the CDU for the 1989 mayoral race again aggressively banked on racism, xenophobia, and bigotry by conjuring up the alleged horrors of "softer" immigration and sanctuary praxis. In the face of a growing nationalist sentiment, the conservative policy toward the new internationalized population of Frankfurt has held the potential for the formation of world-city Frankfurt as a two-class society, split along racial lines.

Selective exclusion also has taken place on the social level. In 1989, there were an estimated 6,000 homeless people; the local housing authority dealt with about 12,000 housing applications. The foreign population currently concentrated in the downtown and surrounding areas has taken the brunt of this housing crisis. Already peripheralized on the housing market, they are the prime victims of gentrification and use changes in the living quarters of the world-city. Instead of counterbalancing the loss of affordable housing, the city under the conservative government all but abandoned public or subsidized housing programs and embarked on a policy of luxury housing provision through "innovative" public-private partnerships, which are feared to be the heart of the local politically-induced gentrification and "yuppification" efforts. While the housing policies of the city made the foreign working class the losers in an environment increasingly regulated by the market, ghettoization processes continue in those downtown areas where gentrification and redevelopment have not yet begun.

World-City Boosterism

The city pursued an aggressive campaign of image production: the image of the "Weltstadt," a concept with a significantly different connotation from that of "world-city." Policy and politics were constructed to fit this image. In return, the image legitimized "by necessity" higher buildings, additional halls on the fair-grounds, and an expansion of the airport. Declarations to that effect read like this:

> Frankfurt's significance in the network of international metrop-olises is growing. Global economic growth has not stopped. The upcurrent in the Asian-Pacific area can be felt in Frankfurt through growing economic contacts and establishments. And this is only part of the world that currently is in development. Financial trade has taken over the formerly leading role of com-merce and drives forward the interweaving of the world economy. One of the nodes of this fabric is Frankfurt, which is on its way from a continental to an international financial cen-ter. (Brueck, 1986:21)

In this sense, world-city Frankfurt became the product of a self-fulfilling prophecy and the boosterist project of the episode of conservative governance in the city that, in spite of its frontier rhetoric, meant hardly more than accepting the inevitable. In contrast to Scholz (1989), who in her analysis of the city's self-mar-keting strategy maintains that Frankfurt actually lived up to the image its government created of the city, we contend that the difference between the postin-dustrial wonderland of the marketing portrait and the post-fordist reality of the world-city is one of the decisive contradictions of the new local system of regula-tion. The open gap between the hoax of the "Weltstadt" and the catastrophic dynamics of the "world-city" ended the conservative interlude in Frankfurt's recent history.

From Selective Exclusion to Selective Incorporation

Election researcher Konrad Schacht, who had predicted a victory of the SPD and the Greens in the 1989 election, pointed to the central problem of the con-struction of a political project in the internationalizing city. "The decisive question is whether the citizens feel the interests of the urban society are represented suffi-ciently against the power of outside investors. Modern local policy in the big city needs to be able to 'listen into' the urban society—and to develop from there a level for negotiations with the investors."[9] It is safe to say that the conservative regime lost this capacity to communicate with the civil society of the city. The peculiar mixture of unrestrained growth (largely by opening the city to international invest-ment) and symbolic politics practiced by the conservatives prefigured the crisis of this particular brand of urban politics in the world-city. The local state became both unresponsive to the demands of the local citizenry and unable to cope with the entire set of contradictions its policies had helped to create. The city government did little to mediate between the interests of any of the class segments that constitute this urban society (except for the inner circle of the growth machine) and the (international) investors who have turned Frankfurt into their playground.

On the eve of the local elections on March 12, 1989, considered strategic by many (including Mayor Brueck), the challenge of world-city formation had finally reached the programmatic statements of the contending parties and began to determine the construction of the political discourse. The SPD and the CDU supported the politics of growth and expansion as they had since World War II. The major difference between them is that the latter unambiguously embraced the further expansion of the "money machine" they helped to turn Frankfurt into in the past, while the former claimed to furnish the "money machine" with a change dispenser for social problems. SPD urban policy in the 1990s in Frankfurt will not constitute a major break with former praxis but will be concessionary.

The Greens, finally, have been split into two camps. A "fundamentalist" wing, opposed to the destructive environmental and social development of the capitalist city, has constructed politics on the level of the neighborhood with utter disregard for the internationalization of the city, while a "realist" wing of the party has embraced the notion of a positive, cosmopolitan urbanism heavily grounded in the middle-class lifestyle-culture of the internationalized, postmodern city. While it seems difficult to make a clear distinction between these two camps, and while the party still holds together displaying an often confusing plurality of programmatic features, it is also true that the current local party power structure is dominated by the more reformist (as opposed to activist, movement-oriented) realos. Their acceptance of citadel formation rests on the belief that it could imply a pluralist cosmopolitan multiculturalism (see Herterich, 1986; Lieser, 1989). This became the political precondition for the current SPD and Green coalition, which was a result of the March 12, 1989, local elections.

The election meant that for the time being the conservative project had been relegated to the status of one out of several possible episodes in the process of world-city formation through local politics. The hegemony of the local authoritarian populist project both fell apart at its right fringe and garnered considerable political resistance on the left end of the electoral political spectrum and in the increasingly politicized urban civil society. While the political mix of development and spectacle had carried the CDU to solid majorities in local elections after 1977, they obtained only 36.6 percent of the vote, 13 percent less than in 1985.[10] Slight gains of the SPD and the Greens opened the possibility for a change in the urban regime through negotiating a coalition agreement between the two parties. Whereas the election clearly demonstrated the vote of the citizens of Frankfurt for a drastic change in policy, the most surprising and terrifying result of the 1989 election was the strong showing of the neoNazi party NPD, which received 6.6 percent of the vote.[11]

Political commentators held various causes responsible for the disastrous defeat of the CDU and the gains of the NPD.[12] Reasons for the latter's success were sought in various areas, ranging from traditional German irrationality at certain historical conjunctures to the crisis of the national CDU government under Kohl to shifts in the socio-economic make-up of West German society. Our interpretation of the 1989 election results, which rests upon our analysis of local politics in the formation of the world-city in Frankfurt since the 1970s, follows:

> In addition to other influences that determined the outcome of this election, the campaigns of the local parties and the voting results reflected the specifics of an emerging world-city politics. The conservative project had constructed the political and social process of the world-city as one of "selective exclusion." During the last weeks before the elections, the CDU staged an all-out attack on the political and human rights of the city's foreign population, using the nationalist-populist slogan: "We Frankfurters are against the right to vote for foreigners." The racist undertones of this explicit statement fell in line with the single-issue campaign of the neoNazi NPD, which basically suggested that foreigners had no place in the city. Thus, the conservative power bloc collapsed because the balance of selective exclusion of Frankfurt's internationalized population came under the attack of racists and nationalists who demanded to replace "selective" by "total."

The government that had made the political suppression of Frankfurt's foreign population a central pillar of their political understanding of how the city was to be organized became a victim of its own dynamics. The CDU had made it politically and socially acceptable for many citizens to think of foreigners as second-class urbanites, holders of the new "dirty jobs," and expendable at the discretion of the capitalists who employed them (or not). The conservatives were finally confronted with the reality that the formation of a world-city, which they had actively pursued for more than a decade, would entail discarding the nationalist and racist parochialism of their policies. When the political right said "Weltstadt," however, they actually meant "Heimat." The conservatives fell short of acknowledging the need for a renewed local system of social and political regulation. While the internationalized working class is here to stay, the CDU proved to be expendable.

While the conservative political project came under attack from the right, the fatal blow was dealt by a combination of the majority vote of liberal, Social Democratic, and Green voters and a growing politicization of the urban civil society. The SPD and the Greens had taken a clear stand in favor of incorporation of the international population into the social and political process of the city.[13] Even though they do not demand a clear-cut departure from the growth-oriented process of world-city formation started by the conservatives, these parties nevertheless captured the uneasiness of the local populace. Voters felt increasingly at odds with the implicit social polarization, the housing crisis, the disregard for resistance against development, the arrogance of the local growth machine in its mediation of international investment, and the empty shell of world-city boosterism. The policies pursued by the new governmental coalition will alter the way in which the local mode of regulation will be constructed in the years to come. The new-structured coherence will be built on the principle of "selective incorporation," which will imply the concessionary approach of the SPD toward international capital and the cosmopolitan multiculturalism of the Greens. Both aspects will be united in a novel configuration of capital accumulation in and through space, which will acknowledge the existence of the "ghetto" of an internationalized working class along the shining globalized "citadel" of Frankfurt's financial and service center.

Conclusion

The analysis of local politics in Frankfurt alone hardly enables us to draw conclusions on the political process in the world-city. Three observations can, however, be made. First, integration of the local, national, and global levels of analysis is a pre-condition for an understanding of current processes of world-city formation there. For this reason, more research using this integrative method needs to be done at other places in order to overcome the methodological dilemma of the world-city hypothesis.[14]

Second, even though the conservative Wallmann regime helped propel the city into the global age, the mode of political regulation that the conservative regime represented is by no means the only possible one. Both modest and radical reform might be able to modify the "inevitability" of growth, economic development, racism and selective exclusion, local powerlessness, and the fetishism of the urban image. Their success will depend partly on the social and political mobilization of their clientele in the civil society of the city. Research on current restructuring processes needs to consider the role of local forms of regulation and local class struggles in space. Our research on Frankfurt has shown that there is considerable room for political negotiation at the local level. Purely economically-informed research and approaches that predict the eclipse of the local political process at the current conjuncture will have to be revised as a result.

Third, the analysis showed that any given system of local regulation, any structured coherence is indeed only a temporary arrangement suffering from a chronic instability (Harvey, 1985). Its spatial borders, its class structure, and its economic base are constantly redefined. Local political struggles, moreover, are crucial to this process. Their capacity to impact the formation of the structured coherence of a world-city ranges from the power of transitory or more stable political projects to open attacks against the structures in formation. The product of these political and economic class struggles in space is a vulnerable phenomenon. The international reach of today's urbanization processes links the local and the global in a previously unknown way and makes local events possible cornerstones of international decisions.

Political conflict over the restructuring of the built and social environment can indicate potential limits to the formation of new types of cities. Political activity of oppositional forces can endanger the growth machine's project of the world-city even though the capacity for co-optation seems unlimited. In addition, real or imagined political threats to the power of the growth machine might be used as ideological weapons in the political struggle over the future of the world-city. In Frankfurt, after the March 1989 election, members of the local growth machine expressed their fears regarding the consequences of the collapse of the conservative regime on the "business climate" of the city. The director of the Chamber of Commerce, Speich, was particularly concerned about the effect of the presence of a fascist party in City Hall: "Things [sic] like the NPD absolutely do not fit into the program of Frankfurt as a commercial center which is open to the world."[15] The mere presence of the NPD raises questions about the reputation of Frankfurt as an international center, a consequence the growth machine cannot accept. The concern of the local bourgeoisie, to be sure, is not about the threat an openly racist party constitutes to the foreign population.

Furthermore, a red-green scare isn't far away. While the catastrophic social problems that have evolved with the formation of the world-city are rarely blamed on the 12 years of world-city building by the CDU, the Green party has become a handy scapegoat for expected and unforeseen difficulties on the world-city frontier. While it seems unlikely that the Green party in Frankfurt, devoted deeply to a strategy of realpolitik, will take a political stance that might seriously threaten the undisturbed process of capital turnover in Frankfurt, there are stirrings on the part of social movements. Local political movements have considerable leverage in this period of internationalization; they help determine the local conditions of global capitalism. While urban reform movements redefine the processes that govern the world-city, radical groups at the periphery of urban social movements begin to disrupt the peace of the "postmodern money-machines" (Dear, 1986), which their cities are being turned into.[16]

Beyond the process of "normal politics" in Frankfurt, resistance to both the expansion of the citadel and the degradation of the ghetto is on the rise. New stirrings of urban social movements can be detected in the city (new coalitions of community groups, resistance against high-rise construction, a fledgling student-housing movement, and militant resistance against plant closings in older industries that are mostly orchestrated by immigrant workers). Through these activities, the entire local political process will be renegotiated: world-city formation in Frankfurt will be turned into the politics of a "different metropolis" where the city becomes more than a use value for international capital alone but for its inhabitants first. As David Harvey reminds us, "real power for today's powerless must be gained from below and cannot be given to them generously from above" (Harvey, 1987:129). In Frankfurt, the search for "forms of praxis for the definition of a language of territorial and class alliances" with regard of a reformulation of local politics in the global city has begun.

Notes

1. By "Modell Deutschland" we mean the special formation of German fordism that came into being in the 1970s as a reaction to the general crises of the postwar regime of accumulation. It was characterized by a close connection between the imperialist role of West Germany and the authoritarian internal political development. This regime was kept together by the peculiar link of power of the social-democratic-liberal coalition and was strengthened by the corporatist support of the labor unions (cf., Hirsch. 1986:9).
2. To a certain degree, recent debates on urban regimes have had similar theoretical thrusts (Stone/Sanders,1987; Fainstein/Fainstein, 1983). The latter, however, deny or ignore the necessity of a major paradigm shift in urban research. For a

more detailed critical discussion of these approaches, see Keil, (forthcoming).

3. Andernacht and Kuhn (1986) have coined the term "Frankfurter Fordismus" in this context. We prefer the term "para-fordism" for this period in order to capture the incomplete character of this regional formation when, indeed, fordism as a national regime had not materialized, yet.

4. One of the slogans that picked up this argument was: "Into the Third World War with a third runway!"

5. The relationship of social movements, alternative social institutions, the parties, the state, and other political institutions has been the subject of much political and academic debate. While it would be going too far here to enter this discussion, it needs to be pointed out that the movement against the runway in Frankfurt was one of the major cases considered (cf., Rucht, 1984:268ff). Hirsch and Roth (1986) have linked the discourse on social movements to the crises of fordism and the emergence of post-fordist arrangements in West Germany. Recent social movement literature has shifted to the "institutionalization of the movement sector" (Roth, 1988; Nullmeiner, 1989) as its focus. In any case, the social movements can now be considered constitutional elements of the new socio-spatial forms after the crises of the "Model Germany"—in our case of the post-fordist world-city Frankfurt.

6. The Startbahn communities in the south of Frankfurt had originally shown enthusiasm for the project. Once it became obvious that they had to take the brunt of the airport's disadvantages (like noise, the cutback of recreational space, etc.), they changed their minds drastically. In contrast to the central city, the state, and the federal governments, these communities started to become adamant opponents of the expansion.

7. This trend shows the political potential of protest and resistance. It does not give any indications whether those voting for the Greens are, indeed, those who are threatened by the consequences of world-city formation, such as, gentrification through expansion of the "citadel." In fact, Green voters often are gentrifiers. The social split in the Green electorate, which even though it does not express an homologous relationship with political attitudes, has often been subject to debate. Esser (1989) has recently made this point for Berlin's 1989 local/state election where he detected two clearly distinctive groups of Green voters: a) middle-class voters who cast their vote for environmental reasons, and b) supporters in working-class areas with alternative infrastructures who chase the Greens for the "anti-capitalist social hope" represented by the party (in Berlin, the Alternative List).

8. The trend towards privatization and public/private partnerships is not unique to

Frankfurt. It has been the pervasive feature of urban restructuring in many cities in Western countries. It is necessary, however, to point to the fact that in Frankfurt the trend towards privatization and urban management coincided with the city's internationalization. It is particularly noteworthy that the local privatized and semi-public institutions emerging and being strengthened after the demise of the social-democratic regime were put to work for the construction of the world-city.

9. "Die entscheidende Frage ist das Gefuehl der Buerger, ob die Interessen der Stadtgesellschaft genuegend gegenueber der Macht der auswaertigen Investoren vertreten werden. Eine moderne, grosstaedtische Kommunalpolitik in einem dynamischen Ballungszentrum muss in die Stadtgesellschaft 'hineinhorchen' koennen—und daraus eine Verhandlungsebene gegenueber den Investoren entwickeln" (Quoted in Horx, 1989:19).

10. Local Elections, City of Frankfurt, May 12, 1989

		(in percent)			
	CDU*	SPD@	Greens	NPD+	FDP#
1977	51.3	39.9	-	0.7	6.0
1981	54.2	34.0	6.4	0.5	4.3
1985	49.6	38.6	8.0	-	2.6
1989	36.6	40.1	10.1	6.6	4.9

(Source, Frankfurter Rundschau, March 14, 1989)
* Christlich Demokratische Union
@ Sozialdemokratische Partei Deutschlands
+ Nationaldemokratische Partei Deutschlands
# Freidemokratische Partei

11. Previously, the NPD had only been in the city parliament once, between 1968 and 1972. Since then, the party had been insignificant, receiving less than one percent of the vote in local, state, and general elections [cf., Hennig (1991) for an analysis of right wing voting patterns in Frankfurt].

12. A good spontaneous reading of the rise of right wing parties in West German and the ensuring public debate is Ely's 1989 article. Particularly interesting for our case is Ely's analysis of the racial foundations of the German discourse on "foreigners" at the heart of the debate: "In the Federal Republic, liberalization is advanced not by naturalizing 'foreigners' so that the state-controlled labor and population policies . . . can first become issues of 'race,' 'ethnicity,' and 'integration.'" Rather, Ely points out, only suggestions to grant the vote to foreigners have been made: "It is precisely at this level that traditional causes for West

Germany's new right radicalism bite deepest."

13. The Greens responded to the CDU slogan against the right to vote for foreigners by putting up posters that read: "We Frankfurters are fed up with the black-brown alliance. Vote them out of office."

14. Cf., Keil (forthcoming) for the application of a similar approach in a case study of Los Angeles.

15. "In das Programm von Frankfurt als weltoffenes Handelszentrum passen solche Dinge wie die NPD absolut nicht hinein" (quoted in *Sueddeutsche Zeitung*, Nr. 61, March 14, 1989:24).

16. Recent examples of other German cities point to this possibility. On May 1, 1987, several thousand people—anarchist youth, punks, welfare recipients, unemployed, foreign workers—rioted in Kreuzberg, the socially most distressed part of West Berlin. Provoked by police who attacked a neighborhood festival, they erected barricades, started fires, and looted stores (Esser, 1987; Homuth, 1987). The event sent shock waves through this city's ruling circles who at the time were caught up in the spectacle of Berlin's 750th Anniversary. In Hamburg, at a congress of 1,300 top managers on August 31, 1988, who gaged the potential of the depressed German coastline as a future location for industry, specifically addressed the alleged danger to their endeavors from the continuing presence of militant squatters in Hamburg's Hafenstrasse (Harbor Street). The head of the corporate Federation of German Industry (BDI), Tyll Necker, said at the occasion: "If Hamburg allows the global symbol of this city—the harbor—with the Hafenstrasse to dilapidate into a synonyme for chaos, the damage to the economy, investments, and jobs will be, if not calculable, yet considerable. One does not mess with symbols" (quoted after Kerner, 1989:103).

Interviews

Wolfram Brueck, Oberbuergermeister Stadt Frankfurt, July 6, 1988.
Christoph Fey, Dezernat Wirtschaft, Stadt Frankfurt, October 25, 1988.
Klaus Kroell, Wirtschaftsfoerderung GmbH Frankfurt, October 26, 1988.
Horstmar Stauber, Flughafen AG Frankfurt, November 4, 1988.

References

Arndt, Rudi (1972) *Mittelpunkt jeder Politik ist der Mensch*. Frankfurt: Presse-
und Informationsamt der Stadt.
Arndt, Rudi (1974) *Zur kommunalpolitischen Situation der Stadt*. Frankfurt: Presse-

und Informationsamt der Stadt.

Bott, Odina (1988) "Das Frankfurter Westend: Bericht ueber einen bekannten Stadtteil aus der Beobachtung Betroffener. Frankfurt.

Brueck, Wolfram (1986) "Eine intelligente Stadt." Frankfurt: CDU-Stadtverordnetenfraktion.

Castells, Manuel (1983) *The City and the Grassroots: A Cross-Cultural Theory of Urban Social Movements.* Berkeley and Los Angeles: University of California Press.

Cooke, Philip (1987) "Local capacity and global restructuring: Some preliminary results from the CURS research program," paper presented at the Sixth Urban Change and Conflict Conference, University of Kent at Canterbury, September 20-23.

Davis, Mike (no date) "Sunshine and the Open Shop: The Urbanization of Los Angeles—1880-1930," unpublished manuscript, Los Angeles.

Dear, Michael (1986) Postmodernism and planning, *Environment and Planning D: Society and Space 4*:367-84.

Dear, Michael J. and Jennifer R. Wolch (1989) How territory shapes social life. In Wolch, Jennifer and Michael Dear (Eds.), *The Power of Geography: How Territory Shapes Social Life.* Boston: Unwin Hyman: 3-18.

Duckworth, McNulty and Simmons (1987) *Die Stadt als Unternehmer.* Bonn: Bonn Aktuell (English translation: The Entrepreneurial American City).

Durth, Werner (1988) Frankfurt. In Werner, Durth and Niels Gutschow, *Traeume in Truemmern.* Braunschweig/Wiesbaden: Vieweg: 465-540.

Ely, John (1989) Republicans: Neo-Nazis or the black-brown hazelnut? Recent successes of the radical right in West Germany, *German Politics and Society Issue 18*:1-17.

Esser, Jochen (1987) *Kommune 53*(9):

Esser, Jochen (1989) Berliner Widersprueche: Rechtsruck und Linksverschiebung, *Kommune 7*(3):6-9.

Esser, Josef and Joachim Hirsch (1984) Der CDU-Staat: Ein politisches Regulierungsmodell fuer den "nachfordistischen" Kapitalismus," *Prokla, 56*:51-66.

Esser, Josef and Joachim Hirsch (1989) The crisis of fordism and the dimensions of a "post-fordist" regional and urban structure," *International Journal of Urban and Regional Research*: 417-37.

Fainstein, Susan, et al. (1983) *Restructuring the City. The Political Economy of Urban Redevelopment.* New York: Longman.

Feagin, Joe R. and Michael P. Smith (1987) Cities and the international division of labor: An overview. In Smith and Feagin (Eds.), *The Capitalist City: Global*

Restructuring and Community Politics. Oxford: Basil Blackwell.

Frankfurter Statistische Berichte (1988), Statistisches Amt und Wahlamt der Stadt Frankfurt.

Friedmann, John (1986) The world city hypothesis, *Development and Change, 17*:69-83.

Friedmann, John (1988) "Environmentalism, civil society and planning." Paper presented at the Second International Congress of the Association of European Schools of Planning (AESOP), Dortmund, November 11.

Friedmann, John and Goetz Wolff (1982) World city formation: An agenda for research and action," *International Journal of Urban and Regional Research, 6*: 309-44.

Friedrichs, J., Hartmut Haeussermann and Walter Siebel (Eds.) (1986) *Sued-Nord-Gefaelle in der Bundesrepublik?* Opladen: Westdeutscher Verlag.

Haeussermann, Hartmut and Walter Siebel (1987) *Neue Urbanitaet.* Frankfurt: Suhrkamp.

Haeussermann, Hartmut and Walter Siebel (1986) Die Polarisierung der Grosstadtentwicklung im Nord-Sued-Gefaelle. In Friedrichs, J., Hartmut Haeussermann and Walter Siebel (Eds.), *Sued-Nord-Gefaelle in der Bundesrepublik?* Opladen: Westdeutscher Verlag.

Harvey, David (1985) *The Urbanization of Capital.* Baltimore: Johns Hopkins University Press.

Harvey, David (1987a) Flexible Akkumulation durch Urbanisierung: Ueberlegungen zum "Post-Modernism" in den amerikanischen Staedten, *Prokla, 17*(69):109-31.

Harvey, David (1987b) Three myths in search of a reality in urban studies,

Haverkampf, Hans-Erhard (1985) Fernsicht auf Frankfurt—Entwicklungslinien der Mainmetropole bis zur Jahrhundertwende, Frankfurter Aufbau AG: Sonderdruck zum Geschaeftsbericht. Frankfurt.

Hechler, Rudi (1981) Das Problem der Air-Base und des Flughafens Frankfurt am Main. In BI gegen die Flughafenerweiterung (Ed.), *Keine Startbahn West.* Offenbach: Verlag 2000:55-58.

Hennig, Eike (1991), *Die Republikaner in Schatten Deutschlands.* Frankfurt: Suhrkamp.

Herterich, Frank (1986) Unsere Stadt—clean, kleinkariert oder kosmopolitisch? *Aesthetik und Kommunikation, 61 and 62*:115-25.

Hill, Richard C. (1986) The spider's web: Transnational production and world urban development. University of Hong Kong, Center of Urban Studies and Urban Planning, Working Paper 21.

Hirsch, Joachim (1986) *Der Sicherheitsstaat: Das Modell Deutschland, seine Krise und die neuen sozialen Bewegungen.* Frankfurt: Syndikat/EVA, 2nd ed.

Hirsch, Joachim and Roland Roth (1986) *Das Neue Gesicht des Kapitalismus: Vom Fordismus zum Post-Fordismus.* Hamburg: VSA.

Homuth, Karl (1987) Identitaet und soziale Ordnung, *Prokla, 68.*

Katznelson, Ira (1981) *City Trenches: Urban Politics and the Patterning of Class in the United States.* New York: Pantheon.

Keil, Roger (forthcoming) Soziooekonomische Restrukturierung und politische Veraenderung in einem neuen Stadttypus: "Global City" Los Angeles. Ph.D. dissertation. JWG-University Frankfurt am Main, Department of Social Sciences.

Keil, Roger and Peter Lieser (1989) Rhein-Main. Die Wachstumsmaschine: Lokale Widersprueche der globalen Oekonomie, *Kommune* 7(3):22-7.

Kerner, Erich (1989) Die Hamburger Hafenstrasse als Investitionsbremse, *1999* 4(1): 101-5.

Leitlinien der Wirtschaftsfoerderung (1987) Frankfurt: Wirtschaftsfoerderungs GmbH.

Lieser, Peter (1989) Multikultur gegen Stadt der Multis, *Kommune* 7(4):12-13.

Lieser, Peter and Roger Keil (1988a) Zitadelle und Getto: Modell Weltstadt. In Prigge, Walter and Hans-Peter Schwarz, *Das Neue Frankfurt: Staedtebau und Architektur im Modernisierungsprozess 1925–1988.* Frankfurt: Vervuert: 183-208.

Lieser, Peter and Roger Keil (1988b) Frankfurt: Die Stadt GmbH & Co. KG, *Stadtbauwelt, 100:* 2122-7.

Lieser, Peter and Roger Keil (1989) "Frankfurt am Main: Global city—Local spaces." Paper presented at the Annual AAG Meeting at Baltimore, Maryland, March 22.

Logan, John R. and Harvey L. Molotch (1987) *Urban Fortunes: The Political Economy of Place.* Berkeley: University of California Press.

Mayer, Margit (1987) Restructuring and popular opposition in West German cities. In Smith, Michael Peter and Joe R. Feagin (Eds.), *The Capitalist City: Global Restructuring and Community Politics.* Oxford: Basil Blackwell: 343-63.

Mayer, Margit (1988) The changing conditions of local politics in the transition of post-Fordism. Paper prepared for the International Conference on Regulation Theory, Barcelona, June 16–18.

Michels, Claudia (1989) "Kommunale Auslaenderpolitik in Frankfurt seit 1980," unpublished manuscript.

Nullmeier, Frank (1989) Bewegung in der Institutionalisierungsdebatte? *Forschungsjournal Neue Soziale Bewegungen,* 2(3-4):8-19.

Peterson, Paul (1981) *City Limits.* Chicago: University of Chicago Press.

Pfotenhauer, Erhart (1988) "Frankfurter entscheidet mit!" Planung und Protest im Aufbruch der siebziger Jahre. In Prigge, Walter and Hans-Peter Schwarz, *Das Neue Frankfurt: Staedtebau und Architektur im Modernisierungsprozess 1925-1988*. Frankfurt: Vervuert: 145-65.

Prigge, Walter (1986) Grosstadtideologien, *Aesthetik und Kommunikation, 61 and 62*:109-13.

Prigge, Walter (1988) Mythos Metropole: Von Landmann zu Wallmann. In Prigge, Walter and Hans-Peter Schwarz, *Das Neue Frankfurt: Staedtebau und Architektur im Modernisierungsprozess 1925-1988*. Frankfurt: Vervuert: 209-40.

Prigge, Walter and Hans-Peter Schwarz (1988) *Das Neue Frankfurt: Staedtebau und Architektur im Modernisierungsprozess 1925-1988*. Frankfurt: Vervuert.

Ross, Robert (1983) Facing Leviathan: Public policy and global capitalism, *Economic Geography, 59*:144-60.

Ross, Robert (1988) "Remaking the state in Massachusetts." Paper presented at the AAG Annual Meeting, Phoenix, Arizona, April 6-10.

Ross, Robert, Don Shakow and Paul Susman (1980) Local planners, global constraints, *Policy Sciences, 12*:1-25.

Ross, Robert and Kent Trachte (1983) Global cities, global classes: The peripheralization of labor in New York City, *Review, 6*(3):393-431.

Roth, Roland (1988) "Entgrenzung von Politik? Zur Bilanzierung der institutionellen Effekte neuer sozialer Bewegungen," unpublished manuscript.

Rucht, Dieter (Ed.) (1984) *Flughafenprojekte als Politikum: Die Konflikte in Stuttgart, Muenchen und Frankfurt*. Frankfurt and New York: Campus.

Sassen-Koob, Saskia (1984) The new labor demand in global cities. In Smith, Michael Peter (Ed.), *Cities in Transformation*. Beverly Hills: Sage: 139-71.

Sassen-Koob, Saskia (1986) New York City: Economic restructuring and immigration, *Development and Change 17*: 85-119.

Scholz, Carola (1989) *Frankfurt—Eine Stadt wird verkauft*. Frankfurt: ISP-Verlag.

Schrader, A. (1950) Wiederaufbau und Exportbedeutung der Frankfurter Industrie. In: *Jahrbuch der Stadt Frankfurt am Main*.

Schwanzer, Wolfgang (1987) "Industrielle Entwicklung in Frankfurt am Main - von der Manufaktur zur weltmarktorientierten Produktion," Fachbereich Wirtschaft der Fachhochschule Frankfurt am Main, Berichte und Informationen.

Scott, Allen and Michael Storper (1986) (Eds.) *Production, Work and Territory: The Geographical Autonomy of Industrial Capitalism*. Boston: Allen and Unwin.

Smith, Michael Peter (1987) Global capital restructuring and local political crises in U.S. cities. In Henderson, Jeffrey and Manuel Castells (Eds.), *Global Restructuring and Territorial Development*: 234-50.

Smith, Michael Peter and Joe R. Feagin (Eds.) (1987) *The Capitalist City: Global Restructuring and Community Politics.* Oxford: Basil Blackwell.

Soja, Edward W., Rebecca Morales and Goetz Wolff (1983) Urban restructuring: An analysis of social and spatial change in Los Angeles, *Economic Geography, 59*(2): 195-230.

Stone, Clarence and Heywood Sanders (Eds.) (1987) *The Politics of Urban Development.* Kansas: University of Kansas Press.

Storper, Michael and Allen J. Scott (1989) The geographical foundations and social regulation of flexible production complexes. In Wolch, Jennifer and Michael Dear (Eds.), *The Power of Geography: How Territory Shapes Social Life.* Boston: Unwin Hyman: 21-40.

Stracke, Ernst (1980) *Stadtzerstoerung und Stadtteilkampf in Frankfurt am Main.* Koeln: Pahl-Rugenstein.

Sueddeutsche Zeitung (1989) vol. 61, March 14: 24.

Timberlake, Michael (Ed.) (1985) *Urbanization in the World Economy.* New York: Academic Press.

Trachte, Kent and Robert Ross (1985) The crisis of Detroit and the emergence of global capitalism, *International Journal of Urban and Regional Research, 9*:186-217.

Wolch, Jennifer and Michael Dear (Eds.) (1989) *The Power of Geography: How Territory Shapes Social Life.* Boston: Unwin Hyman.

Zwerenz, Gerhard (1973) *Die Erde ist unbewohnbar wie der Mond.* Frankfurt:

ECONOMIC CRISIS AND STRUCTURAL ADJUSTMENT: THE CHANGING LABOR MARKET OF SAN JOSÉ, COSTA RICA

Richard Tardanico
Florida International University

Costa Rica has clearly outperformed other Central American countries in resisting marginalization from a restructuring world economy. The comparative performance of Costa Rica seems to be grounded in a complex of features: its stable, social-democratic state; superior economic infrastructure; and, during the regional conflicts of the 1970s and 1980s, strategic importance to the United States. This complex of features manifested itself as well in the performance of San José's labor market in 1979–87, under conditions of economic crisis and structural adjustment. Relative to Central America's other capital cities, what occurred in San José's labor market was not an abrupt, massive reordering but rather a process of moderate change—including much slower than average expansion of informal employment. The fact remains that it involved the growth and restructuring of labor-market inequalities, whose pattern suggests the erosion of Costra Rica's pre-crisis standard, economic growth with improving social welfare.

Among the regional losers in the contemporary world economy is Central America, where the combination of local underdevelopment, local strife, and global reorganization has meant profound economic setbacks since the late 1970s (ECLAC, 1977–91). The countries of Central America are very small and highly dependent on the export of a few agricultural commodities, such as, coffee and bananas. Within this framework, however, the region encompasses striking diversity in its economic, social, and political characteristics (e.g., Dunkerly, 1988; Menjívar Larîn and Pérez Sáinz, 1991; Paige, 1987). Thus, while Central America has suffered deep economic losses, its interplay between local conditions and global restructuring involves varying dimensions and outcomes. Which Central American countries and which urban and rural areas within them, are relative winners and losers in the transformation of the world economy? How are their relative gains and losses manifesting themselves in terms of class, gender, and age inequality?

Costa Rica shares basic disadvantages with its Central American neighbors relative to transnational developments in investment, technology, production, and trade (e.g., Castells and Laserna, 1989; Gereffi, 1989). Yet, compared to its neighbors, Costa Rica's economic performance has been strong. Since the wider Latin American economic crisis of the early 1980s, Costa Rica has attracted significant foreign investment and aid while diversifying into nontraditional agricultural and assembled exports. More exceptionally, it has managed to increase its per capita production (ECLAC, 1984–91; IICA/FLACSO, 1991). So far, then, Costa Rica has outscrambled its counterparts in the struggle to avoid becoming marginalized in a restructuring world economy.

This performance is consistent with the country's trajectory since the 1950s. Several features distinguish Costa Rica's long-range development from that of other Central American countries: political democracy and stability; a superior economic infrastructure; much higher per capita income and greater access to social services; and a somewhat more egalitarian income distribution. These institutional features largely reflect the post-1948 policies of the state's modernizing leadership, in the context of an expanding international economy and the political vulnerability of the traditional rural oligarchy and the lower classes. The state's leadership pursued its development objectives by carrying out a number of key measures: abolishing the standing army, nationalizing the banking system, undercutting the labor movement, and incorporating the poor into large-scale social programs (e.g., Dunkerly, 1988).

Costa Rica's structural adjustment policies of the last decade have facilitated the country's impressive recovery from its economic crisis of 1979–82. Simultaneously, though, they have represented a basic challenge to its long-standing development model (CEPAS, 1990; Dunkerly, 1988; La Nacion, 1991a, b; Lungo, et al., 1991; Torres Rivas, et al., 1987). What has been their impact on the country's socio-economic inequality?

This paper addresses that question by examining the consequences of economic crisis and structural adjustment for the labor market of San José, Costa Rica, 1979–87. In so doing, it represents a step toward three objectives. The first is the understanding of the class, gender, and age patterns of gains and losses associated with economic crisis and structural adjustment in Costa Rica. The second is the understanding of the comparative urban and regional dimensions of these unfolding patterns in Central America, about which little is known (Lungo, 1989, 1990; Lungo, et al., 1991; Menjívar Larín and Pérez Sáinz, 1991; C.A. Smith, 1988). And the third is the consideration of the relative strengths and weaknesses of the gamut of potential development policies (e.g., La Nacion, 1991a, b; Walker, 1991;

Zimbalist, 1988).

The labor-market patterns documented amount not to abrupt transformation but to moderate change. Such change is particularly clear with respect to the growth of informal, or legally unregulated, employment whose expansion was much slower than the norm among Central America's capital cities. San José's moderate pace of labor-market change appears to be related to Costa Rica's state structure and economic infrastructure which, given its geopolitical importance to the United States during the 1980s, favored it among Central American countries during a period of worldwide transformation. Yet, the economy's recovery of 1983–87 included not only a heavier fiscal burden and still reduced public services for most of San José's population, it also seems to have included increased rates of labor-force participation for the city's middle-age and elderly women; the growth of employment inequalities in the formal and informal economies; and regressive shifts in average real wages and wage inequality. This pattern suggests the erosion of Costa Rica's pre-crisis standard of economic growth with improving social welfare.

Costra Rica's Economy: Growth, Crisis, and Adjustment

High coffee prices, advantageous terms of foreign loans, and massive government spending enabled Costa Rica to recover briskly from the world oil shock of 1973–74. Building on momentum established in the mid-1960s, the state's managers greatly enhanced not only its social but also its economic role. By founding and expanding public enterprises, leadership deepened the state's intervention in the development of industry, agriculture, and employment.

Yet, Costa Rica's economy, like that of other Central American countries, was fragile. Manufacturing centered on light-industrial production for the small, domestic market and the limited Central American Common Market. As inefficient production that depended on foreign inputs and capital, manufacturing was buttressed by public subsidies, low taxes on firms, and high protectionist barriers. Agriculture was similarly structured, while imports accounted for a growing share of the consumption of goods and services. This development pattern generated insufficient domestic savings and productive investment. In addition, it generated insufficient employment in the economy's modernizing sectors with public-sector employment, especially for the well-educated, growing in compensatory fashion. Reliance on the earnings of coffee and banana exports, moreover, left Costa Rica at the mercy of the world market. In the 1960s and 1970s favorable terms of foreign and domestic loans masked a chronic tendency toward fiscal and balance-of-payment deficits (e.g., Dunkerly, 1988; Zimbalist, 1988).

In 1977–78, Costa Rica's brittle mid-decade prosperity faltered as coffee prices and private investment dropped. The world oil shock of 1979, soaring interest rates, and the absence of tax reform exacerbated the downward spiral. So did Central America's deteriorating political climate and declining intraregional trade. In 1980–82, production, employment, and the currency plummetted, and the external debt and inflation surged. Not until the summer of 1982 did the state's administrators adopt a coherent plan of economic stabilization (Tables 1–2; García-Huidobro, et al., 1990; Nelson, 1989).

Table 2
Costa Rican GDP by Sector

	Agriculture	Industry	Construction	Services
1977	19.0%	22.0%	5.6%	53.4%
1982	19.9	21.4	3.6	55.1
1987	17.8	22.6	4.4	55.2

Source: Banco de Costa Rica (1988).

The relative severity of Costa Rica's 1980–82 plunge in per capita GDP ranked next to worst among Central American countries, behind El Salvador (ECLAC, 1981–83). By 1983, though, the economy was already responding to the stabilization plan, as U.S. economic aid leaped in the context of regional conflict. This plan included "shock treatment" measures to reduce the fiscal deficit, tighten the currency-exchange market, and encourage international loan agreements. Yet, in the interests of maintaining political stability, the plan also retained some continuity with long-standing policies by including selective measures to cushion the social impact of retrenchment. For instance, it provided food aid and temporary jobs to the poorest families, controlled the prices of key groceries, and favored the lowest-paid workers in raising wages semi-annually (Dunkerly, 1988; ECLAC, 1981–83; García-Huidobro, et al., 1990; Nelson, 1989).

The economy's upturn of 1983–87 which recuperated most of the country's late-1970s levels in areas such as per capita GDP, average real wages, and private consumption placed first in a region that underwent considerable decline. U.S. and multilateral aid as well as local administrative reforms enabled Costa Rican authorities to implement a structural adjustment program marked by gradualism. To be sure, this program included substantial austerity measures, such as, reduced subsidies of basic foods and public services in favor of increased subsidies for exporters of nontraditional commodities. Nonetheless, it additionally included

Table 1
The Costa Rican Economy: Annual Growth Rates

	GDP/PC	Agr.[a]	Manuf.[a]	Infl.	Real Wages	C.Govt. Exp./GDP[b]	C.Govt. Def./GDP[b]	US Econ. Aid	Current Acct. Bal.[c]	Ext. Debt/Exps.[b]
1979	1.8	0.5	2.7	13.2	4.5	19.8	-7.1	109.8	-554	—
1980	-2.2	-0.5	0.8	17.8	0.8	20.8	-8.0	7.6	-658	184
1981	-5.0	5.0	-0.5	65.1	-11.7	16.6	-1.8	9.4	-408	229
1982	-10.0	-4.8	-12.0	81.7	-19.8	17.7	-3.3	227.6	-274	286
1983	-0.3	3.9	1.8	10.7	10.9	20.1	-3.6	279.8	-327	312
1984	4.8	9.6	9.9	17.3	7.8	19.8	-2.8	-14.0	-261	294
1985	-2.1	-5.7	2.0	11.1	9.1	18.2	-2.0	18.2	-299	307
1986	2.4	4.2	7.0	15.4	6.1	18.8	-3.3	-30.1	-193	282
1987	2.5	3.1	5.3	16.4	-9.7	17.7	-2.0	16.9	-445	289
1979–82	-3.9	0.1	-2.4	44.5	-6.6	18.7	-5.1	88.6	-474	—
1983–87	1.5	3.0	5.2	14.2	5.0	22.5	-3.4	67.7	-305	186
1979–87	0.9	1.7	1.9	27.6	-0.2	18.8	-3.8	57.3	-334	273[d]

Source: Banco de Costa Rica (1988); Economic Commission for Latin America and the Caribbean (1985–89);
Inter-American Development Bank (1980–88).
a Annual growth rate of value
b Annual percentage
c Annual value
d 1980–87

selective social policies, such as, continued emphasis on the raising of official minimum wages and the eventual undertaking of a major public-housing campaign. In this setting, economic recovery involved significant foreign aid, reduced debt-service payments, the improved purchasing power of exports, and the U.S.-sponsored, Caribbean Basin Initiative. It likewise involved success in attracting foreign investment and stimulating tourism as well as nontraditional agricultural and assembled exports (e.g., flowers, tropical fruits, apparel, electronics). Even so, limitations of structure and size left the economy vulnerable as the external debt swelled. Per capita GDP wavered between contraction, stagnation, and substantial growth; and most of the population faced heavier fiscal burdens and cutbacks in public services. Inflation cooled before heating up anew, while average real wages recouped most of their lost ground until dropping sharply after 1986. These developments occurred against a background of severe inequality of rural landownership (predominantly small, urban firms) and a weak labor movement [1] (Tables 1–2; CEPAS, 1990; ECLAC, 1983–91; García-Huidobro, et al., 1990; IICA/FLACSO, 1991; Lungo, et al., 1991; Nelson, 1989; Soja, 1989; Zimbalist, 1988).

What were the ramifications of economic crisis and structural adjustment for San José's patterns of laborforce and employment? The following sections examine these questions: first, at the level of short-term trends for 1979–82 and 1983–87, and second, at the level of long-term trends for 1979–87.

San José's Labor Market

A principal theme of the literature on Latin American labor markets before the economic crisis was the region's surprisingly minimal levels of urban unemployment. According to this literature, the reason was not an abundance of employment. It was, instead, that "the poor had to find some income-earning activity, even if it meant 'invented' jobs with minimal productivity" (Portes, 1989:24). From this standpoint, we can expect that the economic downswing of 1979–82 generated major growth in San José's laborforce. We can also expect that it resulted not in a reduced number of jobs, but in the restriction of employment growth to the informal sphere. And, with a swelling mass of informal workers and the relative rigidity of wages in the formal economy, we can expect that the earnings of informal workers fell more severely than those of the remaining formal workers (Bonilla, 1990; Elson, 1989; Hakkert and Goza, 1989; Jatobá, 1989; Portes, 1989; Portes, et al., 1989; Roberts, 1989).

San José's laborforce did indeed expand in the face of economic crisis. This expansion occurred as households mobilized reserve income-producers to com-

Table 3. San José: Population, Labor Force, and Employment

	1977	1978	1979	1980	1981	1982	1983	1984	1985	1986	1987	77-78	79-82	83-87	79-87
Population	563,743	580,652	597,702	614,904	632,266	649,798	667,510	679,432	703,498	721,785	735,499c				
% Growth	3.1	3.0	2.9	2.9	2.8	2.8	2.7	1.8	3.5	2.6	1.9	3.1	2.9	2.5	2.7
%15-59	—	—	—	57.4	57.8	59.1	62.8	58.3	63.4	59.6	65.0				
%12-19	20.3	18.8	19.2	18.0	17.2	17.0	15.9	15.7	15.4	14.9	15.6				
% Female	51.8	52.0	51.7	51.7	50.6	50.5	51.8	52.1	51.9	52.5	51.3				
Labor Force	198,052	210,421	212,752	221,987	227,295	247,371	242,661	241,919	259,554	260,449	281,140c				
% Growth	5.3	6.2	1.1	4.3	2.4	8.8	-1.9	-0.3	7.3	0.3	7.9	5.8	4.2	2.7	3.3
Male	—	5.0	3.5	3.8	1.5	10.2	-3.7	-0.5	5.7	2.0	6.1	4.8	1.9	3.2	
Female	—	8.8	-3.6	5.5	4.3	6.1	1.9	0.0	10.4	-2.7	11.5	3.1	4.2	3.7	
% Female	33.0	33.8	32.3	32.6	33.2	32.8	33.6	33.8	34.7	33.7	34.8				
Employment	187,227	199,014	201,708	210,947	208,400	219,479	221,946	222,896	240,246	244,642	267,584c				
% Growth	6.0	6.3	1.4	4.6	-1.2	5.3	1.1	0.4	7.8	1.8	9.4	6.2	2.5	4.1	3.4
Male	—	5.5	3.4	3.4	-2.1	5.9	-0.5	1.0	6.3	3.2	8.0	2.7	3.6	3.2	
Female	—	7.8	-2.8	6.7	1.0	4.2	4.3	-0.6	10.8	-0.7	12.2	2.3	5.2	3.9	
% Female	32.7	33.1	31.7	32.4	33.1	32.8	33.8	33.5	34.4	33.5	34.4				
Unemployment	10,825	11,407	11,044	11,040	18,895	27,892	20,715	19,023	19,308	15,807	13,555c				
% Growth	-4.9	5.4	-3.2	0.0	71.2	47.6	-25.7	-8.2	1.5	-18.1	-19.3	2.5	28.9	-14.0	5.1
Male	—	-6.3	3.3	15.2	68.1	57.9	-28.2	-15.8	-1.6	-14.0	-23.2	36.1	-16.6	6.9	
Female	—	24.1	-11.1	-21.5	77.4	27.3	-19.8	8.6	6.8	-24.6	1.6	18.0	-5.5	5.0	
% Female	38.3	45.1	41.4	32.5	33.7	29.1	31.4	37.1	39.1	35.9	42.6				
Visible															
Underemp.a	14,965	20,849	33,258	27,162	25,875	46,756	41,344	32,987	35,655	25,418	19,966c				
% Growth	—	39.3	59.5	-18.3	-4.7	80.7	-11.6	-20.2	8.1	-28.7	-21.3	29.3	-14.7	4.8	
Male	—	—	—	—	-6.0	75.7	-9.3	-24.0	1.9	-33.1	-8.0	34.9d	-14.5	-4.0e	
Female	—	—	—	—	-1.9	91.2	-16.0	-12.3	19.3	-21.9	-39.0	44.7d	-14.0	2.8e	
% Female	—	—	—	—	32.1	34.0	33.0	35.5	39.2	43.0	33.0				
Invisible															
Underemp.b	19,479	17,466	15,361	14,031	13,963	46,858	25,913	20,495	19,510	15,195	18,863c				
% Growth	—	-10.3	-9.8	-11.0	-0.4	235.6	-44.7	-20.9	-4.8	-22.1	24.1	53.6	-13.7	16.2	
Male	—	—	-10.0	-21.0	14.1	345.9	-57.9	-11.9	-13.7	-12.3	63.9	82.2	-6.2	33.1	
Female	—	—	-9.6	-3.8	-9.0	154.3	-27.6	-28.3	3.4	-29.7	-14.4	33.0	-19.3	3.9	
% Female	—	58.1	58.2	63.0	57.6	43.6	57.1	51.8	56.3	50.8	35.2				
Employ. Hrs Per Week															
% Less than 47 hrs.	25.1	31.7	35.3	35.5	35.3	37.5	36.6	37.4	38.7	41.2	35.6				
% Less than 30 hrs.	8.2	8.1	8.2	8.4	8.4	10.4	8.7	8.2	8.5	6.6	9.5				

Source: Direccion General de Planificacion del Trabajo y el Empleo (DGPTE), Encuesta de hogares: empleo y desempleo (July 1977-83, 1985-87; March 1984). a Involuntarily employed for less than 47 hours per week; b Employed for at least 47 hours per week but earning less than minimum wage; c Adjusted 1987 data ; d 1981-82; e 1981-87

pensate for reductions in the employment and real earnings of their heads and other members as well as for declining state subsidies[2] (Table 3; see Fields, 1988; Gindling and Berry, 1991; Lavell, 1988; Trejos, 1989). The annual pace of labor-force growth, however, varied markedly and seems to have been slower than during preceding years. Studies need to assess how much of this yearly variation and net increase reflected changes in the economy's growth rate, its sectorial and spatial composition, the state's fiscal and monetary policies, and the population's structure by class, gender, age, and household organization. In comparing labor-force responses by country, geographic area, and social class, relevant too are cultural expectations concerning living standards, job conditions, and the employment of women, youths, and the elderly (e.g., Bonilla, 1990; Jatobá, 1989; Menjívar Larín and Pérez Sáinz, 1991; Roberts, 1989; Smith and Tardanico, 1987; Tardanico, 1991; Ward, 1990).

As expected, employment did not fall. Rather, it increased which it did virtually every year, though more slowly than during the pre-crisis years. Moreover, unemployment soared as the laborforce grew much faster than employment[3] (Tables 3, 5); and, again as expected, an increasing share of employment consisted of downgraded jobs. Yet, contrary to expectations, job growth occurred in not only the informal economy but the formal economy as well. While the expansion of formal employment was unexpected, that of informal employment may well have been slower than anticipated (see Lungo, et al., 1991; Trejos, 1991). Evidence of downgrading in general, and informalization in particular, included the period's sharp upturns in visible and invisible underemployment as well as part-time employment in general.[4] It also included declining public-sector employment and average real wages, as well as the concentration of employment growth in services and nonwaged jobs[5] (Tables 3, 9–13; Tables 4–16, page 86*ff.*)

Research has yet to document the interrelations of firm size, occupational structure, formal and informal employment, earnings, and unemployment across San José's industrial sectors. It is unclear how much of the growth of informal employment involved jobs either linked through subcontracting chains to formal firms in manufacturing and other industry sectors or focused on the provision of petty goods and services (Tables 1, 4, 9–11, 13; Lungo, et al., 1991; PREALC, 1984; Trejos, 1989, 1991; see also Portes, et al., 1989; Roberts, 1989; Ward, 1990). As output in manufacturing and other sectors turned downward, many formal firms likely cheapened their costs and enhanced their flexibility by doing more informal employment subcontracting. At the same time, the growth of "survival," or subsistence, jobs in the provision of petty goods and services (which occupy the lowest rung in terms of skill, productivity, and pay) may have stemmed as much or more from the income-earning needs of households as from consumer demand for cheaper goods and services. Both the subcontracting and subsistence modes of informal job growth were limited by the general downturn in market demand for goods and services, as reflected in the city's rising level of unemployment. They may well have faced cultural constraints as well, given the population's high expectations concerning state regulation of employment and state provision of social services. The class, gender, age, and intra-household distribution of employment options, and their ramifications for socio-spatial structure and socio-political consciousness, is a key research issue.

In 1979–82 nonwaged jobs grew faster than waged jobs in services and manufacturing alike, with construction—plagued by the highest rate of unemployment—suffering a net loss of both types of jobs. Not surprisingly, services continued to have the highest rate of employment, while rising to first in the rate of visible underemployment. Likewise, not surprising, is that manufacturing continued to have the highest rate of waged employment. Yet, manufacturing rose to first in the rate of invisible underemployment, which, combined with its faster growth in nonwaged than waged jobs, was a sign of the sector's short-term restructuring. According to nationwide data, earnings fell most in the swollen informal sector and least in the shrunken public sector, as wage inequality among workers worsened [6] (Tables 4, 7–11; Gindling and Berry, 1991; Trejos, 1989; see footnote 2). This wage pattern is still another trend in line with expectations. Together, the evidence points to more pronounced employment inequalities throughout the formal and informal economies. Job growth seems to have been moderately faster in the informal than the formal economy.

Thus, associated with economic crisis was laborforce expansion, heightened joblessness, not fewer jobs but the modestly faster growth of jobs in the informal than the formal economy, apparently increased job inequalities in both the informal and formal economy, and a more pronounced pay decrease among informal than formal workers. This profile seemed to have taken shape as many of the job market's previous members became either unemployed or more marginally employed in the formal economy, the informal economy, or both. It seemed also to have taken shape as the job market's newly mobilized members tended either not to find work or to find low-end formal and/or informal work. The expansion of the laborforce as the economy contracted was an important factor, therefore, in the swelling rates of unemployment and underemployment. Sectorial differences in unemployment and informal employment call attention to linkages between formal and informal labor, including their variation across the economy (Menjívar Larín and Pérez Sáinz, 1991; Peattie, 1990; Portes, et al., 1989; Roberts, 1989; Ward, 1990).

Gender, Age, and Labor-Force Participation, 1979–82

What were the roles of gender, age, and household organization in shaping the population's responses to the economic crisis? Unfortunately, the published tabular data do not permit the analysis of longitudinal shifts in laborforce participation by individual and household income, industry sector, occupation, education, and household composition. Furthermore, they say nothing about the participation of children under 12-years old. The data do permit, however, the analysis of broad changes in laborforce participation by gender and age for those 12 years of age and older. This allows the framing of hypotheses for case study and comparative study. Regarding such hypotheses, the literature previously reviewed leads us to predict a general upswing in the rate of participation punctuated by substantial class, gender, and age differences.

The data, to repeat, do not address social class. Nevertheless, it should be mentioned that, according to the literature, participation rates should have increased most among those households with the least assets and hit hardest by losses in the following: job and non-job earnings; direct and indirect government subsidies; and other forms of nonmonetary income. Yet, measuring the sum of the economic impact on households, not to mention its relative severity by social class, is far from simple. Moreover, the literature suggests a number of qualifications to its core prediction. These begin with the consequences for household responses of class expectations concerning standards of living and class perceptions concerning the magnitude of economic losses, including whether setbacks are judged as short or long term. They also encompass secular trends and class variation in factors, such as, attitudes about gender and age roles; the constraints and opportunities presented by household organization and community networks; and workforce experience and anticipated returns in entering the labor market.

Leaving class issues aside, the literature predicts a downswing in the participation rates of primary earners—predominantly males of intermediate age—owing to the reduction in suitable employment. Conversely, it predicts an upswing in the participation rates of secondary earners—predominantly females but also youth and the elderly as a whole—as households strived to offset diminished earnings and subsidies. The literature anticipates that employment in general, and informal employment in particular, should have grown faster for secondary earners; that unemployment should have grown faster for primary earners.

In 1979–82, the rate of labor-market participation for the population of 12 years old and more rose. As elsewhere in Latin America, however, this increase was less than what may have been predicted (Tables 3, 5–6, 15; see Fields, 1988;

Horton, et al., 1990; Jatobá, 1989; Portes, 1989). A contrast with predictions is that, using 1978 as a baseline, relative growth in the participation rate was nearly equal for males and females (4.0% versus 3.8%), while employment grew somewhat faster among males (2.7% vs 2.3%).

Data limitations restrict the analysis of age rates of workforce participation to the 1980s (Table 15). The 1980–82 age pattern for males largely conforms to expectations. A measure of economic crisis is that the participation rate decreased for 30–59 year olds, the principal income-earners, while increasing for the oldest segments and the youngest adults. The sole departure from expectations is that the participation rate decreased for 12–19 year olds, probably a consequence of their disadvantages of skill and experience in a crowded job market.

The age pattern of females in the labor market also generally fits predictions (Table 15). The participation rate decreased for the female group of initially highest rank, the 30–39 year olds, while generally increasing for middle-age and older women as well as the youngest adults. As with males, insufficient experience and skill appear to have hampered the participation of the 12–19 year-old females. To the degree that laborforce entry for other females was less burdensome to households, this situation was possibly reinforced by added domestic responsibilities for female adolescents.[7]

Summarizing these trends, proportional growth in the rate of laborforce participation was essentially the same for males and females, though annual employment growth was faster for males. In diverging from expectations, this short-term pattern is of particular interest because it interrupts the long-range pattern of faster gains in female than male rates of participation and employment. As such, it points to comparisons of how households and labor markets interact under differing economic conditions.

The focus of the participation upswing for males and females was, as anticipated, the upper end of the age spectrum and the youngest adults. Another anticipated finding is that unemployment expanded fastest among males, whose rate of unemployment came to exceed that of females. Likewise, as predicted, involuntary part-time work grew fastest among females, whose rate of visible underemployment surpassed that of males. Contrary to predictions, work for less than the minimum wage among the full-time employed grew fastest among males, whose rate of invisible underemployment remained less than that of females. Evidence on unemployment and underemployment shows that the disadvantages of young and old job seekers in general overlapped with those of the newly mobilized females, though age data do not address underemployment (Tables 3, 5, 6). The escalating rate of unemployment for all groups—perhaps the definitive sign of labor-market crisis throughout Latin America (Portes, 1989)—is likely the main reason why laborforce participation rose by less than what may have been expected. Another possible reason is cultural, given the extent of Costa Rica's long-standing reliance on state-provided social welfare.

Also expected is that the growth of male and particularly female employment was most rapid in nonwaged jobs (Table 12). Given the equivocal evidence on the growth rates of underemployment by gender, this evidence seems to say that informalization was fastest among females. The data on waged jobs suggest a degree of female gain and male loss in formal employment. Overall, the female earnings disadvantage worsened (Gindling, 1989).

Labor Force and Employment

Were the labor-market shifts of the crisis years short-term in nature? Or did they endure as part of a larger reorganization process? These questions are essential to gauging San José's labor-market developments under conditions of structural adjustment, as well as to framing them in comparative perspective. Insofar as the economy's upturn reversed the labor-market shifts of the crisis years, at least three sets of change should have occurred. First, the economy's recovery should have reduced the laborforce's rate of growth, based on upturns in the employment and incomes of primary earners as well as in state subsidies. Second, job growth should have been faster in the formal than the informal economy as production revived in major enterprises. And third, not only should real earnings have increased but they should have increased faster for formal and than informal workers. This would have been based on resurgent market demand for skilled workers, coupled with the market surplus of unskilled workers.

In 1983–87, growth of San José's laborforce did in fact decelerate [8] (Table 3). As in 1979–82, though, the period's trend encompassed pronounced growth fluctuations. While standard-of-living indicators substantially improved, among the ones that remained below their levels of the late 1970s were per capita production, average real wages, and the state's real spending on social welfare. We can therefore expect that a greater portion of households than before the crisis continued to face pressure to mobilize extra income-earners. This was particularly true inasmuch as an increased percentage of households consisted of Central American refugees [9] (ECLAC, 1989; Ramírez, 1989).

Still, the labor market improved in terms of the availability as well as the composition of employment. [10] Job expansion became faster, combining with the laborforce's slowed increase to push unemployment below its pre-crisis rate. As average real wages pushed upward, the growth of waged jobs accelerated and the percentage of family employment decreased. Reflecting the dynamism of Costa Rica compared with other Central American economies, manufacturing emerged as the new focus of employment growth, with former leader services dropping to last place. Meanwhile, visible and invisible underemployment decreased (Tables 3–10).

This pattern indicates a reversal of what occurred during the crisis years, including a reduction in San José's proportion of informal employment and low-end formal employment. By 1987, however, a number of countervailing signs appeared (Tables 3–13). After rising for several years, average real wages fell sharply (due to the combination of price inflation and government wage policy; see Gindling and Berry, 1991; Lungo, et al., 1991). The downward trend in invisible underemployment also seems to have reversed itself, with its rate nesting above those of 1977–81. An apparent spurt of expansion pushed the post-crisis growth rate of nonwaged jobs at least to its level of 1979–82. Simultaneously, the post-crisis growth rate of nonwaged jobs exceeded that of waged jobs. This imbalance seems to have occurred not only in construction and services but, to a much lesser extent, in manufacturing as well. Manufacturing remained highest among all industry sectors in the rate of invisible underemployment, while tying construction with the highest rate of unemployment. And in spite of a decline, the percentage of employed population working either voluntarily or involuntarily part time remained higher than in 1977. In this regard, possibly a larger segment of workers than before the economic crisis either sought or resigned themselves to part-time employment. If so, they would have depressed officially measured underemployment without actually reducing the prevalence of informal work and marginal kinds of formal work.

At least through 1985, nationwide wages recovered faster among informal than formal workers (Gindling and Berry, 1991). This trend not only reflects the impact of inflation and the state's wage-setting policies on formal wages. Regarding informal wages, it may also reflect the labor-market withdrawal of the least skilled secondary workers, together with revived demand from consumers and formal enterprises for informal goods and services. Conceivably this wage pattern included expanded demand in the informal economy for subcontracting brokers, employers, and skilled workers (see Lungo, et al., 1991; Trejos, 1991). This would have occurred as a percentage of informal production shifted from the petty services and goods of subsistence jobs toward the industrial activities of jobs created by economic recovery (e.g., informal subcontracting by formal manufacturing firms). As such, the pattern points to the relative attractiveness of informal employment in certain industry sectors or subsectors and certain occupations, such as, some spheres of manufacturing and informal employer or skilled informal employee (see Portes, et al., 1989; PREALC, 1984; Roberts, 1989; on gender consequences, see Ward, 1990). Nationwide data appear to show that the distribution of wages among workers, which became more equitable in 1983–86, became more inequitable for the poorest workers in 1987 [11] (Gindling and Berry, 1991; note 2).

In sum, during these years of economic stabilization and recovery San José's labor market improved but with significant limitations. For instance, the rate of job growth quickened yet the growth rate of nonwaged employment seems to have kept up with or surpassed that of waged employment. The proportion of the workforce with part-time employment remained higher than it was during the pre-crisis years. Average real wages, after climbing for several years, dropped markedly. And nationally, wage inequality apparently worsened for the lowest decile of earners. Such trends suggest that the economy's lingering weaknesses and nascent structural changes were manifested not in a high level of officially measured unemployment but in a pattern of increasing employment inequality.

Finally, national evidence of greater wage recovery in informal than formal jobs, compared with the earnings advantages of the latter during the economic crisis, cautions us against reifying the distinction between the two employment categories [12] (see, e.g., Bromley and Birkbeck, 1988). Such evidence stresses the intersection of the fluid, shifting boundaries of these categories with changes in Costa Rica's institutional matrix, which in turn intersects with the world-scale dynamics of the debt crisis, commodity markets, investment, and aid.[13]

At issue is how these intersecting levels, including the evolving structure of Costa Rican state/class relations, determine which economic sectors and social groups win and lose in structural adjustment. Likewise, at issue is what forms their gains and setbacks take. For example, to what degree is the employment impact of structural adjustment restricted to the formal or informal economy or spread across the two sectors (e.g., the assembly of an industrial product in one sector but not the other; small-firm but not large-firm assembly of the product in the formal economy)? If spread across the two sectors, does this impact take the same forms or different forms in each (e.g., changes in the social relations and technical organization of work; more or less work hours, intensity, instability, earnings, or benefits; shifts in the spatial location of employment)? Does the class, gender, age, and migrant/nonmigrant distribution of gains and losses vary more between or within the formal and informal economy? And what are the implications of such short-term outcomes for long-term social and spatial transformations (e.g., migration; household organization; class location of residence and employment; sociopolitical consciousness; solidarity or disunity of household, community, and class)?

Gender, Age, and Labor-Force Participation, 1983–87

Consistent with the above discussion, a reversion to San José's gender and age patterns of the pre-crisis years would have involved three basic changes. First, the rates of laborforce participation and employment growth would have increased among primary earners—mainly intermediate-age males—as market demand recovered for the most experienced and skilled workers. Second, the rates of participation and employment growth would have decreased among secondary earners—mainly females but also the youngest and oldest age groups at large—as households no longer required that they be employed. Third, the gender and age profile of unemployment and informal employment would have reverted toward its pre-crisis shape. This shift would have stemmed from both improved employment opportunities for primary earners and the labor-market withdrawal of secondary earners. Not to be neglected, however, are the laborforce consequences of secular changes among females in school attendance, household position (i.e., marriage/divorce, fertility, authority), and employment options. Insofar as such changes continued, even the economy's recovery to pre-crisis form would not have simply re-established the labor market's previous gender contours.

In 1987, the city's rate of laborforce participation was virtually the same as in 1982, with that of males ending lower but that of females higher than their 1982 levels (Table 15). In striking contrast to the crisis period, employment grew substantially faster for females than males [14] (Table 3). Whether this shift represented economic improvement over the crisis years—as well as advances in the labor-market position of women—depends on the emerging profile of female participation by age and employment structure.

Conforming to predictions, a comparison of 1982 and 1987 participation rates reveals a net increase for 20–49 year-old males. Yet, the downward slide continued for another age group of primary earners, the 50–59 year olds, as it expectedly did for the age groups of secondary earners. On the female side net increase involved, as anticipated, the 30–49 year olds, a category including primary earners. Unexpectedly, though, the rate also increased for females 60 years old and above. Net decrease generally occurred, as projected, for the rest of the female age groups.

To summarize, San José's rate of laborforce participation in 1987 was virtually equal to that in 1982. The overall rate of male laborforce participation declined, with increases centering—as predicted—on the groups of primary employment age. The overall rate of female participation rose, with increases also centering—as predicted—on the groups of primary employment age. But a possible sign of persistent problems in the economy is that female increases encompassed the elderly as well. Another such sign is that employment increased more rapidly for females than males, though continued secular changes undoubtably shared some of the responsibility in the broader social position of women.

In terms of the predictions, two measures of economic recovery are that the male rate of unemployment tumbled below its pre-crisis level and below the female rate. A less sanguine finding, however, is that the rate of unemployment dropped for all male and female age groups with one pronounced exception: it continued to rise for 40–59 year-old females. This rise may be linked in part to the enhanced laborforce participation that is rooted in the long-term social realignment of gender relations. But the economic conditions of crisis and adjustment seem to be at play as well, causing lingering pressure on households to earn supplementary incomes. Reinforcing this view is the fact that, while underemployment plunged for males and females alike, invisible underemployment for males came to exceed the female level. Perhaps most telling of all was that the invisible underemployment for males reportedly remained above its level for 1980 (Tables 1, 5, 6).

A sign of robust economic recovery is that, compared with 1980–82, waged jobs grew considerably faster for males and females alike. Nonetheless, still another countervailing sign is that the growth of nonwaged jobs for males speeded up relative to 1980–82 and continued to exceed that of waged jobs (Tables 3, 11, 12, 14). A complementary trend surfaces for females if, in controlling for the impact of the 1983's apparent laborforce withdrawal of a high portion of secondary earners, we restrict our attention to 1984–87. In so doing we see that, on the positive side, the growth of female nonwaged jobs plunged relative to 1980–82 (26.7% vs. 12.2%). On the negative side, however, females continued to experience higher growth in nonwagied than waged jobs (12.2% vs. 4.2%). And while the female earnings disadvantage decreased in 1983-87, the latter year was one of increased male/female inequality (Gindling, 1989; Lungo, et al., 1991).

Adjusting downward for the 1987's data problems, what emerges is that non-waged employment grew comparably or faster than waged employment for males and females alike, and that the growth of nonwaged employment possibly accelerated for males but not females. Together with gender and age, evidence on participation, unemployment, and invisible underemployment, the scenario appears to be one of economic recovery combined with a process of labor-market restructuring. This process included some degree of informalization and increased inequality more generally of not only female but also male employment.

Long-Term Trends

What were the consequences of the short-term dynamics of economic crisis and structural adjustment for long-term shifts in San José's labor market? Changes in the city's labor market unfolded as both average real wages and the government's real expenditures on social welfare underwent net decline. Yet, they also unfolded as, following the crisis years, the Costa Rican state fostered significant expansion in export-assembly manufacturing, tourism, and nontraditional agriculture. Against this backdrop, the growth rate of employment slightly outpaced that of the workforce; and by 1987, unemployment and visible underemployment dipped below their rates of the late 1970s. But invisible underemployment remained similar to, or higher than, its rates of 1978–81, and taking into account 1987's data problems, nonwaged employment either modestly increased or maintained its share of total employment (Tables 3–5, 9–11).

So far, we see a reduced rate of unemployment and an augmented or stable percentage of informal employment. In contrast to the rest of Central America, this picture is one not of sweeping transformation but of smaller scale, uneven change. Perhaps most striking is that the growth of informal employment seems to have been much slower than in other major Central American cities (Menjívar Larín and Pérez Sáinz, 1991). And while the growth rates of laborforce participation and employment were faster for females than males, the net changes for women were modest (Tables 3, 15, 16).

Given that the economy's restructuring gained momentum in the late 1980s, the evidence suggests an incremental process of labor-market transition whose features will crystallize over the long run (see Lungo, et al., 1991). Two intriguing signs of such a transition were San José's shifting patterns of invisible underemployment by gender and laborforce participation by middle-age and elderly women (Tables 5, 12, 14, 15).

The 1980–87 surge in invisible underemployment for males contrasted with its considerable decline for females. On the one hand, this pattern implies that a saturated and restructuring labor market depressed the earnings of some males by lowering the pay of their previously held jobs or by pushing them into more marginal jobs. On the other hand, it implies that a growing number of females withdrew from the labor market for reasons of economic improvement or discouragement, and/or that females began displacing males in some segments of the employment and earnings spectrum. Such displacement could have occurred, for example, inasmuch as the composition of manufacturing employment shifted toward low-wage, female labor in assembly activities (see Lungo, et al., 1991; Trejos, 1991). Job growth for males and females alike was more rapid in nonwaged than waged employment. Both kinds of job growth were more rapid for females (Table 12), a trend probably linked not only to economic crisis and structural adjustment but also to long-range shifts in the social standing of women.

Consistent with Costa Rica's secular trend, in 1978–87 San José's rate of female participation grew more in absolute and relative terms than that of males. With respect to laborforce participation by age, a difference between males and females is striking: between 1980 and 1987 the rate of participation decreased for all male age groups except the 20–39 year olds but increased for all female age groups except the 12–19 year olds (Table 15). The degree of seven-year change in the participation rates of females ascended from the lower-adult to upper-age categories starting with a large labor-market group, the 20–29 year olds (2.1%), and peaking with a small group, the 70+ year olds (114.3%). This pattern could simply be an artifact of the comparatively small-size and minimal laborforce participation of the older female age groups as well as of 1987's revised survey. If it is not such an artifact, then the questions concern how such behavior related to structural shifts in the economy and secular changes in the social position of women. They also concern how it varied by social class and household organization.

Clearly, San José's labor-market trajectory featured the incorporation of females, which, if the data are correct, involved a particularly high rate of growth in the participation of middle-age and elderly women. The data do not tell us whether economic crisis and structural adjustment accelerated the longer-term upward trend in female participation or altered the relatively stagnant trend of males. The data do say that, comparing 1979–82 and 1983–87, average yearly growth increased in the female laborforce, as that of males fell. The above considerations also apply in comparing average annual employment growth for the two periods which increased more for females than males [15] (Table 3). Studies need to examine the extent to which economic crisis and/or structural adjustment contributed to such patterns not merely by displacing male breadwinners but also by influencing pre-existing trends in years of schooling, marriage/divorce, fertility, and household organization.

We do not know what portion of the city's expanded nonwaged employment for males and females involved subsistence jobs. For Central America in general, as well as for much of Latin America, it could be hypothesized that such jobs have formed the core of informalization (e.g., Menjívar Larín and Pérez Sáinz, 1991). For San José, however, it is likely that the portion of survival jobs decreased under structural adjustment. This decrease would have taken place inasmuch as secondary earners left the labor market and as the revived economy's leading sectors—such as, export-assembly manufacturing—generated an increasing share of informal employment. Along these lines, "family workers" diminished as a percentage of the employed laborforce; at the same time, the percentage of nonwaged employment apparently rose not just in construction and services but in manufacturing as well (Tables 9–13; see Trejos, 1991).

In any case, a key measure of growing labor-market inequality is that even in manufacturing—the sector where salaried employment grew fastest—job growth appears to have been most rapid in nonwaged employment. Fitting this pattern, the national distribution of wages among workers seems to have become more unequal, with the highest income decile of workers apparently being the only winner [16] (Gindling and Berry, 1991). The nature of sectoral changes in the intersection of formal and informal employment with occupational structure and earnings inequality merits study (see Trejos, 1991).

Finally, from 1977 to 1986 San José's laborforce decreased from 30.2% to 28.6% of Costa Rica's total laborforce. Simultaneously, the city's employment remained at about 28.5% of the nation's total employment. If the data referred to metropolitan San José as economically defined, they would possibly capture a trend of growing concentration of the nation's laborforce and employment. This would not be inconsistent, however, with the long-standing trend (e.g., Lungo, et al., 1991). A basic issue is how the locational tendencies of nontraditional export production may be influencing the socio-spatial dynamics of economy and labor market at the metropolitan and national levels (see Lavell, 1988; Lungo, et al., 1991; Portes, 1989; Roberts, 1989; Smith and Tardanico, 1987). These dynamics center on the evolving territorial pattern of social inequality as expressed in the spatial interplay of investment, production, employment, migration, housing, and services.

Conclusion

Central America is a regional loser in the contemporary world economy based on the combination of local underdevelopment, local strife, and global reorganization. Costa Rica, however, has decisively outperformed its neighbors in resisting marginalization in a restructuring world economy. The comparative performance of Costa Rica seems to be rooted in a complex of features: its stable, social-democratic state; superior economic infrastructure; and, during the regional strife of the 1980s, strategic importance to the United States. [17]

This complex of features appears to have manifested itself as well in the performance of San José's labor market in 1979–87 under conditions of economic crisis and structural adjustment. What occurred in the city's labor market was not an abrupt, massive reordering but rather a process of uneven change. This process was undoubtedly mild relative to the norm among Central America's other capital cities (e.g., Lungo, 1990; Menjívar Larín and Pérez Sáinz, 1991). The fact remains that the 1983–87 recovery from the economic crisis involved not only a heavier fiscal burden and still reduced public services for most of San José's population but it also seems to have involved increased rates of laborforce participation for middle-age and elderly women; increased and restructuring job inequalities within and between the formal and informal economies; and regressive shifts in average real wages and wage inequality. This pattern points to the gradual uncoupling of Costa Rica's pre-crisis linkage of economic growth with improving social welfare.

This paper has raised a host of questions for future research. For example, how do San José's gender and age patterns of laborforce participation of 1979–87 compare to those of previous periods, as well as to those associated with the continued unfolding of structural adjustment? How have such patterns been linked to shifts in state policy, the composition of the city's economy, and the city's economic connections with the nation and world? How have they been related to population trends of growth, age, gender, school enrollment, marriage/divorce, fertility, household organization, and migration? How have gender and age participation varied by class, occupation, economic sector, household organization, and access to programs of education and social welfare? How have earnings been distributed by class, economic sector, occupation, education, gender, and age? Regarding household, community, and class, what do the above dynamics mean for the socio-spatial bases of identity, interests, organization, and action? And what are the implications of the latter processes, not only for local politics and economic development but for extra-local and transnational flows of capital?

These questions lead, in turn, to comparative research on the labor markets of the cities and regions of not only Costa Rica but Central America at large. Central America's official leadership is attempting to establish political stability, revive its common market, and sign free-trade agreements with more developed countries. Even insofar as these efforts are successful, major questions concern the extent and terms of the incorporation of Central America's urban and rural zones into a reorganizing worldwide pattern of investment, technology, production, and trade. The leading economic zones of Costa Rica are the area's most likely candidates to gain a reasonable foothold. Yet, especially given the initiation of more profound austerity measures in 1990, it is unclear how much Costa Rica's post-1982 recovery will translate into enduring development benefits (CEPAS, 1990; La Nacion,

1991a, b; Lungo, et al., 1991; see also Castells and Laserna, 1989; Deere, 1990; Gereffi, 1989). In any event, the consequences of local conditions and global restructuring for Central America's labor markets—and thus for its processes of inequality, conflict, and migration—stand at the center of the research agenda on the area's urban and regional transformations.

Tables 4–16

Table 4
Unemployment and Underemployment
by Economic Sector: Annual Rates

	1978	1982	1987
Unemployment[a]			
Industry	5.8	13.0	4.7
Construction	2.5	20.2	4.7
Services	3.8	14.5	3.9
	1980	**1982**	**1986**
Visible Underemp.			
Industry	15.1	16.9	9.9
Construction	5.9	17.2	5.2
Services	13.6	23.3	10.3
Invisible Underemployment			
Industry	7.5	40.1	9.9
Construction	4.9	34.7	5.2
Services	8.9	22.0	6.9

Source: DGPTE (July 1978, 1980, 1982, 1987).
[a]Excludes first-time job seekers

Table 6
Unemployment by Gender and Age: Annual Rates

	1980	1982	1987
Male	4.9	11.8	4.2
12–19	14.1	27.4	10.8
20–39	4.2	11.5	2.6
40–59	1.9	5.3	3.2
60+	2.8	7.5	3.6
Female	5.1	10.1	5.9
12–19	15.1	24.4	9.7
20–39	3.7	10.0	6.1
40–59	1.3	3.6	4.4
60+	N.A.	N.A.	7.2

Source: DGPTE (July 1980, 1982, 1987).

Table 5

Unemployment and Underemployment by Gender: Annual Rates

	1977	1978	1979	1980	1981	1982	1983	1984	1985	1986	1987
Unemployment	5.5	5.4	5.2	5.0	8.3	11.3	8.5	8.5	7.4	6.1	4.8
Male	4.1	4.5	4.5	4.9	8.2	11.8	8.8	8.8	6.9	5.9	4.2
Female	6.4	7.2	6.7	5.1	8.5	10.1	8.0	8.0	8.4	6.5	5.9
Visible Under [a]	7.7	10.2	15.9	12.9	12.4	21.3	18.6	18.6	14.8	10.4	7.5
Male	—	—	—	13.1	12.6	20.9	19.0	19.0	13.7	8.9	7.6
Female	—	—	—	12.4	12.1	22.1	17.8	17.8	16.9	13.3	7.2
Invisible Under [b]	2.3	8.4	7.5	6.6	6.7	21.4	11.7	11.7	10.2	7.7	9.3 [c]
Male	—	—	—	4.7	5.5	23.7	10.0	10.0	7.1	5.9	9.4 [c]
Female	—	—	—	14.9	13.6	33.2	22.8	22.8	15.4	11.0	9.0 [c]

Source: DGPTE (July 1977-83, 1985-87; March 1984)

a Involuntarily working less than 47 hours per week; percentage of total employment

b Working 47 hours or more per week but earning less than minimum wage; percentage of total salaried employment

c Original data recalculated as percentage of total salaried employment

Table 7

Employment by Institutional Sector: Annual Growth Rates

	1978	1979	1980	1981	1982	1983	1984	1985	1986	1987[a]	79-82	83-87	79-87
Public Sector	10.4	-1.2	3.1	1.8	-6.3	10.8	6.5	5.7	4.6	-.8	-0.7	3.9	1.9
Private Sector	4.8	2.4	5.1	-2.8	8.8	0.8	1.8	8.6	0.9	15.6	3.4	5.5	4.6

Source: DGPTE (July 1978-83, 1985-87; March 1984).

a Adjusted 1987 data

Table 9

Total Wage and Nonwage Employment by Industry Sector: Annual Growth Rates

	1978	1979	1980	1981	1982	1983	1984	1985	1986	1987[a]	79-82	83-87	79-87
Manufacturing	3.7	6.6	0.0	-4.0	3.4	8.9	-2.5	3.5	11.8	14.7	1.5	7.3	4.7
Wage	3.2	2.5	2.7	-4.2	4.0	6.5	-1.3	0.1	14.0	16.5	1.3	7.1	4.5
Non-wage	5.9	25.3	-10.2	-3.3	-0.8	19.4	-7.1	18.1	4.1	7.6	2.8	8.4	5.9
Construction	21.1	-8.0	-2.3	-26.3	15.9	-18.3	0.7	-4.2	27.3	26.2	-5.2	6.3	3.0
Wage	13.6	-1.3	-4.6	-25.3	13.2	-18.6	-8.5	-8.0	53.5	1.6	-4.4	4.0	2.6
Non-wage	50.5	27.6	7.0	-31.0	26.5	-17.2	31.8	4.7	-27.2	134.0	-6.3	25.2	11.2
Services	7.1	-0.9	8.2	1.3	3.6	2.7	1.5	10.9	-3.4	5.3	3.1	3.4	3.2
Wage	6.0	-0.2	9.5	0.0	0.6	3.9	0.9	13.7	-4.0	-4.2	2.5	2.1	2.2
Non-wage	11.9	-3.9	2.6	7.2	16.4	-5.0	3.8	0.0	-0.5	46.2	5.6	8.9	7.4

Source: DGPTE (July 1978-83, 1985-87; March 1984)

a Adjusted 1987 data

Table 8
Employment by Institutional Sector

	1978	1982	1987
Public Sector	24.8%	22.2%	20.6%
Private Sector	75.2	77.8	79.4

Source: DGPTE (July 1978, 1982, 1987).

Table 10
Employment by Nonagricultural Industry Sector

	1978	1982	1987
Manufacturing	24.5%	24.1%	27.5%
Construction	9.3	6.6	6.8
Services	66.2	69.3	65.7

Source: DGPTE (July 1978, 1982, 1987).

Table 13
Nonwage Employment as a Percentage of
Total Employment by Industry Sector

	1978	1982	1987
Manufacturing	18.9%	18.9%	19.7%
Construction	21.1	26.5	34.5
Services	19.4	21.3	23.5

Source: DGPTE (July 1978, 1982, 1987).

Table 14
Nonwage Employment as a Percentage
of Total Employment by Gender

	1980	1982	1987
Male	21.1%	21.7%	25.5
Female	14.8	20.3	17.1

Source: DGPTE (July 1980, 1982, 1987).

Table 11

Nonwage Employment as a Percentage of Total Employment

	1977	1978	1979	1980	1981	1982	1983	1984	1985	1986	1987
Total	19.3	19.4	20.0	19.1	19.7	21.2	20.7	20.8	20.2	19.3	22.6
Self-empl.	—	14.4	13.4	11.3	13.2	13.7	15.2	16.3	15.4	14.9	17.3
Employer	—	3.9	5.0	5.8	4.1	5.6	4.5	3.9	3.9	3.0	4.3
Family empl.	1.9	1.1	1.5	1.9	2.3	2.0	1.0	0.6	1.2	1.3	1.0

Source: DGPTE (July 1977-83, 1985-87; March 1984).

Table 12

Wage and Nonwage Employment by Gender: Annual Growth Rates

	1978	1979	1980	1981	1982	1983	1984	1985	1986	1987[a]	79-82	83-87	79-87
Wage	6.0	0.6	5.9	-2.0	3.3	1.8	0.3	8.6	3.0	4.9	2.0	3.7	2.9
Male	—	—	—	-2.8	2.7	0.1	0.0	8.5	5.5	2.9	-0.5[b]	3.4	2.4[c]
Female	—	—	—	-0.3	4.5	5.3	0.6	9.0	-1.2	8.5	2.1[b]	4.4	3.8[c]
Nonwage	7.5	4.3	-0.7	2.1	13.5	-1.4	1.1	4.5	-2.9	28.3	4.8	5.9	5.4
Male	—	—	—	3.6	-0.2	15.7	0.0	3.5	-4.4	26.3	1.7[b]	8.2	6.4[c]
Female	—	—	—	-2.2	55.5	-35.1	4.6	8.0	2.0	34.2	26.7[b]	2.7	9.6[c]

Source: DGPTE (July 1978-83, 1985-87; March 1984).

a Adjusted 1987 data; b 1981-82; c 1981-87

a Involuntarily working less than 47 hours per week; percentage of total employment
b Working 47 hours or more per week but earning less than minimum wage; percentage of total salaried employment
c Original data recalculated as percentage of total salaried employment

Table 15
Labor-Force Participation by Gender and Age: Annual Rates [a]

	1979	1980	1981	1982	1983	1984	1985	1986	1987
Male	—	50.4	48.6	52.0	50.1	49.3	50.1	50.4	51.2
Female	—	22.7	23.6	24.4	23.6	23.1	24.7	23.1	25.8
Total	35.6	36.1	35.9	38.1	36.4	35.6	36.9	36.1	38.2
	1979	1980	1981	1982	1983	1984	1985	1986	1987
Male									
12-19	—	39.7	33.9	37.2	34.3	29.6	29.7	29.7	32.1
20-29	—	88.0	84.6	88.9	84.7	84.7	86.8	84.1	90.1
30-39	—	98.4	95.0	95.9	97.6	96.5	98.3	95.3	98.6
40-49	—	97.3	95.0	94.8	93.9	92.8	95.7	96.9	94.7
50-59	—	98.7	88.1	86.5	86.2	83.8	85.0	80.6	81.5
60-69	—	50.3	58.8	51.3	50.0	51.1	48.7	49.3	44.0
70+	—	22.4	17.3	28.6	23.6	24.3	21.7	13.6	17.8
Female									
12-19	—	21.5	16.9	17.4	21.4	16.0	17.0	12.7	17.2
20-29	—	44.3	45.1	48.5	44.8	44.1	47.1	45.2	47.5
30-39	—	46.9	46.8	45.9	42.2	47.9	51.6	44.4	49.3
40-49	—	33.4	38.7	34.2	42.3	35.2	39.3	40.5	38.9
50-59	—	18.1	23.5	27.0	24.3	23.0	21.3	23.6	26.2
60-69	—	11.1	12.6	8.3	9.3	11.2	7.5	10.3	17.3
70+	—	2.8	4.4	3.5	2.2	2.9	3.3	2.0	6.0

Source: DGPTE (July 1979-83, 1985-87; March 1984).
a As a percentage of total population by gender

Table 16
Age Structure of Labor Force by Gender

	1980		1982		1987	
	Males	Females	Males	Females	Males	Females
12-19	14.6%	16.7%	12.8%	11.6%	9.6%	10.7%
20-29	31.5	38.1	35.5	40.3	34.8	35.6
30-39	22.3	24.3	22.5	25.8	26.1	29.8
40-49	15.6	12.6	15.0	12.3	16.0	14.3
50-59	10.9	5.5	8.7	7.8	9.7	5.9
60-69	4.0	2.3	3.9	1.7	2.7	2.8
70+	1.1	0.5	1.6	0.6	1.1	0.9

Source: DGPTE (July 1980, 1982, 1987).

Notes

1. The urbanization of Costa Rica's population, which exceeds the Central American average, has proceeded as follows: 1975, 42.2%; 1980, 46.0%; 1985, 49.8%; 1990, 53.6% (IICA/FLACSO, 1991:14).

2. The data on average real wages do not include the job earnings of self-employed workers or other workers not directly covered by social security. Thus, they include neither the lowest-earning workers nor some relatively prosperous segments of the laborforce (see e.g., Portes, et al., 1989).

   Unless otherwise noted, the data reported are from the "metropolitan San José" subsample of DGPTE (1977–87); data for the years before 1977 are either unavailable or not comparable. Based on a 1% population sample, the 1977–87 data cover the population residing in households in metropolitan San José as administratively defined. The data do not include the surrounding zones that have become integral parts of the evolving urban-regional economy (e.g., Lungo, et al., 1991). Though DGPTE does not report the location of employment, officially-defined residents of San José who work elsewhere are classified as part of the city's employed laborforce.

   Among the limitations of such survey data is that they do not capture the fluidity of employment (and unemployment) in the underdeveloped world. This problem involves the prevalence of unpaid work, the frequent changing of jobs, and the simultaneous holding of multiple jobs. The latter involves having jobs that are located in more than one economic sector and that involve contrasts in social relations, technical content, and levels and kinds of earnings. The DGPTE earnings data, however, reflect income derived from primary and secondary jobs.

Another limitation is the intrinsic variability of labor-market data which dictates caution in interpreting short patterns. It should therefore be kept in mind that this paper analyzes such patterns in an effort to suggest questions for macro and micro study. The paper's use of descriptive data rather than statistical analysis is appropriate to this task.

One response to economic crisis seems to have been a 1979–82 reversal of the previous trend of rural-to-urban migration with agricultural employment increasing in 1981–82 (Thery, et al., 1988). Yet, as before the crisis, the out-migration of Costa Ricans to other countries remained insignificant (e.g., Lungo, et al., 1991).

3 . "Employment" refers to a minimum of an hour of work during the survey week to produce goods and services with economic value in the market. Individuals are considered employed if they have jobs but did not work for reasons such as illness, vacation, weather, and labor strikes. On the limitations of this and related measures for the analysis of female work in particular, see Beneria (1988), Bonilla (1990), Elson (1989), and Ward (1990).

4. "Visible employment" refers to employed people who involuntary work less than 47 hours per week. "Invisible underployment" refers to employed people who work at least 47 hours per week but earn less than the legal minimum wage. This measure, then, does not embrace part-time workers (officially those whose employment is less than 47 hours per week), a group whose social characteristics make it vulnerable to earning less than the legal minimum wage (e.g., Bonilla, 1990; Elson, 1989; Portes, et al., 1989; Ward, 1990).

5. For a comparison with nationwide trends, see Tardanico (1992).

The array of measures of employment crises would have been worse if 12–19 year olds—the least experienced and skilled of the labor market's officially-recognized age groups—had not decreased as a percentage of San José's total population. This decrease continued through 1986.

The measures listed, along with data that I do not have on variables (such as, firm size and the age, gender, education, experience, and migrant/nonmigrant status of workers) are commonly used approximations of informal employment as well as low-end, formal employment. Such measures are valid insofar as they capture the least qualified and hence most vulnerable members of the workforce who are the most likely to be engaged in legally unregulated income-earning and marginally formal jobs (e.g., Portes, et al., 1989; Ward, 1990).

Comparative studies show that the informal economy comprises a vast array of income-earning activities, social relations of production, technical content of work, levels of monetary and nonmonetary returns, and ties with the structure of households. Peattie (1990: 34) observes that there is "no such thing as 'the informal sector,' but rather a great variety of informal sectors . . ." As is true of formal employment, the dimensions and consequences of informal employment cannot be separated from specific institutional contexts (see also Bromley and Birkbeck, 1988; Portes, et al., 1989; Smith and Tardanico, 1987; Ward, 1990).

The downgrading of employment may occur through the market and political processes of not only the informal economy but the formal economy as well. The downgrading of labor through the formal economy may involve, for instance, reduced pay and worsened work conditions within the confines of pre-existing, state-enforced regulations. It may also involve the revision of state-enforced regulations themselves. Such revision includes anti-union legislation; the official lengthening of the work day or week; the legal reduction of real minimum wages, job-security safeguards, worker benefits, and health and safety standards; and the creation of free trade-zones that are exempt from many labor regulations.

Nonwaged employment accounted for 20% of all of San José's employment in 1979. This figure does not include "domestic service" which in 1987, the first year for which DGPTE presents tabular data on this category, represented 3.5% of all employment. As of the early 1980s, Costa Rica ranked second to Panama as the least informalized labor market in Central America (PREALC, 1985).

6. The distribution of wages became more favorable to the three upper deciles of workers and less favorable to the other seven, as the Gini coefficient rose from 0.395 in 1980 to 0.42 in 1982 (Gindling and Berry, 1991). Data on wage inequality, which are subject to the same limitations as other labor-market data, convey only part of a broader concept: the distribution of wealth for individuals, households, and social classes.

7. Gindling (1989) observes that in 1980 average years of education were higher for females than males in the Costa Rican labor market. He also observes that Costa Rican females have been disproportionately represented in the economy's higher-paying sectors (see note 14; IICA/FLACSO, 1991; Trejos, 1991) but have earned less on average than males. In 1980–86, the portion of part-time employment hovered around 40–46% for urban, wage-earning females and 32–37% for their male counterparts. The percentage was probably higher for nonwaged workers.

8. Due to various changes introduced in the 1987's employment survey, that year's data on the magnitude of items—such as, San José's population, laborforce,

employment, and unemployment—are underestimates compared to those of previous years. I have therefore extrapolated 1987 figures based on an estimated 1986–87 population growth rate of approximately 1.9%, which averages the 1985–86 and 1987–88 growth rates for San José's population. The distributional features of the 1987 data (e.g., laborforce participation by gender and age; employment and underemployment by industry-sector and gender) remain unchanged. Even so, the data must be interpreted with caution. This is especially true concerning 1987's sharp changes in nonwaged employment (whose increases seem to have been marked in any case), private- and public-sector employment, and, as reported below, earnings inequality among workers. (See notes 11 and 16 for comparisons with 1988 data, and note 10 regarding refugees.)

9. A question for research is the degree to which the reserve employment forces of households acted in either of two ways: by reducing their labor-market participation in view of the revival of the economy and government spending, or by maintaining or increasing their labor-market participation in view of the revival of the fact that the economy and the state's social spending remained below the levels of the previous decade. Alternatively, such household members could have withdrawn from the labor market insofar as their employment opportunities and earnings remained unacceptably low despite a reviving economy.

10. Costa Rica's long-standing flow of rural-to-urban migration, which was interrupted during the economic crisis, seems to have reassserted itself during the post-1982 economic recovery (Hakkert and Goza, 1989).

I have not found data on the relation of migration flows to laborforce patterns including sectorial employment and earnings. By observation, refugees (mainly from Nicaragua and El Salvador) appear to have worked primarily in agriculture and secondarily in urban activities, such as, street vending and construction. According to ENLAC (1989), Central American refugees were important in the rapid expansion of Costa Rica's laborforce in 1987 (see also Ramírez, 1989). Relatively few refugees, however, seem to have settled in San José (see Lungo, et al., 1991).

ECLAC (1989) reports that most of the period's national employment growth was in nontraditional agricultural and manufactured exports. Lungo (1990); (see also Lungo, et al. 1991; Trejos, 1991) observes that in 1986–90 the apparel industry created 36,000 jobs nationally, 61% of all new jobs created by nontraditional exports. Next came jobs in the following nontraditional exports: electronics (12%), agriculture (8%), and tourism (6%).

11. According to Gindling and Berry (1990), the more unequal distribution of wages

among workers involved the lowest share for the bottom decile (1.5%) and the highest share for the upper decile (almost 34%) since 1975. Yet, compared with 1982, the wage distribution became more favorable not only to the upper decile but to four of the five lowest deciles, with the Gini coefficient remaining unchanged at 0.42. This pattern could reflect relatively fast wage growth for skilled workers in the formal and informal economies and for many informal employers; it could also reflect the fact that government minimum-wage policy favored workers in the lowest pay categories which would have especially benefitted formal workers at these levels (see Lungo, et al., 1991; Zimbalist, 1988).

Gindling and Berry detect a similar earnings distribution for 1988. They acknowledge, though, that this two-year finding could be an artifact of changes in the employment survey. Nonetheless, San José's reported incidence of poverty rose from 15% in 1981 to 19% in 1988 (Lungo, et al., 1991).

In 1987 average real wages were 89.2%, and in 1990, 8.7% of their 1982 level (ECLAC, 1991, Jan. 24, 1992). A related matter is that nonwage labor costs (e.g., employer and employee contributions to social security) in the formal sector officially increased in 1983. According to Fields (1988), the rise in employee contributions meant that real earnings were actually lower than reported.
Gindling and Berry (1991; see also Lungo, et al., 1991) observe that the wage advantage of the country's public- versus private-sector workers, which widened in 1980–82, narrowed in subsequent years.

12. The possible income advantages of informal employment for workers must be weighed against the disadvantages of their losing benefits, such as, social security and health insurance. But for low-income workers, the instability of formal employment commonly means the absence of such benefits anyway, while state-provided health care remains widely accessible in Costa Rica regardless of employment status.

13. Employment informalization would possibly have been more extensive during both the economic crisis and these years of structural adjustment if organized labor in San José's private sector had been a strong (or strengthening) political force. Unionized firms would then have had greater incentive to cut costs and promote flexibility by employing workers outside of state-regulated channels (see Portes, et al., 1989). At the same time, informal employment as a household and individual strategy would possibly have been more prevalent if San José's residents had been less accustomed to state-regulated employment and state-provided social welfare.

14. Pertinent to the period's laborforce trends is that in 1982–86 San José's rate of school enrollment for 6–11 year olds fell slightly, from 94.0% to 93.5%, while its

rate for 12–17 year olds fell to a greater extent, from 46.8% to 43.2% (Thery, et al., 1988). Turning to absolute numbers, in 1986 Costa Rica's primary-school enrollment surpassed its 1977 level, but as of 1988 secondary-school enrollment remained below its 1977 level. In contrast, Costa Rica's university enrollment, which merely stagnated during the early 1980s, expanded substantially in 1985–88. Gindling and Berry (1991) discuss the regressive implications of the comparative trends in secondary and university enrollments.

In 1987, 9.8% of San José's employed females worked in domestic service and 23.9% worked in the public sector. As for employed males, 0.2% worked in domestic service and 18.9% worked in the public sector.

15. According to the preliminary data reported in DGPTE (1988), San José's rate of laborforce-participation continued to rise, from 38.2% in 1987 to 39.2% in 1988; females accounted for 60% of the national laborforce's expansion. The following growth-rate data for 1988 are relevant for comparison with the extrapolated 1987 data: laborforce, 3.8%; employment, 1.1%; public-sector jobs, 13.4%, and private-sector jobs, 1.4%; waged jobs, 3.2%; and nonwaged jobs, 6.7%.

16. The relative gain of the highest-earning decile of earners was from 31.01% in 1980 to 33.99% in 1987. The share of wages accruing to the fifth lowest earning decile of earners remained virtually unchanged from its 1980 level. In line with note 11, Gindling and Berry (1991) stress that the 1987 data are inconsistent with those of previous years and thus require cautious interpretation.

17. In wider international perspective, the weakness of organized labor in Costa Rica—including the weakening of its public sector stronghold and the development of private-sector "solidarity" associations— is a contributing factor as well.

References

Beneria, L. (1988) "Conceptualizing the Labour Force: The Underestimation of Women's Economic Activities." In R.E. Pahl, ed., *On Work: Historical, Comparative & Theoretical Approaches*. Oxford: Basil Blackwell.

Bonilla, E. (1990) "Working Women in Latin America." In *Economic and Social Progress in Latin America: 1990 Report*. Washington, D.C.: Inter-American Development Bank.

Bromley, R. and C. Birkbeck (1988) "Urban Economy and Employment." In M. Pacione, ed., *The Geography of the Third World: Progress and Prospects*. London: Routledge, Kegan & Paul.

Castells, M. and R. Laserna (1989) "The New Dependency: Technological Change and Socioeconomic Restructuring in Latin America." *Sociological Forum*, 4(4).

CEPAS [Centro de Estudios para la Accion Social] (1990) "Ajuste estructural y desajuste social." *Documentos de analisis*, no. 11.

Deere, C.D. (1990) "A CBI Report Card." *Hemisphere: A Magazine of Latin American and Caribbean Affairs*, (3)1.

DGPTE (Direccion General de Planificacion del Trabajo y el Empleo) (1977-88) *Encuesta nacional de hogares: empleo y desempleo*. San José.

Dunkerly, J. (1988) *Power in the Isthmus: A Political History of Central America*. London: Verso.

ECLAC (Economic Commission for Latin America and the Caribbean) (1977-91) *Economic Survey of Latin and the Caribbean*. Santiago, Chile: United Nations.

Elson, D. (1989) "How is Structural Adjustment Affecting Women?" *Development*, 1.

Fields, G.S. (1988) "Employment and Economic Growth in Costa Rica." *World Development*, 16(12).

Garcia-Huidobro, G., et al. (1990) *La deuda social en Costa Rica*. Geneva: OIT/PRE-ALC.

Gereffi, G. (1989) "Rethinking Development Theory: Insights from East Asia and Latin America." *Sociological Forum*, 4(4).

Gindling, T.H. (1989) "Women, Earnings and Economic Crisis in Costa Rica." Presented at the Congress of the Latin American Studies Association, Miami.

Gindling, T.H. and A. Berry (1991) "Labor Markets and Successful Adjustment: The Case of Costa Rica." Unpublished paper.

Hakkert,R. and F.W. Goza (1989) "The Demographic Consequences of Austerity in Latin America." In W.L. Canak, ed., *Lost Promises: Debt, Austerity and Development in Latin America*. Boulder, CO: Westview.

Horton, S., Kanbur, R., and D. Mazumdar, eds. (1990) *Labor Markets in an Era of Adjustment*. Washington, D.C.: Economic Development Institute, The World Bank.

IICA/FLACSO [Instituto Internacional de Cooperacion para la Agricultura/Facultad Latinoamericana de Ciencias Sociales] (1991) *Centroamerica en cifras*. San José.

Jatoba, J. (1989) "Latin America's Labour Market Research: A State of the Art." *Labour and Society*, 14(4).

La Nacion (1991a) "Fallas en los PAE retrasan ajuste." San Jose, September 23.

La Nacion (1991b) "Lo que le falta al PAE III." San Jose, September 24.

Menjivar Larin, R. and J.P. Perez Sainz, eds. (1991) *Informalidad urbana en Centroamerica: entre la acumulacion y la subsistencia*. Caracas: FLACSO/Nueva Sociedad.

Lavell, A. (1988) "Economic Recession and Urban Labour Market Dynamics in Costa Rica, 1977-1984." Presented at the Conference on the Demography of Inequality in Contemporary Latin America, University of Florida, Gainesville.

Lungo, M. (1989) "La investigacion urbana en Centroamerica." In M. Lungo, ed., *Lo urbano: teoria y metodos*. San Jose: Editorial Universitario Centroamericano.

Lungo, M. (1990) "Tendencias del proceso de urbanizacion en Centroamerica en los '80." Presented at the Conference on Change and Quantity in Urban and Regional Development, Gilleleje, Denmark.

Lungo, M., M. Perez, and N. Piedra (1991) "La urbanizacion en Costa Rica en los 80: el caso del area metropolitana de San Jose." Presented at the Conference on Caribbean Cities at the Threshold of a New Century, Latin Amercan and Caribbean Center, Florida International University, May-June.

Nelson, J. (1989) "Crisis and Reform in Costa Rica." In B. Stallings and R. Kaufman, eds., *Debt and Democracy in Latin America*. Boulder, CO: Westview.

Paige, J.M. (1987) "Coffee and Politics in Central America." In R. Tardanico, ed., *Crises in the Caribbean Basin*, vol. 9, *Political Economy of the World-System Annuals*. Newbury Park, CA: Sage Publications.

Peattie, L.R. (1990) "Real-World Economics." *Hemisphere: A Magazine of Latin American and Caribbean Affairs*, 3(1).

Portes, A. (1989) "Latin American Urbanization during the Years of the Crisis." *Latin American Research Review*, 24(3).

Portes, A., Castells, M., and L. Benton, eds. (1989) *The Informal Economy*. Baltimore: The Johns Hopkins University Press.

PREALC [Programa Regional del Empleo para America Latina y el Caribe] (1984) *Costa Rica: caracteristicas de las micro-empresas y sus duenos. Documentos de Trabajo*, 253. Santiago, Chile.

PREALC (1985) *Cambio y polarizacion ocupacional en Centroamerica*. Santiago, Chile.

Ramirez, M.A. (1989) *Refugee Policy Challenges: The Case of Nicaraguans in Costa Rica*. Washington, D.C.: Center for Immigration Policy and Refugee Assistance, Georgetown University.

Roberts, B.R. (1989) "Urbanization, Migration, and Development." *Sociological Forum*, 4(4).

Smith, C.A. (1988) "Enhancing Research on Central America." In M.B. Rosenberg, ed. (1988) *Central American Studies: Toward a New Research Agenda. Occasional Papers Series Dialogues*, 110. Miami: Latin American and Caribbean Center, Florida International University.

Smith, M.P. and R. Tardanico (1987) "Urban Theory Reconsidered: Production,

Reproduction and Collective Action." In M.P. Smith and J.R. Feagin, eds., *The Capitalist City: Global Restructuring and Community Change.* Oxford: Basil Blackwell.

Sojo, A. (1989) "Actual dinamica socioeconomica costarricense." *Sintesis*, 8(May-August).

Tardanico, R. (1992) "Labor-Market Transitions: Costa Rica in Comparative Perspective." In J.M. Malloy and E.A. Gamarra, eds., *Latin America and Caribbean Contemporary Record.* New York: Holmes and Meier.

Tardanico, R. (1991) "Social Dimensions of Structural Adjustment: Households and Employment in a Costa Rican Barrio." Unpublished paper.

Thery, A., E. Kritz, E. Karp, and M. Perea (1988) *Costa Rica: Social Equity and Crisis.* Report prepared for the Agency for International Development. Washington, D.C.: Anita F. Allen Associates, Inc., and International Science Technology Institute.

Torres Rivas, E. et al. (1987) *Costa Rica: crisis y desafios.* San Jose: DEI.

Trejos, J.D. (1989) "Caracterizacion del sector informal urbano de Costa Rica." *Documentos de Trabajo.* San Jose: Instituto de Investigaciones en Ciencias Economicas, Universidad de Costa Rica.

Trejos, J.D. (1991) "Informalidad y accumulacion en el Area Metropolitana de San Jose, Costa Rica." In R. Menjivar Larin and J.P. Perez Sainz, eds., *Informalidad urbana en Centroamerica: entre la acumulacion y la subsistencia.* Caracas: FLACSO/Nueva Sociedad.

Walker, I. (1991) "El ajuste estructural y el futuro desarrollo de la region centroamericana." Postgrado Centroamericano en Economia y Planificacion del Desarrollo, Universidad Nacional de Honduras, *Documentos de Trabajo*, no. 2.

Ward, K., ed. (1990) *Women's Work and Global Restructuring.* Ithaca, NY: ILR Press.

Zimbalist, A. (1988) "Costa Rica." In E. Paus, ed., *Struggle against Dependence.* Boulder, CO: Westview.

THE BUBBLING CAULDRON: GLOBAL AND LOCAL INTERACTIONS IN NEW YORK CITY RESTAURANTS

Louis Amdur, Janet Baus, Philana Cho, Dalton Conley,
Stephen Duncombe, Herman Joseph, Daniel Kessler,
Jennifer Parker, Huaishi Song, and Sharon Zukin*
City University of New York

The restaurant industry, including hotels, is the largest employer in the U.S. service economy. With rapid turnover, low wages, and low-skill kitchen jobs it attracts immigrant workers who participate in an ethnic division of labor reflecting both global and local patterns of change. In the largest U.S. cities, especially New York, the restaurant work force is also recruited from arts producers, who are drawn to centers of the service economy and markets for their creative work. Ethnographic study and interviews at four restaurants in New York City show that restaurants play a significant role in reproducing the international labor markets and "artistic mode of production" typical of a global city. At the same time, restaurants' internal hierarchies reproduce the ethnic and social divisions of labor typical of the larger society as well as the economic polarization of the city as a whole. Global and local forces equally shape cuisine, labor recruitment, entrepreneurial mobility, and clienteles suggesting that the study of transnational space should focus on both economy and culture in changing urban institutions. This study also questions a number of macroeconomic assumptions about immigrant labor markets and transnational capital flows.

The development of the restaurant industry in New York is inextricable from global processes of change. Not only does it respond to the general growth of services, especially high-level business services, in a global city but it also reflects interregional capital shifts and a steady supply, since the immigration laws of 1965 and 1986, of "new" immigrants. Restaurants generate a large number of low-wage and "dead-end" jobs that are often filled by immigrants who lack English language skills and U.S. educational credentials (Bailey, 1985). These factors, and the restaurant industry's traditional barriers to unionization, make this a pliable labor force. Restaurant jobs in turn support the structural inequality described as polarization, which divides haves from have-nots in the urban economy by work, wages, and prospects for advancement. Whether it is truly industrialization for export in sending countries that encourages immigration (Sassen, 1988) or a variety of internal economic and political processes that push out a relatively skilled part of the population, restaurants in receiving countries (and the hotel and travel industry more generally) represent an employer of first and last resort. Significantly, restaurants are among the fastest growing sectors of the service economy in the United States as well as in New York City.

Analyzing these connections requires a new perspective on the restaurant's social role. While seemingly among the most "local" of social institutions, a restaurant is also a remarkable focus of transnational economic and cultural flows. As an employer, a restaurant owner negotiates new functional interdependencies that span local, regional, and global scales. Moreover, a restaurant, as a place where cultural products are created and reproduced, effects the transnational diffusion of cultural styles. Along with the household, community, state, and "cities' transnational linkages" (Smith and Feagin, 1987), the restaurant is a "transnational space" that processes new social identities. This applies to a restaurant's laborforce as well as to various groups of restaurant consumers.

Most research on the local impact of globalization has focused on industrial sectors (e.g., Sassen, 1987; Perry, 1987; Scott and Storper, 1986; Hill, 1989). But the services, which account for a greater proportion of job growth even among unskilled workers, are a logical site of inquiry. Small firms in the services, especially in global cities, may simultaneously represent a conduit of global capital, global patterns of labor mobilization, and formation to some degree of global products and a global clientele. They also serve complex functions for both urban natives and immigrants. In short, services relate even more directly than manufacturing to the simultaneous processes of global and local social reproduction that characterize many urban populations today. Studying small firms in the services should illuminate some of these processes.

This study seeks to innovate in yet another way by incorporating ethnographic research and structural analysis. In light of its long history in the social sciences, ethnography needs no justification. The very "minutiae" of ordinary people's lives permit us to reconstruct the texture of social experience. Their voices convey both the lived history of structural change and the ambiguities of geographical and cultural displacement. By profiling their careers, we can suggest some of the costs of social mobility and question, as well, traditional categories of social class, race, and gender. Thus, we also join in the search for a "new" narrative of space and society that pays equal attention to context and analysis (Sayer, 1989).

Appropriate Models

There are several models for analyzing the connections between global and local processes of economic, cultural, and social change. One of two starting points for our study of restaurants in New York is to consider economic organizations, including firms and markets, as a complex product of social and cultural processes (Zukin and DiMaggio, 1990). The other is to consider the urban political economy in terms of both a global and local division of labor.

Smith and Feagin (1987) emphasize that cities function in a "new international division of labor." Both labor recruitment and capital flows are enacted with increasing disregard for national borders. The demand for labor in specific places is shaped to a large degree by the internal decisions and clustering practices of transnational firms. These actions create new concentrations of industry and labor, including "global cities" that coordinate capital flows while attracting workers with varied social, economic, and cultural skills. Migrants are absorbed by the growth of the advanced service sector and the expansion of high technology industries as well as by all the support services (clerical, retail, personal, and domestic) that a heterogeneous laborforce requires. Thus, the study of global centers (such as, New York, London, Tokyo, and Los Angeles) often focuses on the dichotomy between highly-skilled, native migrants and less-skilled, immigrant workers [Sassen, 1988; cf., Waldinger (forthcoming)].

While internationalization produces extensive urban restructuring, it may also deepen economic, social, and spatial cleavages (e.g., Soja, 1987, 1991). The cumulative legal, linguistic, and educational disadvantages of immigrant workers are reproduced by income polarization and a "dual city" division of labor markets. On the one hand, certain expanding sectors, such as, FIRE (finance, insurance, and real estate), generate a small number of extraordinarily high incomes. On the other hand, the dual city model strongly relies on a racial and ethnic division of labor. Although some researchers blame racial polarization on a jobs/skills mismatch that especially affects urban blacks (Kasarda 1985), others have found persistent racial differences at every income level that reflect ghettoization of the employment structure (Fainstein, 1987). Another criticism of the polarization and skills mismatch hypotheses is that they ignore the heterogeneity of minority populations and, thus, cannot account for differential occupational and economic mobility among groups (Bailey and Waldinger, 1991). Within groups, moreover, polarization may divide those with full-time employment from a rising number of people who are excluded from the laborforce. Bailey and Waldinger (1991) do not pinpoint growth in the service industries as a cause for the differential experiences of native and immigrant minorities. Yet, small businesses, particularly in the service sector, may escape regulations associated with affirmative action policies. Further, the face-to-face nature of some service work—e.g., in retail sales and restaurants—may lead employers to hire applicants from certain racial and ethnic categories and exclude others. Thus, polarization may divide workers in the "front" and "back" regions of service firms.

These limitations of opportunity in the service economy lead to questions about the nature of full-time employment at the bottom. Particularly in restaurants, it may provide dead-end jobs that absorb a pool of surplus labor or access to the mainstream economy in terms of on-the-job training and opportunities for entrepreneurship (Bailey, 1985; Waldinger, 1990). For both owners and employees, restaurants may offer a chance to accumulate economic and cultural capital.

Yet, migration to global cities provides a laborforce of cultural workers who already arrive with cultural capital. These artists, actors, and other creative personnel enter different labor markets. While many are employed in business services connected to corporate capital (advertising, graphic design, journalism and mass media, public relations, publishing), others are often unemployed or underemployed in their chosen cultural field. Thus, they become a reserve laborforce for part-time or full-time work in new service industries. Indeed, global capital creates a dynamic marketplace for all kinds of cultural capital. All the arts contribute to the production of new symbols which constitute both a language and a currency for the transmission of information, innovation, and social status. While political economists are mainly concerned with these processes as examples of intersectorial shifts of capital investment or flexible accumulation (Harvey, 1989), they are arguably part of a long-term Artistic Mode of Production (AMP) that complements the new service economy in major cities (Zukin, 1989: 176–92).

The Artistic Mode of Production transforms urban space from manufacturing to service-sector use by establishing a built environment for the performance, display, sale, and production of cultural symbols. Such space ranges from art galleries and museums, including "alternative spaces," to artists' lofts, theaters, and public places that feature the large-scale installations typical of "public art." More generally, urban design, the expansion of a large workforce of cultural producers, and conspicuous investment in art work—including architecture—support the growth of cultural consumption (Zukin, 1990). Restaurants are an important part of this process.

Restaurants as Cultural and Economic Institutions

Restaurants in global cities link cultural production and consumption with corporate capital in several ways. First, they offer jobs waiting on tables to an underemployed arts laborforce. Restaurants in Manhattan and Los Angeles—which are centers of theatrical, film, and TV production—are known to hire actors as waiters. Second, investors from the corporate sector or the professions actively seek promising young chefs to establish in their own restaurants. Although this form of investment is generally not so profitable and was greatly reduced after the stock market crash of October 1987, it still attracts publicity. Third, restaurants contribute to the exciting cultural milieu and image that many corporate executives prefer (Brake, 1988). The more corporate expense accounts are concentrated in a city, the greater the resource base to support both *haute cuisine* and *nouvelle* alternatives (cf., Zukin, 1991, ch. 7).

Moreover, restaurants provide a place for corporate patrons, culture industry executives, and artists to meet. They are sites where new trends are discussed, gossip is exchanged, and deals are made. Restaurant staff—especially waiters—who have direct contact with customers present themselves along with the menu. They may be seen as potential employees or as trendsetters by culture industry executives. The way they talk and dress provides a large part of the restaurant's ambiance. Waiters thus not only provide a backdrop for business meetings, they also contribute to the production, circulation, and consumption of symbols. A restaurant's style, especially in Manhattan, is both implicitly and explicitly negotiated by waitstaff and management. The accents and appearance of waiters affirm distinctions between restaurants as surely as menu, price, and location.

Waitstaff are not the only source of a restaurant's role in facilitating the accumulation of cultural capital. Restaurants indicate social class and other distinctions. Being seen in a particular restaurant, or with a certain person, or occupying a "good" table are all indicators of power and status in a city or an industry. By the same token, customers establish a restaurant's relative status. A restaurant that attracts social elites, celebrities, or industry leaders in any field gains luster. Restaurant design also contributes to the production of a city's visual style. Architects and interior designers, restaurant consultants, and restaurant industry magazines diffuse global trends that are adapted to local styles. Owners are amenable to submitting their own vision to these agents' mediation and even hire publicists to further the presentation of a specific image. Restaurateurs often appear as a cultural synthesis of the artist, the entrepreneur, and the social organizer. The restaurant itself is both theater and performance. It serves and helps constitute the

Artistic Mode of Production.

In a curious way, restaurants also synthesize the global and the local. They receive culinary styles of preparation and trends from other parts of the country and the world and institutionalize them in their menus. Yet, they also adapt strange food to local tastes and eating patterns. Moreover, they form agglomerations by restaurant type, which then become neighborhood institutions (Little Italy, Chinatown). In New York restaurant cuisine, the local reterritorializes the global.

Restaurants similarly bring together a global and local laborforce and clientele. The industry's labor market mobilizes immigrants and natives whose networks—both cultural and economic—influence a restaurant's style. The division of labor along ethnic and national lines generally parallels the division into "front" and "back" regions with higher or lower social status, with the exception of high-status chefs. Moreover, a restaurant's status is influenced by the cultural style, economic level, and ethnicity of global and local clienteles. While some restaurants serve the tourist trade, others are appropriated as meeting places of an international business class or for maintaining ethnic contacts. In other words, in a global city, restaurants bring together global and local markets of both employees and clientele (see Figure 1).

New York Restaurants

The restaurant industry, one of the fastest growing industries in the United States, employs over 5 million people nationwide, including 130,000 at more than 5,000 restaurants in New York City (U.S. Department of Labor, 1989). During the 1980s, the New York restaurant industry alone added 20,000 jobs. Over 33% of the workforce in New York City restaurants are immigrants, not including increasing numbers of undocumented immigrants (Winnick, 1990). There are no data on the number of cultural producers working in restaurants.

Despite growing numbers of jobs, average wages in the restaurant industry have continually fallen below average weekly earnings across all industries. Both "front" and "back" employees earn low wages. While "front" employees typically earn more than "back" employees, excluding chefs, most of their income comes from tips. "Back" employees rely only on their wages. Average weekly earnings of restaurant employees increased only slightly less than $130 from 1978 to 1988 (from $144.83 in 1978, and $190.11 in 1983, to $271.93 in 1988), while wages across all industries increased more than $400 (from $281.86, and $426.11, to $684.38) (State of New York Department of Labor, 1988). Therefore, restaurant employees' average weekly earnings show an overall decline as a percentage of

Figure 1
Analysis of the Restaurant Service Sector
Labor and Clientele Markets: The Global and the Local

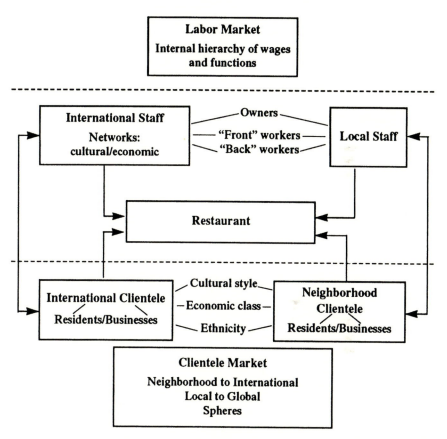

average weekly earnings across all industries in New York City (from 51.4% in 1980, and 44.6% in 1984, to 39.7% in 1988). (See Figure 2.) Part of this decline can be accounted for by the dramatic increase in a small number of high-paying jobs in financial services, skewing the total average wage.

To examine the global and local influences on the entire range of New York

Figure 2
New York City Restaurant Employment and Wages

Top line: % of NYC average wages earned by restaurant workers

Bottom line: % job growth in restaurant industry of total NYC job growth

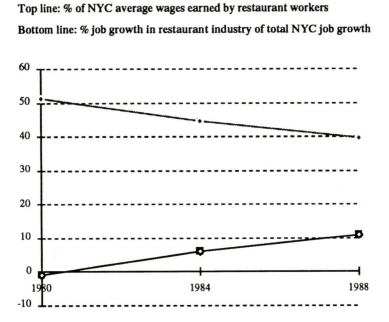

Sources: *Annual Labor Area Report*, NYS Dept. of Labor, 1986, and
Occupational Supply and Demand, NYS Dept. of Labor, 1990.

City restaurants would require a huge research effort. For a preliminary study, a sample of four restaurants in Manhattan and Queens was constructed. The selection of restaurants was guided by three main criteria: price, location, and "local character." We chose "tablecloth" or "full-service" restaurants in the moderate-price range because we believed they would approximate a mainstream model of restaurant markets. We excluded both franchise restaurants, regardless of price, and expensive restaurants, with entrees priced at $20 or more, on the assumption that they would show highly-specific labor patterns and would also be less connected to a local community. We therefore also rejected restaurants that mainly attract a tourist clientele. We chose restaurants in mixed residential and commercial areas which all carry a strong local character because of the type of residents (by ethnicity or social class) or local businesses. Three of the four restaurants are in Manhattan: one on the Upper West Side north of 72nd Street, one in the Flatiron district of lower Fifth Avenue south of 23rd Street, and one in the Gramercy Park area around 20th Street on the east side. The fourth restaurant is in Astoria, Queens.

These restaurants were in some crucial way accessible to the research team, either because one of the group had eaten there frequently or knew the owner and staff. The other side of accessibility is rapport. Particularly because of the often illegal nature of employment practices in the restaurant industry with respect to immigration and wage laws, an investigation of restaurant work may be seen as intrusive. For this reason the research team tried to establish a rapport with owners and employees when making the initial contact. Even then, it was necessary to reassure both groups that the survey would not be forwarded to the Immigration and Naturalization Service or the Department of Labor. A small number of employees denied interview access despite these assurances. All owners were interviewed.

Two questionnaires were constructed for owners and employees. They included around 20 questions on the global recruitment of the restaurant laborforce, education, occupational background, the expectations and real conditions of restaurant workers, the organization of work, hiring preferences, access to jobs, living and commuting arrangements, earnings, and aspirations. All interviews were done at the restaurants, using English, Spanish, and Chinese. To highlight the cultural context of restaurant work, we necessarily describe these restaurants, their owners, and their employees in some detail.[1]

The first restaurant, Aperture, is designed to be an "artsy" place where its clientele, drawn from the photographic, graphic arts, advertising, and publishing industries in the Flatiron district, can feel at home. Larry, one of three co-owners, designed the restaurant himself. Theatrical track lighting with colored gels casts warm hues on the white walls. Jazz, Motown, and Europop tapes—mixed by Larry—create a musical backdrop to conversation. The restrooms are built into hollow false columns that imitate the area's loft structures. A "curator" who is not on the restaurant staff chooses monthly art exhibits, and there is an "opening" for each show. Larry is in his early thirties, a native New Yorker, born in Astoria, and raised in a solidly middle-class community of Queens. He and his father own the Queens restaurant in our sample. Although Larry has been a co-owner of that restaurant with his father for several years, he exercises control over most daily aspects of Aperture. His two co-owners at Aperture are Egyptians, one in his late-twenties and the other in his thirties. One is the chef and the other the manager. Aperture seats 62 with 10 more chairs at the bar. The restaurant was opened in 1985.

Mia, the second restaurant, is a Chinese restaurant near Gramercy Park, the only private square in New York City. This is a middle-class neighborhood bordering a commercial area with banks, insurance company headquarters, advertising firms, and a college. Mia's modern exterior and sleek decor create a posh "American" atmosphere. There are none of the stereotypical red tables and dragon paintings of U.S. Chinese restaurants. Instead, Mia has black-top tables with small vases of fresh flowers, black and white, ceramic floor tiles, and a slick, black bar. The only Chinese references are the menu, which includes Szechuan style food, the chopsticks on the table, and a sole Chinese on the waitstaff. The owner, Lee, comes from Taiwan. His family has owned a restaurant in Taiwan for many years, and his brothers run several restaurants in New York. Mia seats 60 and 10 at the bar and was opened in 1985. Lee makes all menu decisions and designed the restaurant with his family.

Rain Forest, the third restaurant, was opened in 1987 on the Upper West Side not far from Lincoln Center and the gentrified shopping areas of Broadway and Columbus Avenue. Despite its Brazilian motif and menu, the owner, Don Pedro ("Pete" to his customers), is neither Brazilian nor Portuguese but Spanish. Stylized murals on white walls depict forest scenes from the Amazon. The restaurant attracts a middle- and upper-middle-class clientele of Americans from the neighborhood and Latinos from around the city, as well as, members of the Latino diplomatic community. Pete formerly owned another Brazilian restaurant in New York, which he sold when the rent was raised. He then worked as a headwaiter at another Brazilian restaurant, from which he took several waiters and a chef to open Rain Forest. Pete makes all the decisions on decor and menu design as well as management. The restaurant seats 107.

Our fourth restaurant, Neptune's, originally opened as a seafood restaurant in Astoria more than 50 years ago. It seats 60. The present owner, John, bought Neptune's 20 years ago after it had closed. An immigrant from Italy as a child, he turned it into an Italian restaurant but kept the original name because of the restaurant's reputation in the neighborhood. John initially had three partners; in 1985, his son Larry bought out the remaining two partners and joined John as co-owner. Neptune's is located on a busy commercial street under the elevated subway tracks, a 20-minute ride from Manhattan. Inside, the restaurant has dark wood paneling, mirrored walls, glass brick partitions, and track lighting that create a subdued, elegant effect. Fishing nets and seashore objects complement an earlier theme, but Larry is in the process of redecorating with "French country" fabrics, wicker baskets, fresh flowers, and paintings. The new decor is somewhat at odds with the menu of traditional Italian dishes and adaptations of nova cucina. Bottles of mineral water are set out on the tables bearing price tags. Since becoming co-owner, Larry has made all the decisions concerning menu and decor. Astoria is historically an immigrant community. In the past 10 years, however, the Irish, Italian, and Greek populations have been supplemented by new immigrants from Asia and Latin America. Besides the new residents who resemble gentrifiers, a new source of Neptune's business has been a lunchtime crowd of people who work at a nearby television production center for film, advertising, and television.

Restaurant Employees

Thirty-five respondents come from 17 different countries in North Africa, the Middle East, Asia, Scandinavia, the Caribbean, North America, and Latin America. Ranging in age from their late-teens to their mid-forties, except for one owner in his late-fifties, they include: two busboys and a cleaner from Bangladesh; a bartender and two waiters from Brazil; a delivery man, waitress, chef, and take-out manager from China; a waiter, bartender and two owners from Egypt; a cook from Haiti; a manager from Hong Kong; a waiter from Israel; an owner from Italy; a cleaner, a cook, and a salad man from Mexico; a busboy from Morocco; a waitress from Norway; a waiter from the Philippines; a waiter from Portugal; an owner from Spain; and an owner from Taiwan. Those who migrated to New York from other states include four waitresses from Ohio, Michigan, and Missouri, and a bartender from California. There are only three native New Yorkers in our sample. They were born in Queens and work in the restaurant in Queens. One is Larry, co-owner of that restaurant.

Common to all these countries is the growing number of service jobs in relation to industrial and agricultural employment. In 14 of these countries, service employment far outweighs any other kind of employment. Only a few of our respondents came with industrial skills and experience—an electrician from Brazil and an engineer from Egypt. However, many respondents did come with experience in service occupations. They include a waiter from Brazil, a chef and busboy from Egypt, two office workers from China, a restaurant worker from Haiti, a dishwasher and other low-skill kitchen staff from Mexico, a salesperson from the Philippines, a social worker from Israel, an airport host from Morocco, and a dancer from Norway. A few had professional experience, such as, a real-estate manager from Portugal (now a headwaiter) and an agricultural engineer from Egypt (now a bartender). Eight were students in their country of origin before they immigrated.

Nine respondents expected to find work in a restaurant in New York. They either had restaurant experience—as in the cases of a previous restaurant owner from

Haiti who now works as a cook, a dishwasher from Mexico who is also a cook, and a waiter from Brazil who is still a waiter— or they had been informed about restaurant job opportunities by friends or relatives from their country of origin who had moved to New York City. The rest of the respondents seem to have gravitated into restaurant work. It is relatively easy to get and keep a restaurant job in New York. The flexible work hours enable employees to support primary interests in the arts or university studies.

Most of the employee respondents, 17 out of 29, got their jobs through personal connections—a friend or relative—or they had worked with the owner or chef before. The second most relied-upon method was simply walking in off the street to ask for a job.[2] Seven of the respondents obtained their jobs this way. A few of the immigrants, unlike the native New Yorkers and U.S. migrants, found their jobs through a newspaper ad or an employment agency (see Table 1).

Table 1
Access to Restaurant Jobs for Immigrants, Migrants,
and Native New Yorkers (n = 29)

Geographical Origin	Personal Connection	Newspaper Ad	Walked in	Agency
Immigrants	10	3	4	2
Native New Yorkers	2	–	–	–
U.S. migrants	5	–	3	–

Looking at the type of jobs employees do and their educational attainment confirms a degree of polarization in the restaurant between those who work in the "front"—i.e., the dining room/bar area—and those who work in the "back"—i.e., the kitchen. Out of 19 "front" respondents in our sample, 12 are immigrants, 3 are U.S. migrant artists or actors, and one is an immigrant dancer from Western Europe. The majority of those who work in the "front" and who come in contact with customers hold college degrees or are in college now, while no one who works in the "back" has any college education. Out of 13 waitstaff, four have a bachelors degree, one has an acting degree, and three have some college education. Only five have no higher education. Out of 3 bartenders, one has a bachelor's degree, one has an engineering degree, and one has no college education. Out of 3 busboys, one has a bachelor's degree, one went to bartending school, and one has no college or restaurant education. A respondent who works as a host has an associate's degree in hotel management. Of the two managers interviewed, one has training in TV production and the other has no higher education. Although college graduates in our sample include both immigrants and U.S. citizens, the respondents with no higher education are all immigrants except for one native New Yorker.

Native-born employees who migrated from out-of-state generally expect to pursue careers in the arts or professions. The immigrants and native-born New Yorkers, on the other hand, tend to expect to make careers in the restaurant industry.

While most of the immigrant employees live in the outer boroughs (Queens and Brooklyn), the arts employees mainly live in Manhattan, followed by Brooklyn and Queens. All employees who live in Brooklyn work in restaurants in Manhattan. Queens residents in our sample work in Queens as well as in Manhattan. The arts employees and those in professional schools tend to live with non-relatives. However, most immigrants in our sample live with family members, although some live alone. Owners live in the suburbs. One bartender and one chef own their own homes. The rest rent apartments (one busboy rents a room). There is no correlation between immigrants, country of origin, and residence in Manhattan (see Table 2).

Table 2
Place of Residence of Immigrants and Arts Workforce (n = 29)

Place of residence	Immigrants	Arts
Manhattan	7	3
Outer Borough	15	3
New Jersey	1	–

The Social Division of Labor

The differences between immigrants and the arts workforce parallel differences between the front and back regions of the restaurant. Four vignettes of respondents who work at Aperture and Neptune's in different positions (the waitress Linda, the busboy Hassan, the salad man Jesus, and the chef Medhat) indicate the contrast in their expectations of restaurant work and the cultural capital they bring to it. They also suggest contrasts in the labor markets of immigrants and cultural producers who work in the service economy. We intend these few profiles of respondents to illuminate differences among them. Profiles also make good use of incomparable qualitative data.

Linda

Linda is a 23-year-old, white waitress at Aperture. She was raised in a midwestern suburb. After graduating from college with a degree in theater arts, she moved to New York in 1990 to look for a job in the musical theater. She found work as a telemarketer but was laid off after three months. Linda walked into Neptune's because she lives in an apartment nearby and got a job on waitstaff despite having no restaurant experience. She was given on-the-job training by the other waitresses. The owner suggested she apply for a job on waitstaff at Aperture, his restaurant in Manhattan.

Linda now has a role in a national touring company production of a Broadway hit that will soon be on the road. She has no plans to continue in the restaurant industry. She has met many theater people at Aperture and finds the job good for making business contacts.

Linda lives in Astoria with her boyfriend and has a 25-minute commute to work by subway. She has no health insurance, works 36 hours a week, and makes $400 in a good week. None of her family are in the restaurant business. Her father and brother are "corporate types."

Hassan

Hassan has worked as a busboy at Neptune's for four months. He is unusual there in that he found his job through an employment agency. Moroccan by birth, Hassan immigrated to the United States in 1986. He had worked in "hospitality" at an airport in Morocco and thought of restaurant work as a quick entry into the U.S. economy. "If I can find something better, it will be welcome for me. But the first thing is that you have to earn a living. The fastest way is the restaurant because you don't need too much knowledge about anything." With his recently earned certificate in bartending and improved English-language skills, Hassan hopes to move up in the restaurant industry. He is in his late-twenties.

Like the waitstaff, Hassan earns $10 per eight-hour lunch or dinner shift and another $250-$400 a week in tips. He rents a room by himself in Astoria. He has a sister and brother in France and parents in Morocco. His friends—who are Moroccan, Egyptian, and Brazilian—reflect the ethnic diversity, tolerance, and numerical strength of immigrants that he prizes here. He lived in Florida before coming to New York.

Jesus

A 22-year-old man from a small town in Mexico, Jesus has lived in New York City for six years. He works as a salad man at Aperture, having worked his way up from the entry level position of dishwasher: "Everybody come don't know English, so started like that." The chef brought Jesus with him from Neptune's where they had worked together. He has been at Aperture 15 months.

The chef is slowly teaching Jesus how to cook. Jesus believes that in nine or ten years he may become "a chef or a nice cook." He plans to climb the restaurant ladder by degrees. Since his English-language skills are limited and his time is fully occupied with work, he depends on the chef for his advancement. Jesus left school in Mexico planning to work in the restaurant business. He has taken some English classes but is not confident about his ability to converse. Jesus doesn't have great interest in the restaurant industry but lacks alternative plans.

Jesus makes $320 for a six-day week. He has no health insurance. His commute to Manhattan from a suburb in New Jersey takes one hour each way. He lives with his mother and father, who is also a salad man. He plays guitar in his spare time and relaxes "because the work is really hard." Jesus doesn't like New York and misses home. He is friends with other Mexicans in New York but can't socialize with them easily because they live far away. In the future, Jesus "would like to do something out of the kitchen" (i.e., in the "front").

Medhat

Medhat is the chef at Aperture and one of three co-owners. He learned how to cook in a two-year restaurant apprenticeship in Cairo after he graduated from high school. He was trained to prepare Continental cuisine and is not familiar with Egyptian cuisine. He reads cooking magazines and attends trade shows in search of new ideas. Medhat designs the menu at Aperture. As executive chef, he is responsible for ordering the food and managing the kitchen. He also has general supervisory duties. The owner brought Medhat with him from Neptune's when he opened Aperture.

Medhat pays for his own health insurance. Although his income and hours vary depending on business, he says that he is not making good money because of the high cost of living. He lives with his wife, an immigrant from Central America, and newborn child in Astoria. He says they would like to move away from there but cannot afford to so. He has no time for hobbies. Medhat is 27 years old and plans to stay in the restaurant industry or enter another entrepreneurial field. His family in Cairo are professionals. Medhat came to New York hoping to get rich.[3]

These four vignettes illustrate both the precariousness and flexibility of restaurant employment. While job applicants who have cultural capital (approximated by English-language skills and middle-class background) find their way to jobs in the front of the restaurant or at the top of the kitchen hierarchy, it is possible for others to work their way up from entry-level positions. Ultimate career goals, however, differ. For cultural producers, restaurants are always a temporary job, even though other interviews we have done with waiters indicate that they generally continue working in the restaurant industry for many years. For immigrants, restaurants offer both entry-level jobs and access to entrepreneurial opportunities. As they perfect their language skills and become knowledgeable about the industry, restaurants provide their own ladder for internal promotions. Yet, waitstaff and kitchen staff all depend on their personal relations with the chef and owner. They lack health insurance, cannot anticipate promotions, and earn less than the minimum wage.

The Ethnic Division of Labor

It is important to note that all four restaurants in our sample hire an ethnically diverse workforce, although those that feature an "ethnic" cuisine do tend to hire a large percentage of employees from that ethnic group. Ethnicity does not entirely predict the positions for which people are hired. It is true that American-born whites occupy "front" positions rather than work in the "back." Only two black employees appear in these restaurants, and they are both at the Chinese restaurant, Mia. One, an American-born actress, is on waitstaff in the "front." The other, a man who ran a restaurant in the Caribbean, works as a butcher and cook. At the Chinese restaurant, the owner, manager, take-out manager, delivery man, and chefs are Chinese, as is one of the waitstaff. The other waitstaff are native-born Americans or other Asians, and the bartender is from the Middle East. By contrast, at the Brazilian restaurant the owner is Spanish and the cook is Mexican; both lived in Brazil, where they learned the cuisine. The waiters (who double as busboys) are Brazilian, and the headwaiter is Portuguese, so all the "front" employees speak Brazilian. Hiring patterns at these two ethnic restaurants suggest that cultural experience is necessary to prepare the cuisine, but this experience may be achieved by a learning process as well as ascribed by group membership.

John, the owner of the restaurant in Queens, refers to the staff as a "United Nations." The restaurant hires a large percentage of Middle Eastern employees. The deployment of the staff indicates a de facto ethnic division of labor that is typical of many mid-level restaurants in New York. A host and a waiter are the only native New Yorkers. Another waiter and a busboy are from the Middle East; the bartender is from Brazil; a busboy and two cleaners are from North Africa, Mexico, and Bangladesh; and the Italian-born owner is the chef. The owner states that he does most of his hiring from the neighborhood. According to his son, "In Queens it is easy to find a waiter because they all know each other. When they hear of a job opening they'll come in droves." Nevertheless, he also says he hires waiters through an employment agency. For his other restaurant in Manhattan, he claims he places an advertisement in the Village Voice or the New York Times.

In fact, the staff at the Manhattan restaurant is predominantly either U.S.-born arts workers who got their jobs by walking in off the street or Middle Eastern immigrants who knew the owner from working at the restaurant in Queens, or walked in off the street. Both arts workers and immigrants work in the "front." In the "back," there are a Mexican salad man (Jesus) and an Egyptian chef (Medhat).

The owner's son indicates the difference between employees at Aperture and Neptune's by contrasting Manhattan and Queens. "In Manhattan, you have a lot of actors, artists, or those who are aspiring to be. In Queens, you get all kinds who are looking to be in the business." He emphasizes the importance of hiring "front" staff who adequately represent the cultural capital invested in the restaurant. "If a waiter is not what you perceive the restaurant to be, the customer's perception will be completely distorted. So they mold the restaurant. They turn the restaurant into what it is supposed to be." For this owner, there is no possibility of exchanging the cultural capital of different groups of workers: "If I had my Manhattan waitstaff in Queens, it wouldn't work. Some of my waiters in Manhattan are gay, but it is okay there, whereas it wouldn't work in Queens. It would be offensive."

Yet, workers in the "back" are interchangeable in the owner's eyes. Their lack of skills and English language, and their inability to get other kinds of jobs, enable them to establish an ethnic monopoly over the low-pay positions, at least for a time. "I have a good set of boys," the owner says of Neptune's staff.

For porter, you get a certain ethnic group that seems to go into that. Maybe five-six years ago it was a different ethnic group. Now we're coming into a Mexican domination of that position. Five years ago, it was an influx of Slavic people. You cannot get an American boy or young man to wash dishes or be a porter. It's beneath them. One summer we tried the Youth Program, to give a job to a needy youth. They sent a few boys over and as soon as they heard they had to clean or wash dishes, they said, 'Oh, we won't do that.' Well, what did they expect to do, become a brain surgeon in a restaurant?

So you have to depend on one ethnic group. Who knows who it will be after the

Mexicans? Lately, a fellow from Bangladesh started working here, kind of out in left field, but he happens to be a very good worker. They all get along very well.

Restaurant industry talk confirms that Mexicans have begun to dominate the lowest-skill kitchen positions, perhaps because most Mexican immigrants in New York come from rural areas and lack urban job skills. Besides Neptune's, Mia, the Chinese restaurant also has two Bangladeshi busboys who were students in that country and now live in Queens. We can speculate that Bangladeshi immigrants, like Mexicans, lack English-language skills, "urbane" manners, and the European or culturally "white" appearance that would appeal to owners for positions in the "front." Mexicans and Bangladeshi contrast with Egyptians, North Africans, Brazilians, and Colombians; that is, "Europeanized" immigrants from former European colonies or settlements are mainly hired for "front" jobs and as chefs, especially in mainstream restaurants. Alternatively, as recent immigrants, Bangladeshi and Mexicans lack the contacts and internal entrepreneurs that slightly older immigrant groups have developed. Yet, certain Middle Eastern and Latin immigrants have objective or subjective characteristics that other groups lack. On the one hand, Egyptians (but not Brazilians) in our sample have either done apprenticeships in Continental restaurants or attended college before they immigrate; most come from middle or upper-middle-class backgrounds. On the other hand, they have the culturally "white" persona and middle-class manners that many restaurant owners like; "We have Egyptian waiters," the owner of Neptune's says. "They have class. They're great waiters. They have great table manners. They're all that way."

By the same token, these immigrants with cultural capital make up a pool of relatively loyal labor for promotion. Lacking investment capital and family connections in this country, they are dependent on their employers for giving them access to entrepreneurial opportunity. As the owner of Aperture says about his two Arab co-owners, who get a share of the profits if there are any, "I feel very comfortable with them. I knew they weren't going anywhere when they were working for me before, but they were working just as hard so I knew I could have faith in them." All three derive benefits from the co-owner arrangement. For this owner, "it is good because I have the loyalty and initiative I wanted from them to sustain the business without my having to be there (all the time). For these two guys, I would say they may be able to save for five or six years and eventually open up their own restaurant."

For potential immigrant entrepreneurs, the restaurant industry is both an easy and a difficult point of entry into the mainstream economy. The failure rate of restaurants in Manhattan is said to be 75 per cent during the first year of operation.

Rents are high. Providing a decor is expensive and may require periodic changes. Moreover, immigrants who prove successful in mainstream restaurants must already have cultural capital.

Nevertheless, the lure of entrepreneurship is as strong as the dream of return. The Egyptian manager, one of the two immigrant co-owners of Aperture, is an ambitious man who completed three of the four required years of law school in Egypt. He began working in restaurants in New York because he chose to become an illegal immigrant by staying in the city after his visa expired. He was promoted from dishwasher, a typical unskilled entry position, to busboy, waiter, and waiter's captain as he moved from restaurant to restaurant. He became a manager at Neptune's before moving to Aperture with the owner. He lives alone in Astoria, works six days a week, 13–14 hours a day, and has no social life. He plans to pay off his debts in New York, go back to Egypt, and finish law school.

Similarly, the cook, headwaiter, and a waiter at the Brazilian restaurant all plan to open their own restaurants one day. Another waiter expects to remain a waiter. Although they have lived in the United States far longer than the other immigrants in our sample (13 to 18 years), they also plan to return to their country of origin.

Restaurant Owners

Five out of six owners in our sample are immigrants originally from Italy, Egypt, Taiwan, and Spain. This is a somewhat higher percentage than in the New York restaurant industry (Bailey, 1985). The sixth owner is the son of the Italian immigrant owner and was born in Queens. Capital for starting the restaurants has come from personal savings as well as mortgages and loans from local banks. Except for Lee, it appears capital was not obtained outside New York City. Five out of six owners had extensive job experience in the restaurant industry before becoming owners. Thus, restaurants are a primary source for earning and saving the necessary capital to become an owner.

Don Pedro, the Spanish owner of the Brazilian restaurant, first immigrated to Brazil, and then in 1961 came to New York City where he worked as a waiter, engaged in some business ventures, and got mortgages and bank loans to open up a Brazilian restaurant. Lee, the Chinese owner of Mia, has family in the restaurant business in both Taiwan and New York City. Three years after immigrating to New York in 1973 and working at his brothers' restaurants, he decided to open up his own restaurant. He relied mainly on bank loans for capital. John, the owner of the restaurant in Queens, immigrated to New York City from Italy as a child before World War II. He was a hairstylist in Astoria for 10 years before buying the restaurant at a very low cost with three partners. His son, the only non-immigrant owner, worked with a large restaurant chain and started his own catering business in Manhattan, which provided him the capital to join in partnership with his father at the restaurant. He eventually opened two more restaurants in Manhattan, one of which is in our sample. His two Egyptian co-owners began their restaurant careers in New York City as low-skill kitchen workers and eventually became waiters at the restaurant owned by the father-son team. They saved their earnings as restaurant employees and have bank loans.

Small restaurants are a projection of the owner's personality and family ties. These owners exercise daily operating control over most aspects of their restaurants. They also determine the highest level to which staff can rise, which is limited by family or individual ownership. A seemingly individual expression, such as, a restaurant's decor or theme, may in fact reflect a collective family decision. Lee says that his restaurant's modern motif was "designed . . .according to the tradition of my family and my own idea." All the familys' restaurants bear the name of one of the family members; Mia is the English name of one of Lee's sisters. The co-owner of Aperture and Neptune, however, prides himself on choosing the menu and decor at both restaurants by himself. He pays equal attention to restaurant trends as reported in industry magazines, seminars, and food shows; his local customer base; and his personal desire for change. He has to be careful that the people he hires translate without violating his vision of what the restaurant should be. He expects his "excellent cooks" (not "chefs") to cook a recipe the way he gives it to them. The owner wants a certain amount of skill in this job, but he also wants pliability and won't pay high wages. "This position requires someone with not too much talent and not too little talent, so it is a tough position to fill." In fact, this is the job description that most chef-owners give for a chef's position. Unlike an elite restaurant, however, a moderate-price, mainstream restaurant will hire mainly from an immigrant workforce for their chef's positions.[4]

The restaurant owner does not often fire people. Yet, he or she can be a harsh taskmaster and does not necessarily command the workers' respect. Owners do not want a unionized workforce, so they have to tread a fine line between paternalism and bureaucratic rationality. "I don't want a union house," the co-owner of Aperture and Neptune's says.

If they took a vote and voted in a union I would have to sell the restaurant or just close it down until I could get rid of the union. So, what I try to do is run the restaurant as close to a union house as possible without it being a union. Therefore, when we fire someone we give them three warnings—union rules—and we write personal letters after a vocal warning. It's more so in Manhattan than in Queens.

People are more transient in Manhattan and thus less 'into' the job.

The personalism that restaurant owners who function as managers show with their staff carries over to their relations with customers. John and Don Pedro develop a "name" relationship with steady customers. Lee, however, who employs several types of managers, refers to regular customers who eat at the restaurant every day but does not emphasize personal relations with them. A personalistic style of labor and customer relations to some degree reflects the long hours owners put in and their face-to-face interactions with both workforce and clientele.

As this implies, most restaurant owners define their business in terms of the surrounding neighborhood. However, they develop different strategies to service the neighborhood without sacrificing profits.

Neptune's varies their menu and prices to suit four markets: an older, local customer base in Astoria, steady customers who drive into Queens from the Long Island suburbs to eat there, new customers from the neighborhood who work in high-status, white-collar jobs, and culturally sophisticated people who work at the nearby film studios. The restaurant features "traditional Italian" dishes at moderate prices as early bird specials for the older customers, but it also spotlights as "specials" newer, lighter preparations with more exotic ingredients. Unlike an elite restaurant, however, they offer the same specials two or three days in a row. The younger owner has learned from the trade magazines that people now prefer "real food" to nouvelle cuisine. So, he has changed the menu to include "a lot of stews, mixed grills, soups, homemade pasta, a lot of cheeses, goat cheeses, a lot of oils in my sauces." Without ever losing the original seafood theme (for health-conscious customers) or the Italian theme (that according to industry magazines has "soul") the restaurant in Queens offers an amalgam of cooking traditions. The menu seeks to appeal to both a local clientele of ethnic customers and a cosmopolitan clientele of knowledgeable consumers.

The Chinese and Brazilian restaurants are somewhat different. On the one hand, their product is a single ethnic cuisine. On the other hand, their owners believe in not changing the restaurant. (Lee is adamant on this point.) Yet, their menus are not strictly "ethnic." Mia's dishes are sophisticated and light preparations, including salads of Chinese dishes over greens that appeal to American palates. They have no stews, dim sum, or inexpensive traditional ingredients like chicken feet. Unlike Chinese restaurants in New York that cater to Chinese, the menu lists dishes in English only. The Brazilian restaurant offers a weekend brunch for its Upper West Side customers. The restaurant's appeal is international rather than specifically Brazilian or Latin, and it draws a high-status Latino clientele rather than low-income Latino immigrants.

While most restaurants serve a mainly local clientele, owners interpret this function in different ways. They are influenced by the cosmopolitanism or traditionalism of those local residents who can afford to eat in the restaurant and the economic conditions that affect different parts of their customer base. If the neighborhood changes, the owner must decide whether and how to adapt to the change (cf., Wheaton, 1990). The clientele at Neptune's, for example, has become more diverse ethnically, culturally, and economically over the past few years. As the younger owner describes these changes,

We started with the people in the neighborhood, typical Queens middle- to lower-middle-class. They were very New York Post (a tabloid) type of people— Daily News (another tabloid) people, the type of people that were only interested in what is happening on a daily basis in and around the neighborhood. . .. Now what we have evolved to is what the neighborhood has evolved to. A lot of people that are Times readers, affluent people, people who read the Wall Street Journal for financial purposes. A type of people who are much more educated, (who live here) because of what is affordable. We get a lot of people from (Long Island), New Jersey, and Manhattan who travel to come here. I see a lot more doctors, professionals in general. I know that is what my customer base is because when we got hit with the 1988 recession, (after) Black Monday (when the stock market crashed in October 1987), we got hurt.

An overextension of cultural capital (in terms of menu and decor that reach toward a global, cosmopolitan clientele) may force a restaurant to scale back to a local market.

By the same token, a restaurant owner in Queens plays a different role in the local social and professional community than a restaurant owner in Manhattan. The Queens owners describe Manhattan restaurant owners as engaging in cutthroat competition. They see Queens owners as more cooperative, especially in their neighborhood and on their shopping street. Restaurant owners in the borough exchange information rather than withhold it as a trade secret. Further, with the interest in food that has developed in the past few years, a restaurant owner can engage in "outreach" activities that help mold the local community's tastes. The younger owner writes articles for the weekly neighborhood newspaper, most recently on the nutritional value of fish. Partly this just extends the local merchant's community functions. Partly, too, it expands the restaurant's potential local clientele. "A guy from Queens who goes into Manhattan and is (served) buffalo meat is going to eat it and say it is great, but if they eat the same thing (in Astoria) they are going to say something is wrong with it," the younger owner says.

Among our owners, only the Chinese owner brings investment capital transnationally into the New York restaurant industry. The aspirations of immigrant employees, however, both to open restaurants and return to their country of origin, suggest it is important to trace capital flows from the U.S. restaurant industry to other countries.

Local/Global Implications for Economy and Culture

A brief exploratory study using qualitative techniques can only tentatively suggest generalizations and implications. Nevertheless, interview material and observation indicate three categories of questions for further investigation: the relation between the internal culture of restaurants and their contribution to forming a global culture, the nature of employment and entrepreneurship in the restaurant industry, and macroeconomic consequences of immigrant predominance in the restaurant workforce. These questions transcend the boundaries between economics, urban political economy, and cultural studies.

Full-service restaurants owned by immigrant entrepreneurs may offer an intermediate menu between ethnic and "American" cuisines. Despite the difficulty of defining an American cuisine, especially in New York City with its strong immigrant contributions to urban culture, immigrant owners are clearly capable of conceiving a menu and decor that appeal to American tastes outside their ethnic group. This suggests that the division between immigrant-sector and full-service restaurants that some researchers base on immigrant ownership and labor patterns is not so clear-cut as they think (cf., Bailey, 1985). Moreover, a full-service restaurant's menu and decor demonstrate an interesting interaction between a local and global laborforce, market trends, and clientele. Restaurants in turn help shape a global culture. They do this, first, by bringing exotic foods into an American mainstream. This process differentiates transnational cuisines by the cultural capital invested in their presentation rather than by the national origins of their primary consumers. Second, restaurants diffuse the culinary amalgam they develop if and when their workforce return to their countries of origin and establish their own restaurants.

We hesitate to call this process acculturation rather than globalization. Yet, an immigrant workforce also learns English in the restaurant as well as an organization of work, recipes, and—as far as their positions permit them to observe—strategies of dealing with clientele.

This study also suggests many further questions on the nature of employment and entrepreneurship in the restaurant industry. Opportunities offered to various groups in a global city clearly contrast in terms of permanent employment and "front" or "back" responsibilities. Immigrant groups that are considered to have developed successful entrepreneurs in the restaurant industry must adapt to continual changes in the global sources of labor supply. The Chinese restaurant owners' association in New York, for example, has recently organized to offer training to the many new Chinese immigrants who arrive in the city with very low skills ("New York Chinese Restaurant Association Initiates a Self-Salvation Movement," Sing Tao Daily [(Jih Pao), June 6, 1991, p. 26]. Moreover, the high cost of opening a full-service restaurant in Manhattan (optimally, $250,000 to $1 million) precludes many immigrant entrepreneurs from transcending the immigrant sector of the industry.

Rigidities in the ethnic and social division of labor in the restaurant industry raise questions about the industry's continued strategies of labor recruitment as well as the polarization of job opportunities in the city. The lack of interchangeability between groups of "minority" employees (immigrants, teenagers, women) that predominate in different sectors of the industry (Bailey, 1985) does not apply to some groups of immigrant men. The objective and subjective conditions in which groups do become interchangeable (Mexicans and Bangladeshi, Egyptians and Brazilians) must be explored. This is especially important in light of the continued underrepresentation of American-born blacks in full-service restaurants, which researchers attribute to job expectations, institutionalized racism, and weak ties to entrepreneurs and labor markets. Special training programs that target blacks and others in prison populations and drug treatment programs are very new and depend on employers' willingness to change existing hiring patterns ("Seeing Beyond Burgers and Soapsuds," *New York Times*, June 12, 1991, p. C1).

Moreover, the underrepresentation of native New Yorkers in our sample emphasizes the industry's dependence on continued migration and immigration. If New York loses the dynamism of a global cultural center, the industry risks losing a labor supply of artists, actors, and other creative producers and performers who migrate to New York from other parts of the country and the rest of the world as well.

Our small qualitative study also raises questions about both the national and global impact of immigrant subcultures and their formal and informal institutions. We believe that in the absence of much detailed research, there are great discrepancies between theorized macroeconomic models and economic and social reality.

First, general economic models must assume an open U. S. economy which is increasingly affected by the rational economic decisions of businesses and governments of other countries around the world. In specific economic sectors, such as restaurants, researchers must disaggregate data by immigrant groups. Qualitative data must be collected on cultural capital, motivation and sentiments, and ability to get access to the local economy. The growing "Quiet Sector" of formal and informal networks demands new research strategies. Immigrant access and mobility rely, for example, on employment agencies that specialize in undocumented workers and nonpermanent residents, as well as on inter-firm mobility that in turn depends on personal ties through work experience. These issues are significant not only to studies of labor and immigration but also to domestic and transnational monetary flows.

The continued expansion of the restaurant industry by hiring undocumented and off-the-books workers forces us to confront the issue of "leaks" in standard macroeconomic models. Leaks are generally understood to be channels through which money "gets lost" and is not directly recirculated back into the economy as models would predict. The visibility of the informal service sector in New York has not yet resulted in its documentation. Its size, the countries of origin of participants, and the volume of monetary transactions that pass through the sector remain to be shown. In addition, because this economy is untaxed and outside the social security system, analysts must research its overall effect on the fiscal crisis of local governments, as well as on government transfer programs and social services. Moreover, social scientists should trace the formal and informal institutions that aid immigrants in investment and sending money overseas (e.g., Urgente Express, Western Union, South American Express, American Express, check-cashing services, travel agencies that provide a multitude of services, etc.).

The conditions under which immigrants work in restaurants raise a major concern with the welfare and future of unskilled immigrants. We need a better conception of the impact of such work on immigrants' quality of life, as well as upon the broader public. We must define the social and economic costs of neglecting human capital investment by underemploying highly-skilled and educated immigrants in both secondary and informal labor markets. A critical analysis may aid in adjusting the data on unemployment and underemployment and calculating their severity.

Finally, many international monetary policies and general programs of "development" were drawn from macroeconomic models that rely on quantitative economic and social indicators. However, as we suggest, quantitative analysis omits many significant factors. Ethnographic and qualitative survey research should enter new factors into current models and suggest new modes of analysis. Even small micro-level studies can develop realistic assumptions about rational economic decision-making by producers and consumers and indicate the processes by which a global economy and culture are produced.

Notes

*The authors acknowledge the participation of Julia Butterfield and Ramona Hernandez.

1. All restaurants and respondents appear under a pseudonym. Supplementary information on the restaurant industry comes from ongoing interviews with owners, chefs, and waitstaff by two of the authors (Zukin and Parker).
2. Some respondents who said they walked in off the street may have heard about the job through personal connections. Those who had worked with a chef or owner obviously got their first job by other means.
3. Several weeks after being interviewed, Medhat died of a heart attack.
4. Chef's positions in elite New York restaurants are still dominated by West Europeans (mainly French) and white Americans. Very occasionally, sous-chefs in elite restaurants are Asians, native-born blacks, or European Latin Americans. Elite chefs tend to be "professionals," i.e., those who have completed a traditional European apprenticeship, graduated from a vocational cooking school, or had some college education and "switched careers" by doing apprenticeships in other elite kitchens. By contrast, immigrant cooks in full-service restaurants get on-the-job training in food preparation.

References

Bailey, Thomas and Waldinger, Roger (1991) "The Changing Ethnic/Racial Division of Labor." In Manuel Castells and John H. Mollenkopf (eds), *Dual City: Restructuring New York*, New York: Russell Sage Foundation.

Bailey, Thomas (1985) "A Case Study of Immigrants in the Restaurant Industry," *Industrial Relations* 24, no. 1 (Spring):205-21.

Brake, K. (1988) Phonix in der Asche-New York verandert seine Stadtstruktur, in Beitrage der Universität Oldenburg Zur Stadtund Regionalplanung, no. 5, Oldenburg: BIS.

Castells, Manuel and Mollenkopf, John H. (1991) "Introduction." In *Dual City*.

Fainstein, Norman (1987) "The Underclass/Mismatch Hypothesis as an Explanation for Black Economic Deprivation," *Politics & Society* 15, no. 4: 403-51.

Harvey, David (1989) *The Condition of Postmodernity: An Enquiry into the Origins of Cultural Change*, Oxford: Basil Blackwell.

Hill, Richard Child (1989) "Comparing Transnational Production Systems: The Automobile Industry in the USA and Japan," *International Journal of Urban and Regional Research* 13: 462-80.

Kasarda, John (1985) "Urban Change and Minority Opportunities." In Paul E. Peterson (ed), *The New Urban Reality*, Washington, D.C.: Brookings Institution.

Perry, David C. (1987) "The Politics of Dependency in Deindustrializing America: The Case of Buffalo, New York." In *The Capitalist City*.

Sassen, Saskia (1987) "Growth and Informalization at the Core: A Preliminary Report on New York City." In *The Capitalist City*.

——(1988) *The Mobility of Labor and Capital: A Study in International Investment and Labor Flow*, Cambridge: Cambridge University Press.

——(1991) "The Informal Economy." In *Dual City*.

Sayer, A. (1989) "The 'new' regional geography and problems of narrative," *Society and Space* 7:251-76.

Scott, A. J. and Storper, M. (1986) *Production, Work, Territory*, Boston: Allen and Unwin.

Soja, Edward W. (1987) "Economic Restructuring and the Internationalization of the Los Angeles Region." In *The Capitalist City*.

——(1991) "Poles Apart: Urban Restructuring in New York and Los Angeles." In *Dual City*.

Smith, Michael P. and Feagin, Joe R. (eds) (1987) *The Capitalist City: Global Restructuring and Community Politics*, Oxford: Basil Blackwell.

State of New York Department of Labor (1988) *Fiscal Year 1986 and Industry Profile 1988*.

U.S. Department of Labor; Bureau of Labor Statistics (1989) *Employment Hours and Earnings, States and Areas, 1972-1987*, Volume III, Minnesota-New York (March) Bulletin 2320.

Waldinger, Roger (1985) "Immigration and Industrial Change in the New York City Apparel Industry." In George J. Borjas and Marta Tienda (eds), *Hispanics in the United States Economy*, Orlando: Academic Press.

——(1990) "Immigrant Enterprise in the United States." In S. Zukin and P. DiMaggio (eds) *Structures of Capital: The Social Organization of the Economy*, Cambridge: Cambridge University Press.

Wheaton, Dennis Ray (1990) "The Busy Bee: Homes Away From Home," *The Journal of Gastronomy 6*, no. 1:16-23.

Winnick, Louis (1990) *New People in Old Neighborhoods*, New York: Russell Sage Foundation.

Zukin, Sharon (1989) *Loft Living: Culture and Capital in Urban Change*, 2nd ed., New Brunswick, NJ: Rutgers University Press.

——(1990) "Socio-Spatial Prototypes of the New Organization of Consumption: The Role of Real Cultural Capital," *Sociology*, vol. 24:37-56.

——-(1991) *Landscapes of Power: From Detroit to Disney World*, Berkeley and Los Angeles: University of California Press.

Zukin, Sharon and DiMaggio, Paul (eds) (1990) *Structures of Capital: The Social Organization of the Economy*, Cambridge: Cambridge University Press.

ETHNICITY, RACE, CLASS, AND IDEOLOGY COME TOGETHER IN L.A.

Allen David Heskin
University of California, Los Angeles

Los Angeles is a living laboratory of economic restructuring. The restructuring expresses itself in the city's increasing multiethnicity. Yet, like most U.S. cities it is highly segregated both by ethnicity, race, and class. There are areas of the city that are exceptions. In those internationalized zones ethnicity, race, and class meet each other. A group of housing co-operatives formed in one those areas of Los Angeles is a model of the dimensions of that encounter. Issues of ethnic identity become both highlighted and blurred by class and the introduction of U.S. concepts of race. Language as both a symbol of identity and as a physical barrier to communication becomes of paramount importance. Racism and the suspicion and distance created by the racial state is omnipresent and tears down whatever modicum of community is constructed. How to create a whole out of these disparate pieces, a kind of multiculturalism, becomes the challenge. What the whole would look like becomes a matter of discourse and debate. Only by passing through layers of understanding do we see the possibilities.

This article examines the intersection of ethnicity, race, class, and ideology in five unusual multiethnic, working-class housing co-operatives, known as the Route 2 Project, located in the Silverlake/Echo Park district of Los Angeles.[1] The five co-operatives were formed from property acquired in the 1960s by Caltrans, the State of California Transportation Agency, to expand the Route 2 freeway. When Caltrans decided not to build the extension in the mid-1970s, the residents of the state-owned property organized and after many years of struggle, purchased the property and formed the co-operatives. The residents won the right to purchase the property in the early 1980s. The property was purchased, rehabilitated, and the co-operative formed between 1981 and 1985.

During Caltrans' ownership much of the Route 2 Corridor housing acted as port-of-entry housing. The primary in-migrants have been Latinos from some fourteen Latin American countries who make up more than sixty percent of the co-operatives' population. Other parts of the world are also represented in smaller numbers in the immigrant population. Among the immigrant Latinos there are variations in racial terms from white to black or, in ethnic terms, from European to African.2 There is also great variation in the class backgrounds among the Latino immigrants, for example, middle- and upper-class, college-trained, urban Cubans, and poor, rural, Mexicans with third grade educations. These immigrants are usually referred to as Latinos in the Route 2 co-operatives, regardless of these variations, as opposed to the remainder of the population which is referred to as Americano. The Americano population is equally divided between Anglos and a mix of native-born minority groups including African-Americans, Asians, and as is discussed below some Chicanos. It should be noted that although these definitions are the dominant ones in the co-operatives the dimensions of the term Latino have been the subject of conflict. Regardless of this debate the terms Latino and Americano have from time to time been important in the lives of the co-operatives and have been employed at various times as symbols of conflict and division.

Los Angeles is very a multiethnic but segregated city (Research Group on the Los Angeles Economy, 1989). Latinos from various countries concentrate in East Los Angeles, the inner ring around downtown, and the eastern portion of the San Fernando Valley; African-Americans concentrate in the south-central part of the city and the eastern portion of the valley; and Asians concentrate in various ethnic enclaves bearing the names of their nationalities. The multiethnic character of the city's population has increased due to an in-migration of nearly two million people from third world countries over the past twenty years (Soja, Heskin, and Cenzatti, 1985). The national racial minorities have become a local majority (Adler, 1983a p. 482).

A few areas in Los Angeles differ from this general pattern. Many of these are transitional zones where ethnicities mix, and intermarriage is common. These open areas also often serve as ports-of-entry for different national groups. Schools in these zones typically report that their student population speaks more than fifty languages and dialects. The Route 2 Corridor is in one of these uniquely diverse and internationalized zones.

I became involved with the Route 2 Project in 1979 when I was asked to serve on the board of directors of the project's newly organized community development corporation. The corporation had the task of purchasing and rehabilitating the property and organizing the co-operatives. In 1985 I moved into one of the co-operatives that resulted from the corporation's efforts, where I have resided since. I have observed the interactions of the residents of the project in countless situations and interviewed and engaged in lengthy discourse with many of the residents of the project over the years on the subject of this paper. I have made notes and tapes on occasion, periodically written papers on my observations, and shared my observations with the subjects of the study to obtain further reactions. I have been more than a participant-observer of the process of the project. It might be more accurate to say I have been a "partisan-observer," as the term was used by Leroy Ellis (1969).

I, like many other outsiders, was drawn to the project by its exceptional multicultural image.[3] This same image has attracted many liberal politicians and professionals who supported the project. Internally, issues of ethnicity, language, racism, and class have been omnipresent. They are endemic to such a multiethnic working-class and immigrant environment and denote that interaction is taking place. At their best these tensions are representative of a dynamic process of creation.

Ideology

The internal conflicts have been accentuated by ideological divisions within the project's leadership which do not perfectly match ethnic or racial differences. There have been two prevalent ideologies in the Americano population, progressive populist and pluralist, while the leaders in the immigrant Latino population have tended to be clientelist in their approach. Each of the ideological groups has had different reactions to the project's multiethnicity. Early on a progressive populist leadership approached the multiethnicity of the project as an opportunity for multiculturalism. Multiculturalism in their minds is a form of social relations in which different ethnicities "maintain their identities, but engage in extensive interaction and mutual influence." When multiculturalism occurs, "relations between single minorities and the dominant culture are complemented by organized interaction among minorities," and members of ethnic groups become "able and willing to communicate and cooperate across cultural boundaries" (Heskin and Heffner 1987, p. 526). In the process each group's identity is continually enriched and reconstructed.

This progressive populist approach must be distinguished from the color blindness claimed by current-day conservatives sometimes referred to as "authoritarian populists."[4] The Route 2 populists are quite aware of ethnic differences and celebrate the differences rather than ignore them. To many of the populists multiculturalism is not an approach to a problem, the problem of multiethnicity, but an attraction that keeps them living in and working on the project. In their view the co-ops which have many mixed ethnic families as members should be an oasis from the racial state outside the project.[5] A nondiscrimination pledge has been repeated over and over again in the project, and the relations among the Americanos of all ethnicities reflect its intention. The relations between the Americanos and the immigrant Latinos have not been as healthy. The gap has proved more difficult to bridge.

Americano ethnic pluralists in the co-operatives, reacting to years of experience with racism, see minority ethnic and racial groups as bases of power for fighting historical and continuing oppression. They emphasize the importance of communication between groups rather than between individuals. Multiethnicity or multiculturalism is not valued per se. Pluralists believe multiethnicity should be managed with full consciousness of the needs of each ethnic group. In their focus on needs of competing groups, however, the needs of outside groups are not of primary concern. Some theorists characterize this primary focus on the needs of one's own group as nationalism or cultural nationalism (Omi & Winant 1986, pp. 103-108).[6]

Also in the co-operatives, particularly within the immigrant population, are people who approach the co-operatives as clientelists. The immigrants' national identities and class differences can push them apart, reflecting old national and regional feuds and class conflicts. At the same time their current immigrant status in a strange land can build unity emphasizing their commonalities of language and culture. Part of the Latin American political tradition is clientelism. The essence of clientelism is captured in the seemingly unchangeable relationship between the landed patron and the peasant (Powell 1970).[7] Clientelism is centered on family and reciprocity, and it, along with immigrant status, carries a heavy obligation to family members and fellow countrymen particularly those undergoing the immigrant process. Strong elements of what may in other contexts be called nepotism come into play. While immigrant Latinos dominate this group, the clientelist position is not without resonance in elements of the Americano working-class population of the co-operatives.[8]

The clientelist immigrants in Route 2 undergo a process of identity reformulation as they integrate into this country.[9] They learn about racism in this country, their position within the racial state, and the country's racial rhetoric. In the process they develop common ground with the ethnic pluralists. In the co-operative there has been a counter force which has limited this cross-identity.

Who's a Latino?

Although the terms Latino and Americano are primarily used in the project as I described above, within the inner circles of the pluralist and clientelist leadership in the Route 2 project there is great disagreement on the dimensions of the term Latino and the requirements for "true" ethnic membership. This has added great confusion and created substantial conflict between the two groups of leaders. The pluralists, like the emergent group of Latinos discussed by Felix Padilla in his book, Latino Ethnic Consciousness (1985), define Latinos by activism while the clientelists, like Padilla's traditional group of Latinos, use much more of a cultural definition.[10] This has allowed the ethnic Americano-Latinos among the pluralists, for example, to organize a Latino caucus with the active immigrant leadership and at the same time attempt to delegitimize and exclude non-participating immigrant Latinos from their definition of Latino. The clientelists in turn have excluded ethnic Americano-Latinos (Chicanos), regardless of activity, who have assimilated into U.S. culture particularly if they have lost the Spanish language. A further twist on this theme has been the clientelist inclusion of Anglos who speak Spanish and are identified with the immigrant group's problems, to what amounts to honorary Latino status.

Class

The division between Americanos regardless of ideology or ethnicity and the vast majority of Latino immigrants is further complicated by the factor of class. The corridor population while overwhelmingly working-class is composed of various strata of the working class. Certainly the Americano leadership whether populist or pluralist tends to be skilled workers with many union members. A few of the leaders have moved into administrative positions and are approaching membership in the professional-managerial class. In contrast, a great deal of the corridor's immigrant and clientelist population works in the secondary labor-market with garment workers, domestic workers, and contract labor in significant numbers. Because of the tendency of labor-market membership to be coterminous with immigrant/ethnic status, many of the class-strata-based conflicts in the corridor are perceived by residents of co-operatives as ethnic or race conflicts with some African-Americans, Asians, and delegitimated Latinos as well as some Anglos on the Americano side.[11] Among all the possible foci of conflict in the Route 2 Project, ethnicity has stood out as the major issue visible if, for no other reason than language, a primary element which divides the population and prevents full, direct interaction. Monolingualism is common across the population including both large numbers of English-speaking-only and Spanish-speaking-only individuals. Race, on the other hand, is an issue that seems to have been superimposed on the setting and although it has appeared from time to time, it has not stuck as a central issue.

Within the diverse Americano population it has rarely been an issue. It appeared as a programmatic issue only as the immigrant Latino population was integrated into the racialism of U.S. society. However, because of the class fragmentation of the Latino population, ethnicity or race as analytic categories do not perfectly fit the Route 2 Project situation. Examples of the misfit are found in the sometimes frayed relations between Chicanos in the project and the immigrant Latinos, and the fact that the Latinos in the project come from fourteen different countries and contain a range of racial and ethnic variations.

Although ethnicity has been dominant in the rhetoric of conflict in the co-operatives, the categories the immigrants used, Latino and Americano, while having significant ethnic content, actually more clearly divide immigrant from non-immigrant in class terms than ethnic or racial groups from one another. The emphasis on immigrant status represented in the Americano/Latino categories in the Route 2 Project echoes a distinction described by Robert Miles (1982). Although Miles is writing about England, much of what he has written seems to apply to the Route 2 Project.[12] He argues that race (as opposed to racism) has no objective basis in the current historical period and is, therefore, an inappropriate category to be employed in understanding social relations. He sees race instead as a social construction of the racial state that is employed through the practice of racism to divide the working class.[13] Ethnicity on the other hand has material characteristics such as language and presents a real, rather than ideological, category. This has certainly been the case in the Route 2 Project. Beyond this Miles argues that the immigrant process itself is central to understanding social relations, particularly its role in the fractionalization of the working class.

The central role of immigrant status is demonstrated in the Route 2 Project. The tendency for the Latinos and Americanos to have different positions in the laborforce introduces a number of structural elements into the project beyond the obvious one of variation in financial resources.[14] Workers in the primary laborforce usually work nine-to-five, five-day-a-week jobs. Workers in the secondary economy have much more irregular hours (Sassen-Koob, 1985). Some of the more marginalized workers in the co-operatives are day laborers who cannot easily control their work hours or plan their free time. In this setting establishing meeting times is difficult. The Americanos usually want to meet on week-day nights. The Latinos are often unavailable on these nights and prefer instead either Friday night or weekend meetings. Friday night meetings are a particular anathema to the Americanos.

Scheduling meetings is not the only problem. Autonomy in the work place is also a factor. Having access to a phone during work hours is important to conducting the business of the co-operative. Since the Housing Authority is primarily a nine-to-five office with phone hours between 10:00 AM and 12:00 PM and 1:00 PM and 4:00 PM, the opportunities for communication are limited. Many of the Latinos work in very regulated environments with little opportunity to communicate with the outside world or take time off for meetings. Workers in the primary laborforce have more freedom during working hours. Certainly those members of the co-operatives with administrative positions have a great deal more freedom.

This clarity is not perfect. Class also emerged clearly within the Latino, meaning Latino immigrant, population. Different countries have sent various classes to the corridor or sent more people with rural rather than urban backgrounds. For example, the Cubans in the project tend to be from major cities with petite-bourgeoisie or professional-managerial backgrounds and college educations. The Mexicans in the project tend to be rural and have minimal educations. The class educational divisions have resulted in language fights over the style of Spanish to be used and in other episodic conflicts. More than once the charge of racism has been leveled by one Latino against another.[15] The charge suggests that the offender has separated him- or herself from the group and considers him- or herself better than other Latinos.

Class difference was a major factor in a conflict that emerged when a group of very low-income, Mexican residents, who lived in overcrowded quarters without open space, felt deliberately snubbed when they attended an organizing party held in a much higher-income Cuban neighbor's backyard on a hot summer night rather than in the host's spacious house.[16] The party was held outside due to the heat and because the varnish was drying on the newly refinished floors inside. The Mexicans had held meetings in their modest apartments and didn't understand why they were meeting outside. The reasons did not satisfy the offended. Why did the host have to refinish his floors that weekend? Weren't they good enough to be invited inside?

Communication[17]

While many of the issues present in the co-operatives are structural and not particularly amenable to local response, these problems can be exacerbated by the very material problem of language difference and communication across languages.[18] The co-operatives share much with other forms of organization. They can only function if they successfully achieve a formal arrangement for interaction toward common goals. To be effective the participants in these organizations must communicate; to communicate, they must have both the ability and the motivation to do so (Taylor & Simard, 1975). Interpersonal conflict or class and culture-based rivalry and differences in norms, values, and perceptions can all interfere with communication.

The issue of effective communication held particular importance in the organizing and development phases of the Route 2 Project because of the dominant populist leadership. The populists insisted that problems ordinarily lightly passed over in the name of expediency be confronted and solved in an open, participatory fashion.[19] Solutions could not be imposed from above (Adler, 1983b, p. 362; Harris & Moran, 1979). They insisted upon having an open debate and relied on it as a check on their actions. Individuals affected by issues were expected to participate. Language and culture can disrupt the smooth working of this process. They do in the Route 2 Project.

The early leadership approached the communication problem in two ways. They sought to operate as bilingual an organization as possible by providing all notices, newsletters, and key co-operative documents in both English and Spanish and providing translation between English and Spanish at meetings.[20] Secondly, they hired Latino and Chicano bilingual organizers to work with the residents. The organizers would not only do their jobs as organizers but would also act as translators and multicultural mediators when needed (Taft, 1981). The leadership was not very sophisticated about the meaning of this scheme in practice. Little was known about the requirements of bilingualism and interpretation, and few organizers were available who had experience in the type of organizing needed in the corridor. More organizers know about conflict-oriented organizing than about populist multicultural community building. Further, it is difficult for a multiethnic group to attract many of the best Latino and Chicano organizers. Many of these organizers are nationalists and, therefore, want to make their talents available to support their own group.

Ability

In the multiethnic-monolingual world of the Route 2 resident, cross-cultural interpretation is certainly an essential element of communication. Cross-cultural interpretation requires a greater skill level than is usually available within groups such as those in the Route 2 Project. Interpretation requires more than switching the words in one language for those in the other. The interpreter must convey a speaker's tone and gestures and the context. Interpretation is situation-specific and requires considerable familiarity with all the differences of culture, class, and gender contained in the audience (Seleskovitch, 1976). In a technically sophisticated project like Route 2, it also requires technical proficiency with the language not readily available.

In the search for situational and audience-specific equivalents, an interpreter must call on a knowledge of the contextualization cues that allow listeners from different backgrounds to sort out the ambiguities inherent in all language. Disastrous confusions of meaning can result from misuse or misunderstanding of (1) nonverbal signals such as posture, gaze direction, facial expression, and body movements; (2) paraverbal signals such as intonation, tempo, and loudness of speech; and (3) the implicit semantics of technical jargon or dialect. The sum of these cues, together with strictly verbal content and presuppositions drawn from the context (physical location, social setting, history of encounters between the participants), will determine the specific meaning drawn from what is said (Gumperz, 1982, 1976; Conklin and Lourie, 1983, p. 262-76; Brislin, 1980). Over and over again this reality has been demonstrated in the project. Publishing a newsletter is extraordinarily difficult. On one memorable occasion four separate translations of a newsletter were completed before an acceptable version was obtained. Translators for the articles were sought from the Route 2 population. Several residents who volunteered claimed to be fully bilingual, but these individuals proved to be only partially bilingual and not up to the task. A supposedly professional hired translator was also unsuccessful. Finally, a professional was located who could do the job. This was not an isolated incident. It took time to find people with sufficient skills to do similar tasks.

There was also a running debate about what style of Spanish should be used in the project. At one point, the debate erupted into a near violent argument over whether the formal urban Spanish of the Cubans or the more informal rural Spanish of Mexican peasants should be used in fliers and newsletters. The Cubans felt Spanish would be defiled by the rural style. Others worried the mass of the residents would be unable to read the more formal Spanish text. Periodically, committees of Latinos from different countries were set up to decide what style of Spanish should be used and what words should be employed for the very technical terms of the housing co-operatives. Usually the board would have to intercede by asking the committee to come to a resolution so the project could proceed.

In the early organizing period of the Route 2 Project, before funds were available to hire translators, the groups had no choice but to use members with varying degrees of bilingual skills to interpret at meetings. The job usually fell upon one of the bilingual members. When organizers were hired, they often took over the job. As was later learned, the organizers' skills at interpretation also varied greatly. In the life of the project ten people held organizer jobs, only one of whom had ever served as an interpreter before. In this period interpretation was often by summary or by whisper to a group on the side of the meeting. In large meetings, sequential translation was provided to the best of the translator's ability. Much later in the process, professional interpreters capable of simultaneous translation were hired for meetings. Even later in the process translation equipment (head sets) was sometimes employed.

Motivation

The Route 2 Corridor population is no different than other groups. Some people are eager to participate and others are not. Also, some people who are willing to participate will make the extra effort required to communicate across cultures while others will not. An effective organizer must be able to bridge the intergroup biases and differences contained in the organization and bring the membership to active participation while recognizing and developing organic leadership. Various authors have described organizers as stimulants, catalysts, mobilizers, enablers, and trainers (Alinsky, 1971, 1969; Fellman, 1973; Kahn, 1970; Molina, 1978; Twelvetrees, 1982). There is always a danger that the population will become dependent on the organizer and that the organizer will be drawn into a leadership position. In theory, once the political/managerial skills are imparted to the residents and experience begins to accumulate, full responsibility for the organization devolves upon the resident leadership.

The multicultural mediator role that the organizers are expected to fill only further complicates the organizers' task. Mediators must understand expectations about the behavior and roles appropriate to given situations and resolve issues, such as, who approaches whom, whether an appeal is to reason or sympathy, whether demeanor is assertive or humble, whether etiquette is formal or casual, whether topics are intimate or impersonal (Taft, 1981, p. 56). Errors in communicative deportment of this kind are especially serious, because they will be seen, not as simple misunderstandings, but as breaches of conduct attributable to attitude or character.

The mediator is the person who determines the intentionality of a cultural *faux pas*, as in the case of the outdoor party, and leads the group either in rage or friendly laughter in such moments. It is not enough to abstractly appreciate that a remark is an insult or a joke. The mediator must feel the insult or get the joke and ensure that everyone understands its meaning. It is this ability that allows the mediator to bond with all elements of the membership and bring them closer to bonding with each other (Taft, 1981).

The job of a multicultural mediator is to grasp and convey meaning beyond the limits of an interpreter's competence. Equivalents for everyday objects, events, and stereotypes that depend on shared experience require the mediator's intervention. To find semantic equivalents for metaphors or allegories requires the mediator's knowledge of the actual conditions of living in a specific culture, as distinct from the interpreter's knowledge of its linguistic conventions (Sechrist, et. al, 1982).

The Organizers

The first organizer in the Route 2 Project was not hired until the early 1980s. Two likely candidates applied for the organizer job. One was an Anglo man with limited organizing experience who had spent time in Latin America and was bilingual. The other was a Mexican woman, educated in this country, with about the same level of experience. The man had more technical knowledge of housing, but the woman was chosen for the position. It was felt that both her gender and her ethnicity would help her do a better job.[21]

Over the next five years, the group obtained additional funding from various foundations to hire additional organizers. At one time, there were three paid people serving as organizers. The organizers came from various ethnic backgrounds: the next two people hired were Chicanas; two later people who worked part-time were Cubans, and then a Puerto Rican was hired. These organizers were followed by a largely monolingual English-speaking, Anglo woman and a Salvadoran man. Two Chicanos were the last full-time, paid organizers in the project.

Only the Anglo woman was a professionally-trained organizer although several other organizers had held jobs that involved organizing. The Latinos were capable of varying degrees of bilingualism with some stronger in English and others in Spanish. The degree to which they served as bridges between the groups and cultural mediators also varied. Some of the organizers were better at this function than others, although evidently as a group they did not successfully serve this function. The technical complexity of the project as well as the intercultural dynamics discussed earlier made this role difficult. Some of these organizers also seemed to see themselves more in pluralist terms, as monocultural advocates and brokers, rather than mediators.

Learning About the Requirements of Communication

The organizing board of the co-operatives, although multiethnic, was primarily made up of Americanos. This meant there was a largely English-speaking, non-immigrant Latino board leading a majority immigrant Latino, largely Spanish-speaking population. In this period the leadership was expanded, with the help of the organizers, but very few immigrant Latinos were among those added. While the property was purchased and rehabilitated, the Latino population, in the main, went along with the process, but at a distance.

The most vocal Latinos to emerge in the early period were leaders of the dissent group. The experience of fighting off the revolt by this group began to acquaint the English-speaking populist board members with the means to involve the Latinos. Several Cuban residents, along with an African-American resident of the multifamily property, led a largely Latino dissident group that wanted to buy the property they lived in as individuals with the limited-equity restriction. The project leadership decided to hire a professional translator for the meeting that grew out of this conflict because of its importance and expected complexity. A court-certified interpreter was hired and contributed extraordinarily to the well-attended and intense meeting, creating clarity and calming people down to the point that communication was possible.

The leadership noted the value of having a "real" interpreter and lamented not being able to afford such a person at all their meetings. Once, with the encouragement of an organizer, a Spanish-speaking Latino resident came to a meeting to ask that an "independent" translator be provided at meetings. Unfortunately, the leadership reacted defensively to the request and did not seek to find out what the person really wanted. They had hired Latino organizers to do the translation and didn't know what else to do. They did not control what the organizers said in the translations and felt they had gone more than half way in reaching out to the Latinos. They felt unjustly accused of somehow biasing the translation. The organizer who encouraged the Latino to come to the meeting was silent and did not mediate the misunderstanding. It took some time for the leadership to gain a full understanding of what the Latinos wanted and change their position.

As was discussed earlier, the everyday problem of language at meetings was complicated by the populists' approach. The meetings took hours to gain a word-by-word understanding of every document, lease, contract, or regulatory agreement that was to be involved in the project. As the leadership became more knowledgeable, newcomers had an increasingly difficult time understanding the discussions at the meetings. Some English speakers did overcome this hurdle through patient listening and asking questions; Spanish speakers did not.

It must have been very difficult for the Spanish speakers attending the meetings to tell whether their lack of understanding was due to technical and language barriers, personal inability, or deliberate exclusion of Latinos. Tenacity and faith in the process was required to stay long enough to overcome both the technical and language barriers. The discussions required a high level of technical sophistication with both languages. The lack of trained knowledgeable interpreters made the Latinos' task unsurmountable.

Given the barriers to Latino participation, mediation was necessary to assure the Latinos that they were not being deliberately excluded and that Americanos were doing their part to bridge the cultural gulf. As in the case of the request for the independent translator, the organizers were not able to provide the mediating element and doubts about the intentions of the non-Latinos went unchecked.

Interviews with Latinos in the project during this period disclosed much confusion and suspicion about the development of the co-operatives. For example, many of those interviewed were very upset that their children could not inherit their homes. As one person put it, "her children would be put out if she died." In fact, children were not excluded from inheritance. A lengthy debate had been held on this subject early in the process, and it had been agreed that children should have the right of inheritance. The documents affirmed inheritance rights, but the affirmation was buried in many pages of technical legal documents. The word did not get down to the members. About half of those interviewed attributed some problem either real or rumored to anti-Latino bias in the project.[22]

As the co-operatives began to take on more operational substance, the lack of Latino leadership became more serious. The rehabilitation and operation of the co-operatives presented complex policy questions that directly affected the residents' lives. There were hard choices to be made and much resident participation was necessary to make them. In two almost entirely immigrant Latino groups, one of the co-operatives and a rental project known as Imogen, which was built to relieve overcrowding in the co-operatives and was to be a sixth co-operative, stable leadership did not develop. The growing belief that the two leaderless groups would fail as co-ops and the increasing operational burden on the non-Latino leadership in the other four groups created an atmosphere of crisis. The leadership put increasing pressure on the organizers to solve the Latino leadership problem. Under this pressure, one of the organizers, a Chicana, left the project. It was a critical time, and the board was becoming desperate for someone who could do the job.

A trained professional organizer was working on the rehabilitation staff as a bookkeeper. Although she was Anglo and had little facility with Spanish, she had worked for a multiethnic organization and had successfully organized a Latino neighborhood community in Los Angeles.[23] She was committed to multiculturalism and felt the responsibility to solve the problem. Under the urging of staff and board, she was pressed into service.

The former bookkeeper and the remaining Puerto Rican organizer, who had started with the organization as a rehabilitation trainee, responded to the pressure for success in organizing the Latinos with a demand for higher pay and the professionalization of their function. In addition to their organizational and leadership development responsibilities, they had been involved in many minor tasks generated by the rehabilitation, such as, getting signatures on documents or arranging for temporary relocation during fumigations. They wanted to be freed from this responsibility so that they could concentrate on organizing. The board acquiesced to both demands, raising the organizers' salaries and creating a new position to carry on the rehabilitation work.

At this point the board intended that the English-speaking organizer would work with the four ethnically-mixed, functioning co-operatives. The Puerto Rican organizer, with support and training from the new, professional organizer, would concentrate on the two troubled, primarily Latino, Spanish-speaking co-operatives. It soon became obvious that this strategy did not sufficiently address the needs of the two troubled co-operatives and pressure to solve this problem was, again, brought on the organizers, particularly the Puerto Rican organizer.

Again, the response to the pressure was a demand for more money for the Puerto Rican organizer. However, this time the board lost its temper and fired the Puerto Rican organizer, who, in their eyes, had not successfully switched from his position as a rehabilitation trainee to a professional organizer. His firing generated a crisis that proved to be another important step in learning how to solve the problem of communication.

The fired organizer attempted to rally the people he had been working with against his firing. Many of the Latinos were afraid of what would happen to them when he was gone. As one person said, he was our "only link" to the leadership group. Once again, the leadership responded by calling a mass meeting. Again, the professional interpreter was called in to translate. The Latinos supporting the organizer demanded that he be reinstated pending a full evaluation of Latino participation and his performance. If this were not possible, they demanded full participation in the selection of his replacement.

The meeting was very painful, but productive. In the anger of the meeting, yelling and shouting, the English-speaking leadership felt that for the first time they had participated in a direct conversation with the Latino residents. They saw, again, the value of the professional interpreter. They did not want the organizer to be the Latinos' only link. They became concerned that the organizers, by virtue of their monopoly on interpretation and cultural mediation, had been playing a gatekeeper role not proper to the organizer function. They wanted a mediator, not a broker, and more than that they wanted to talk directly to the residents.

The leadership refused to reinstate the fired organizer, but willingly accepted full participation of the Latinos in hiring the next person. During the hiring process, conversations between the Americanos and Latinos began to take place. It was learned that one of the problems with the past organizing was that the organizers were not good translators. Some of the Latinos were sufficiently bilingual to know that what was said in Spanish was different from what was being said in English. This made them suspicious of the organizers and the overall co-operative process.

The leadership learned that when the Latinos had called for independent translators, they were not attacking the board but the low quality of the organizers' translations. What the Latinos really wanted was competent translators. For the first time, as a result of what it learned and its increased desire to talk directly to the Latinos, a translation budget was created. Perhaps in anger and somewhat out of necessity, it took the money from the organizing budget and adopted a policy requiring that professional interpreters be present at all "significant" meetings.

A primarily Spanish-speaking Salvadoran, who had recently moved into the co-operatives and who had been a labor organizer in his country, was recommended by the interviewing committee and hired. The work of the two organizers was no longer divided along language lines. The new plan was for the two organizers to work as a team. Working this way, they began to make headway. They exploited the organizational potential of small and large crises that took place in the co-operatives by holding building meetings and teaching the people about how to take charge of their situation.

They saw the various crises that occurred in the co-operatives as opportunities rather than problems. For example, in one dispute over the allocation of backyard space they encouraged and assisted in setting up a committee of representatives of the twenty-four properties in the co-op to analyze the distribution of space, recommend a solution for the immediate crisis, and head off future problems. The co-operative was two-thirds Latino, and there was heavy Latino participation on this committee. The incident initiated more active Latino participation in that co-operative.

Latino participation was increasing in all the co-operatives and organic Latino leadership was being identified in the four functioning co-operatives, but the leadership problem in the two troubled groups did not materially improve. The organizers assembled boards that held together temporarily, but in both co-ops family problems overwhelmed the elected presidents and they dropped off the boards. The problem was greater than mere instability in Imogen. Unlike the co-operatives, Imogen had a federally required deadline for purchase of shares and formal conversion. The deadline for sale of the shares and the conversion to a co-operative passed without the required sale.

The Imogen residents suffered from years of failed organizing and Latino isolation. The firing of the Puerto Rican organizer split the group between those who had come to trust the leadership and its process and those, still suspicious, who did not. There was not enough time for the new organizing effort to heal the wounds of the past, and at the time the sale was required each faction approached the organizing board with the desire to buy the other out. Since this was not possible, the project remained a rental.

The failure of Imogen to convert drove the organizers even harder to find a solution to the problem of the remaining leaderless co-operative. The organizers concluded that internal leadership development was not possible under the urgent operational pressures facing this co-operative. They believed that the educational level of the particular immigrants in this co-operative was too low and their economic marginality too great for them to carry out the tasks needed to operate the co-operative without years of preparation and training. Their solution was to look outside the co-operatives for potential leadership.

There were about fifty vacancies in the five co-operatives after the rehabilitation was completed, including half a dozen in the troubled co-op. The organizers began to encourage organizationally active Latinos they knew to get on the waiting list. A number of these people signed up. Next, the organizers focused on membership selection, particularly in the troubled co-op. Their efforts and the choices made by the co-operative boards brought in a significant number of people with the leadership skills and the educational background to understand how to operate the co-operatives. Several of these people were organizers themselves. Quite a few had full bicultural Latino-Americano membership and were fully bilingual. Although the goal of the organizers had been to find caretaker leadership, they had, in fact, recruited people into the ranks of the residents who for the first time had the qualifications to act as multicultural mediators.[24]

The recruitment of these multicultural mediators provided a major missing element in the achievement of multiculturalism. For a period of time, it looked like the strategy would work. The pressure of operating the co-operatives transformed the Latino caucus from a primarily political body into an educative body. The group focused on how to get the job done, and the initial Latino advocacy focus was moderated by a concern for who was a good worker and who wasn't, regardless of ethnicity.

In this period, the policy to employ paid professional interpreters was implemented. Many individuals were tried but did not prove up to the job. Each interpreter selected different equivalents for the co-op words and confused the process further. Finally, a capable individual was hired regularly to translate as many evenings as he could, with other paid translators and volunteers filling in where necessary. With the addition of the new bilingual leadership, this seemed to work.

The bilingual activists monitored the quality of the translation and ensured the uniformity that had been missing. But they did not want to translate; they wanted to participate in the meetings and could not do both. However, they often interrupted the translation with discussion of how to translate various concepts. Sometimes the translator would shout out for help, and one of the bilingual people would make a suggestion.

Besides assuring uniformity and correctness in translation, the new activists made the discussions accessible to different cultural groups, in particular the less-educated and rural Latino immigrants. They were able to illustrate and explain technical concepts by reference to agrarian metaphors and stories from local oral traditions. They could find the cultural equivalents for jokes, puns, and role references. They could detect the intention behind a clumsy phrase, a potential insult, or an inappropriate gesture, and ensure understanding on all sides.

In sum, the bilingual activists performed the whole spectrum of functions that the theoretical literature assigns to the cultural mediator. Unfortunately, this period did not last. Two problems emerged. First, among the imported leadership were the pluralists who became impatient with the caretaker role and began to exclude inactive long-time residents from their area of concern. This problem was accentuated by their inability to solve long-standing problems faced by the co-operatives and some unfortunate decisions that worsened the situation. Second, the new leadership began to fight among itself.

Currently, the ease of communications with the co-operatives varies. Feelings of separation and racial difference still exist. There is, however, more communication between the Latino and Americano population. Membership committees have begun to favor bilingual applicants, and direct communication within the multiethnic population has increased. Time has also passed, and people have become more familiar with each other.

Racism

The very existence of multiethnicity in the project coupled with its location within the racial state gives rise to the question of the existence of racism among the corridor population. Certainly the fact that the leadership of the development phase of the project was, while multi-ethnic, Americano created the suspicion of racism in the Latinos' mind. This situation should lead any researcher to ask whether one group is favored over another. Does the structure of the project result in an unequal distribution of benefits or burdens? Is that look of disapproval or other action racially motivated? Every time a significant question is answered, the answer is subject to scrutiny for racist behavior or result. Who was elected to the leadership positions? Whose unit was repaired or improved? Who was selected for a vacant unit? The issues never end. After discussing these and similar questions in general, I will examine a case involving the selection of a new member of one of the co-operatives.

Discrimination can be intentional behavior or the unintentional product of the particular structure within which an act takes place (Feagin and Feagin, 1986). There were isolated incidents of intentional racist behavior in the project, but these were not the rule. Overt racism is not acceptable behavior in the project. At one point in the development of a co-operative, a group of Anglo residents demanded their co-operative be divided into two areas with one largely Latino and one largely Anglo. The Anglos rationalized the split would provide internal cohesion. The largely Americano leadership saw the Anglos' request as racist. The failure to include the two areas in the co-operative would have made the purchase of the largely Latino area financially infeasible. The leadership insisted that everyone should benefit and no one should be displaced. The co-op was not divided.

The issue of structural racism is more complex, but by the most obvious measures one would have to say that the Latinos received more of the benefits of the project than the Americanos. Certainly an analysis of subsidy dollars would lead to that conclusion. All families in need received Section 8 subsidies, but the Latino families tended to have a greater need for these subsidies. All overcrowded families received units appropriate to their family size, but the Latino families tended to be more overcrowded than the Americano families. A high percentage of rehabilitation funds were spent creating large bedroom apartments out of smaller ones. Four, five, and six bedroom apartments were created for specific Latino families. These benefits, however, also indirectly benefitted the Americanos. They made it possible for everyone to avoid displacement and become part of the co-operative.

The analysis is also complex when the burdens are considered. The Americanos did most of the work that made the project possible even though they received less of the direct benefits. These burdens, however, are balanced by the fact that the Americanos tended to have nicer units than the Latinos to start with. This contributed to their greater willingness to participate. Also, the Americanos suffered less of the inconvenience of the rehabilitation including the inconvenience of moving. Americanos are more likely to pay a monthly charge that while higher in a dollar amount (the maximum) represents a smaller percentage of their income than the members on Section 8. They are less likely, moreover, to suffer the indignities of participating in a subsidy program. Research has shown that some people value their privacy over housing quality and affordability (Hollingshead and Rogler, 1963). A researcher could find this sentiment in the Route 2 Corridor. Although the Latinos gained the most, they also had to give up more of their privacy to the Housing Authority and HUD regulations.[25]

Any unevenness to benefits and burdens in the project cannot be isolated from the greater variance in the larger society. The structural racism of the larger society penetrates the project creating inherent inequalities in the corridor population that no project by itself could overcome. One of the most salient elements of this is that the United States is not officially a bilingual nation. English speakers have an extraordinary advantage over non-English speakers in the society. The lack of bilingualism in the larger society has created a constant pressure to have a native English speaker as president so that person can represent the co-operative to the outside world. In dealing with the politicians or the Housing Authority on complex matters such as Section 8 regulations, English is virtually a requirement. Recently the Latino majority on the board of an eighty-percent Latino co-operative pushed to have Americanos be president and vice-president of their board. Only at the insistence of the Americanos did a Latina, who was unsure of her English but who was the acknowledged leader of the co-operative, assume the presidency.

The advantage conveyed by the ability to speak fluent English exists when dealing with co-operative business as well as in each individual's economic life. Monolingual Spanish speakers are likely to be shuttled to the secondary economy while the English speakers are more likely to find a place in the primary economy. This secondary place in the economy carries with it other structural disadvantages in dealing with co-operative business.

Who is the Racist?

Residents addressed the issue of racism in selecting a family to occupy a two-bedroom, non-Section 8 unit vacated by an Americano family in one of the co-operatives. The co-operative had to choose between three families: a Chinese family consisting of a mother and teenage son; a Latino family consisting of a husband and wife and two young children; and a mixed family consisting of a pregnant Anglo wife and a Latino husband. The Chinese woman was an accountant with a substantial income, although still within the moderate income requirements; the Latino husband was a sheet metal worker; and the Anglo wife, the spokesperson for her family, was a bilingual school teacher with an organizing background in Latino communities and her Latino husband was an artist. The Latino family was a friend of a Latino member of the board and the Chinese and Anglo applicants were friends of an Americano member of the board.

This co-operative had become increasing Latino over time and some of the Americanos were worried about the co-operative losing its multiethnic character. Many people who moved into the co-operatives whether Americano or Latino were friends of current residents. Some of the Americanos saw the increasing Latinoization of the co-operative through these friendship and kin networks as a problem. When friends of Americanos were chosen for membership over friends of Latinos, some Latinos saw this as a problem and there were murmurs of racism. The non-Section 8 case brought the issue to a head.

Three Latino and three Americano members of the co-operative acting as the membership committee and the two Latino neighbors of the vacant unit interviewed the applicants. Of those present four people were on the board, two Latinas and two Americanas. Only one person at the meeting, an Americano, backed the Chinese family. He argued that the accountant had skills the co-operative desperately needed and that over the time the co-operative had been interviewing no one with this skill level had applied. A Latino member replied that the family didn't need the apartment since the woman had plenty of income and could live anywhere. The Americano said that was exactly the point. The accountant wanted to live in the co-operative and would work for it. If need was the primary criteria, particularly in non-Section 8 cases, the co-operative would soon be without the skills to operate.

All the Latinos in the room including the neighbors backed the Latino candidate. The friend of the Latino applicants had been on the phone recruiting support and brought another friend to the meeting whom she had previously and successfully supported for admission to the co-operative. Since this person had not attended a meeting for several years, her presence at the meeting angered some of the Americanos who felt the meeting was being stacked. The Latinos argued that the Latino family needed the apartment more than the other families and that the husband's skills would be valuable in supervising the maintenance of the co-operative. He had also promised to do the repairs himself. The husband and the family's friend said the wife in the family had secretarial and accounting skills, but the wife was very quiet and spoke very little in the interview.

The Anglos reacted by saying that they had heard the man's speech before and that very few of those making this speech ever kept their promise to work. The co-operative had a lot of men with manual skills who failed to be active. This made the applicants' friend angry; she declared she knew the family and promised it would work for the co-operative. She put her credibility on the line. Underlying the Americanos' reaction but unspoken, however, was the memory of two friends of this member who had previously been admitted after promises but who had not kept their word.

The remaining two Americanos (one Anglo and one not) backed the mixed Anglo/Latino family. They believed that like the Latino family the mixed family needed housing. In addition, however, they saw the organizing skills of the wife in the mixed family as more important to the co-operative than any other skill. Active co-operative members needed help encouraging participation in the co-operative. The woman's bilingual and teaching skills could be employed to prepare a newsletter. The co-operative had wanted a newsletter for some time, but few people had the skill to prepare a bilingual newsletter and none of them had made it their priority.

An Americana populist at the meeting believed the Anglo woman applicant would also encourage multiculturalism in the co-operative and act as a multicultural mediator. The Americana did not see the husband in the Latino family in that role, although he was also bilingual. In the Americana's mind, the Anglo woman's marriage to a Latino and her long-time involvement in Latino communities confirmed her abilities for the role. She regarded the husband in the Latino family as part of the Latino culture and not likely to be a prime mover towards multiculturalism. Since the Chinese family was not bilingual, it also could not bridge the gap between the cultural groups.

The tense meeting became tenser when one of the Americanos, reacting to the perceived attempt to stack the meeting, asked whether the Latinos at the meeting were voting for the Latino applicants because they were Latino. The Latinos answered the question negatively and reiterated their reasons for supporting the family: the family was the most in need, the family's skills would be useful to the co-operative, and they were the neighbors' choice.

The Latino family received a majority of the votes at the meeting, but among the attending board members the vote was split two to two. Consequently, the three members of the seven-person co-op board who did not attend would have to make the final decision. Two of the three remaining board members were Latino. It was decided at the committee meeting that the highest ranking member of the board in attendance, the Americano vice-president, should hold a meeting with the absent board members the next night to make the final decision.[26]

One of the Latino members could not attend the meeting. The other two members came at different times and ended up talking individually with the vice-president. She described the three applicants. Both of the board members voted for the mixed family, and the family was awarded the unit.

The Latino member of the board who had supported her friends was clearly upset at the decision. She felt she made a mistake allowing the Americana to convene the meeting and that pressure had been put on the Latino member to vote for the mixed couple. She withdrew from activity in the co-operative, but after several talks with the Americanos involved (talks that would not have likely taken place at an earlier point in the development of the co-operatives) resumed full involvement. The board resolved to create a new waiting list for the non-Section 8 units to reduce the chances of such a problem recurring.

Almost everyone involved in this event believed initially that racism played a part in the interview meeting. There was no agreement about the nature of the racism. The Latinos saw the Americanos as anti-Latino and voting for their own, and the Americanos saw the Latinos as biased in favor of Latinos and voting for their own. The Latino members viewed the Latino member who broke ranks and voted for the mixed family as a "dupe" of the Americanos, a term which had been applied before in the history of the project to Latinos who consorted with the Americanos. They were regarded as tokens or only Latinos on the outside. In the most dramatic incident a Latino distributing fliers in his co-operative had been accused of being paid by the Americanos. He had to go home and get his pay stub to convince his accusers that he had another job and was just volunteering to help the co-op.

What the charge of racism means in a multiethnic organization like a Route 2 co-operative is not entirely clear.

If the intentional bias charges were both true —

In the larger society, Anglos are the majority and as a group the purveyors of the racial state and racism. Minority groups who suffer from racism and the racial state are seen by some as having a legitimate right to assert their group interests in the larger society and to demand affirmative treatment to redress past and continuing wrongs (Omi and Winant, 1986).[27] In the co-operatives, the division between the majority immigrant Latinos and minority Americanos confuses the usual societal debate.

National minority groups that are subject to discrimination in the larger society, including Chicanos, form a minority Americano population in the co-operatives. Can the immigrant Latinos claim an affirmative action preference for immigrant Latinos within the project without being seen as racists? To a U.S. African-American member of the co-operative, for example, the preference for Latinos can look like a new version of the same racist game. The Americanos claimed not to be anti-Latino but promulticultural. Can Americanos support a claim for affirmative action for Americanos on the grounds that they are seeking multiculturalism in the co-operative? If they are saying in effect that the Latino quota was filled by past practices which increased the percentage of Latinos in the co-operative, that this unit was an Americano unit, and vote against a Latino for that reason, are they being racist? Can a bias for multiculturalism be seen as racism?

If nepotism controlled judgment —

It may be that intentional bias had nothing to do with the decision and that one or both sides were simply favoring their friends and received the support of their friends in their effort. The reality of the situation in the project and in the larger racial state is that each ethnic/racial group is likely to have people of their group as friends. Trying to help a friend and friends helping friends who are helping friends is likely to have a biasing effect. The activity may have no racial motive, be unintentional, but have the effect of creating biased results. It has been argued that nepotism in this form, the "good-old-boy network," is the basis of racism (Feagin and Feagin, 1986). Here the story is only complicated by the presence of numerous groups that suffer from exclusion from these networks.

If different criteria controlled judgment —

The Latinos stressed the applicants' level of need in their discussion. As one of the Latinos put it, "helping people in need is what the co-operative is all about." The Americanos emphasized the skills of the applicants and the needs of the co-operative. Their position is that once eligibility is established, skills need to be considered primary or there will be no co-operative to help people in need. Here the issue becomes one of structural racism. Structurally Latinos have less economic and educational opportunity than Americanos, particularly Anglo Americanos (Barrera, 1979). If the Americano criteria of skill level is used, then selection is likely to favor Americanos. Conversely if the criterion is need, the opposite is true. Selection results are less clear when national minority groups are brought into the picture.

Given the limited number of vacancies in the co-operative there is no external reason for structural racism to express itself in the co-operative. Here, however, the issue was not just skill, but a particular type of skill; the Latinos considered manual labor skills important while the Americanos stressed mental labor skills. When the type of skill becomes a criteria and a choice is made from an applicant pool largely representative of the present representatives in the co-operative, the likelihood of this structural tendency to express itself is greatly enhanced. The claimed importance of mental skills is certainly subject to skepticism by the listener whose group will be negatively affected by its application.[28]

The issue of skill level as a criterion also raises the question of the training of members of the co-operatives. Whose responsibility is the training? Who designs the training and who does the training? Do the residents with greater skill levels have a special responsibility to train the less skilled members or is it an overall co-operative responsibility? Training has taken place from time to time. Members who participate are becoming more sophisticated over time. The issue is partly one of short-term versus long-term participation. In the long term, people can be trained; in the short term, the skills are needed.

If stacking the meeting and the reaction controlled judgment —

In the co-operative, majority rules. The populists, however, believe the rule of the majority should be part of an open process where decisions are based on meritocracy.[29] Can the societal history of racism justify stacking the meeting? I have been in groups where it has been argued when there have been complaints against such tactics that "its about time Anglos understood what it feels like." Can the Americanos' definition of meritocracy be seen as biased in itself and justify stacking a meeting? What is usually argued is that merit is only a proper criteria up to that necessary to do the task. Beyond that, affirmative action can come into play (Maquire, 1980). If the meetings were stacked, can the Americanos justify violating their own rule of meritocracy and vote against the stacker's friends? This would seem to corrupt the process even further.

Conclusion

The residents of the Route 2 co-operatives faced the necessity of solving problems of race, ethnicity, ideology, and class which are becoming increasingly common in major cities in the United States. Through persistence and good fortune, they discovered a partial solution to a portion of their problem. They learned in this case that an organizer's dedication to multiculturalism may be more important than bilingualism or particular ethnic membership. When it came to interpretation, they learned how loosely the term bilingual is used and that their situation called for a very high level of bilingualism. In a multiethnic situation with a substantial number of monolingual individuals, great care must be taken to ensure that the person assigned this role has the requisite ability.

Residents also realized that in multicultural organizations there are both practical and organizational risks in combining the organizer, translator, and mediator roles. On the practical level, it is difficult to find a person with this multiple competence. On the organizational level, the organizer may not be able to maintain the neutrality necessary to satisfy the requirement of interpretation. Moreover, the gatekeeper potential of the roles may inhibit direct contact between ethnicities and undermine the development of democratic institutions within the organization.

The residents also discovered the central importance of resident multicultural mediators. They learned how fragile multiculturalism can be. Without mediating individuals in the community to build trust between ethnicities, many misunderstandings can overwhelm good intentions. They also learned about the dangers of injecting mediators into a community devoid of such resources.

Even with this knowledge, in the populist sense, multiculturalism is not easily attained. The implication of bias is possible in nearly every significant act. The whistle cannot be blown, and everyone cannot simply agree to avoid behavior that could be interpreted as racist. The suspicion and distance created by the racial state cannot easily be overcome. The existence of racism in the racial state is omnipresent and tears down the community constructed within the co-operatives. As people get to know each other, the words for communication are found and distance is reduced.

Still with the group, however, are the structural issues of class and the conflicts it engenders. These issues are difficult to address because class issues are masked by the ethnic and racial categories that seem inevitable given the multiethnic nature of the corridor population. Only recently has the role of class begun to become clear to the residents and a subject of discussion. Whether they can sort out the basis of the conflicts in the co-operatives and find a solution to them remains to be seen.

Notes

1. The obvious missing characteristic is gender. The role of gender in the project is discussed in Chapter 6 of *The Struggle for Community*, Allan David Heskin (1991).
2. Racial differences among the Latinos have generated charges of racism within the Latino populations. One dark-skinned Latina often made charges of racism against fairer Latinos.
3. This statement should be qualified. The multicultural image was largely in the Anglo world. Among Chicano activists in the city, the project was often char-

acterized in the early days as a Cubano project because of the original Cuban leadership.

4. For a discussion of the authoritarian populist rather than progressive populist approach, see Omi and Winant (1986), p. 120.

5. For a discussion of the racial state see Omi & Winant (1986). Omi and Winant set out the long history of racism in the United States and discuss the role of the state in the establishment, maintenance, and redefinition of racial categories, what Miles (1982) calls racialization. Their position is similar to those theorists who see the state as the locus and product of class struggle and, therefore, relatively autonomous from the bourgeois (Carnoy, 1984). Omi and Winant see the racial state as a focus of "racial" conflict in which distinct state institutions intervene in a contradictory fashion as pressures are placed on them. Overall, however, as with the relative autonomy theorists position on class, their position is that racism underlies the state's actions.

6. The racial state and the attack on ethnic groups requires self-defense. The stress on one's own needs is an inevitable result. The creation of the category "race" and the fractionalization of the working class is the result (Miles 1982).

7. The patron is a "gatekeeper" who stands between the community and the state and connects the peasant to the larger market (Powell 1970). John Powell indicates that the patron's "basic function is to relate to community-oriented individuals who want to stabilize or improve their life chances, but who lack economic security and political connections, with nation-oriented individuals . . . ." (p. 413). The test of reciprocity is the ability of the patron to improve the life chances of the individual or more likely the family. Empowerment in this context is a term often used to evaluate the ability to survive and not, as the pluralists use it, to compete (Friedmann 1988, p. 116).

8. For a discussion of this see Fellman (1973).

9. This is true even with immigrants who believe they will return to their country of origin. To some extent they have to adjust to conditions in the United States.

10. Padilla sees the traditionalists as pluralists and the emergent group in another category. On this point we disagree; I see the difference between the groups being a matter of tactics. They both seek benefits from the state. What is different is that the traditionalists play more within the rules and the agenda set by the state than the emergent group.

11. I say some because the issue is identification with the culture as much as ethnicity. See discussion following in the text. There is certainly voluminous material on the subject of ethnicity, race, and class. See, for example, the excellent collection of articles in Rex and Mason (1986).

12. The global phenomenon of restructuring contributes to making this juxtaposition possible. See Soja (1989), p. 188.
13. For a further discussion of this point and its implications see Fields (1982). It is important to note that Miles sees *racism* as important if not central to societal analysis. If, however, I am correct that racism is not a primary internal factor in the Route 2 Project, then racism itself does not come into play.
14. This is somewhat offset internally by the subsidization of the monthly carrying charges of the lower income residents. The housing in Route 2 is sometimes treated as transitional housing on the way to unregulated ownership and is employed as part of the immigration process. Over the years that Caltrans owned the housing, many immigrants moved on as they successfully integrated into the economy. This process contributed to a collection and over-representation of those who did not have this success. The Americanos have also gone through a similar process of passing through this housing on their way to unregulated ownership, however, they tend to have a head start in the process.
15. Interestingly, I rarely heard the charge publicly made against an Americano although the feeling existed in the Latino population.
16. Nationalism is also a factor in Route 2. Long held national animosity clearly played a role in motivation. How one approaches a problem is a result of history. Nationalism in this context shares a great deal with racism.
17. Much of this section is adapted from Heskin and Heffner (1987).
18. "Organizations as a separate, competitive monocultural group or bloc have not always offered a completely satisfactory alternative route to full social entitlement: externally, racism limits entry into the central arena of power, while internally ethnic groups are divided by socio-economic class, national origin, citizenship status, length of residence in the U.S., and degree of assimilation into the dominant Anglo culture.

    For Angeleno Latinos particularly, the mechanisms for assimilation into the dominant culture have been weak: language and cultural maintenance are supported by ethnic segregation, the physical proximity of Latin America, the continuous inflow of migrants, and by a dense network of Latino businesses, communications media, and social institutions of all kinds (Conklin & Lourie, 1983; Giles, Bourhis & Taylor, 1977).

    Importantly, many of the goals of low-income groups (such as crime prevention, adequate housing, and access to public services) are shared with the contiguous or intermingled communities of other ethnic groups. Organization along strict ethnic lines means fragmentation and competition for scarce resources. Each minority must direct its demands, in isolation, to the dominant culture thus minimizing minority interaction and contributing to the maintenance of the status quo. To be truly effective, in a multiethnic environment such as Los Angeles, organizing must have the capacity to employ multiculturalism.

Active community organizers have stated this new multicultural imperative quite dramatically and generalized it to the national scale. Jose M. Molina (1978) writes that "as a breath of fresh air blowing throughout the organizational field, a new trend is now in motion in this country—in San Francisco, Los Angeles, Cleveland, Arkansas, North Carolina, Connecticut, and elsewhere. I am referring to multiethnic, multiracial-majority, constituency organization." Other organizers, such as, Miller (1974) and De Leeuw (1974) concur. Heskin and Heffner (1987).

19. See Chapter 2 of *The Struggle for Community*, Allan David Heskin (1991).
20. The reference to key documents indicates the structural limits of what a group can do in a non-bilingual environment. For example, HUD does not provide its material in multiple languages. To translate all HUD regulations and appropriate statutes to Spanish would have been an impossible task. Corporate documents, rental agreements, disclosure statements, and the like were translated. Handouts and training material were also translated.
21. Most of the initial organizing would be done at the residents' homes. Women were home more than men, and it was felt women residents would be more comfortable with a woman. It was also believed that a woman would have a better chance of getting in the home to talk to the residents.
22. Interviews with 20 active and inactive Latinos from a variety of countries were conducted by Lupe Compean between July and August of 1984. An example of a real problem that existed was the overt racism of the some employees of the contractors hired to rehabilitate the property. Several incidents took place as verbal attacks on Latino co-op members by these workmen. Complaints were filed with the contractor and the problem lessened.
23. The organizer was trying to get away from that kind of work and develop professional skills that would allow her to make a decent living. Organizers are traditionally underpaid.
24. Part of the organizers job in a multiethnic situation is to identify and develop "natural cross-links" in the population (Molina, 1978). They could not find these people and instead recruited them into the project.
25. One of the biggest issues in the research and in the Route 2 Project involves how many people live in a home. The Section 8 Program has regulations on overcrowding and being underhoused. Those in the Section 8 Program can be forced to move from their existing homes to an "appropriate-sized" unit.

26. The other board members at the interview said they were too busy to come to yet another meeting that week.
27. For a discussion of the affirmative action debate see Maguire (1980).
28. There is some basis for the argument that need alone will detrimentally effect co-op participation. The boards of the co-operative tend to be made up of people who are either non-Section 8 residents or people towards the top of the Section 8 income criteria. In the co-operative in question, for example, the majority of the residents on the board are non-Section 8 members. Among those who are Section 8 eligible all but one are in the higher income group. That one person just suffered a personal tragedy which greatly reduced the family's income. Whether mental versus manual skill is preferable is more debatable although clearly both mental and manual skills are required to make the co-operative work. It should be made clear that the Americanos are talking about skill and not capacity. However, either interpretation could be made by a listener to the argument.
29. See discussion in Chapter 2 of *The Struggle for Community*, Allan David Heskin, 1991.

References

Adler, Nancy J. 1983a. "Domestic Multiculturalism: Cross-cultural Management in the Public Sector." In: William B. Eddy (ed.) *Handbook of Organization Management.* New York: Marcel Dekker.

___. 1983b. "Organizational Development in a Multicultural Environment." *Journal of Applied Behavioral Science.* 19(3):349-363.

Alinsky, Saul D. 1971. *Rules for Radicals.* New York: Random House.

Barrera, Mario. 1979. *Race and Class in the Southwest: A Theory of Racial Inequality.* Notre Dame: University of Notre Dame Press.

Brislin, Richard W. 1980. "Expanding the Role of the Interpreter to Include Multiple Facets of Intercultural Communications." In: Larry A. Samovar and Richard E. Porter (eds.) *Intercultural Communication: A Reader* (3rd. ed.) Belmont, California: Wadsworth Publishing.

Carnoy, Martin. 1984. *The State and Political Theory.* Princeton, New Jersey: Princeton University Press.

Conklin, Nancy Faires and Margaret A. Lourie. 1983. *A Host of Tongues: Language Communities in the United States.* New York: The Free Press.

De Leeuw, Barbara. 1974. "Learning to Build Majority Organizations," *Just Economics.* 2(1):2.

Ellis, Leroy. 1969. *White Ethics and Black Power.* Chicago: Aldine Publishing

Company.

Feagin, Joe R. and Clairece Booher Feagin. 1986. *Discrimination American Style.* Malabar, Florida: Robert E. Krieger Publishing Company.

Fellman, Gordon. 1973. *The Deceived Majority: Politics and Protest in Middle America.* New York: Dutton.

Fields, Barbara. 1982. "Ideology and Race in American History." In: J. Morgan Kousser and James M. McPherson (eds.) *Region, Race, and Reconstruction.* Oxford: Oxford University Press.

Friedmann, John. 1988. *Life Space and Economic Space.* New Brunswick, New Jersey: Transaction Books.

Giles, Howard, Richard Y. Bourhis, and Donald M. Taylor. 1977. "Towards a Theory of Language in Ethnic Group Relations." In: Howard Giles (ed.) *Language, Ethnicity, and Intergroup Relations.* London: Academic Press.

Gumperz, John Joseph. 1982. *Discourse Strategies.* Cambridge, England: Cambridge University Press.

Harris, Philip R. and Robert T. Moran. 1979. *Managing Cultural Differences.* Houston: Gulf Publishing.

Heskin, Allan David. 1991. *The Struggle for Community.* Colorado: Westview Press.

_____, and Robert A. Heffner. 1987. "Learning about Bilingual, Multicultural Organizing," *The Journal of Applied Behavioral Science.* 23(4): 525-541.

Hollingshead, A. B. and L. H. Rogler. 1963 "Attitude Towards Slums and Public Housing in Puerto Rico." In: Leonard Duhl (ed.) *The Urban Condition.* New York: Simon and Schuster.

Kahn, Si. 1982. *Organizing.* New York: McGraw-Hill.

Maguire, Daniel C. 1980. *A New American Justice.* Garden City, New York: Doubleday and Company.

Miles, Robert. 1982. *Racism and Migrant Labor.* London: Routledge and Kegan Paul.

Miller, Mike. 1974. *Putting People Power in Action: Reader in Mass Organization.* San Francisco: Organize.

Molina, Jose M. 1978. "Cultural Barriers and Interethnic Communications in a Multiethnic Neighborhood. In: E. Lamar Rodd (ed.) *Interethnic Communication.*

Omi, Michael and Howard Winant. 1986. *Racial Formation in the United States: From the 1960's to the 1980's.* New York: Routledge and Kegan Paul.

Padilla, Felix M. 1985. *Latino Ethnic Consciousness: The Case of Mexican Americans and Puerto Ricans in Chicago.* Notre Dame, Indiana: University of Notre Dame Press.

Powell, John Duncan. 1970. "Peasant Society and Clientelist Politics." *The American Political Science Review*, 64, 2: 411-425.

Research Group on the Los Angeles Economy. 1989. *The Widening Divide*. Los Angeles: UCLA Graduate School of Architecture and Urban Planning.

Rex, John and David Mason (eds.). 1986. *Theories of Race and Ethnic Relations*. Cambridge: Cambridge University Press.

Sassen-Koob, Saskia. 1985. "Capital Mobility and Labor Migration." In: Steven E. Sanderson (ed.) *The Americas in the New International Division of Labor*. New York: Holmes and Meier.

Sechrist, Lee, Todd L. Fay, and S. M. Zaidi. 1982. "Problems of Translation in Cross-Cultural Communications." In: Larry A. Sanovar and Richard E. Porter (eds.) *Intercultural Communications: A Reader*. Belmont, California: Wadsworth Publishing.

Seleskovitch, Dancia. 1976. "Interpretation: A Psychological Approach to Translation." In: Richard W. Brislin (ed.) *Translation: Applications and Research*. New York: Gardner Press.

Soja, Edward W. 1989. *Postmodern Geographies*. London: Verso.

_____ , Allan D. Heskin, and Marco Cenzatti. 1985. *Los Angeles Through the Kaleidoscope of Urban Restructuring*. Los Angeles: UCLA, Graduate School of Architecture and Urban Planning.

Taft, Ronald. 1981. "The Role and Personality of the Mediator. In: Stephen Bochner (ed.) *The Mediating Person: Bridges Between Cultures*. Boston: Schenkman Publishing.

Taylor, D. M. and Simard, L. M. 1975. "Social Interaction in Bilingual Settings." *Canadian Psychological Review*. 16,4:240-254.

Twelvetrees, Alan. 1982. *Community Work*. London: British Association of Social Workers.

APARTMENT RESTRUCTURING AND LATINO IMMIGRANT TENANT STRUGGLES: A CASE STUDY OF HUMAN AGENCY

Nestor P. Rodriguez
University of Houston

Jacqueline Maria Hagan
University of Houston

Houston's 1982–1987 recession created a severe crisis in the city's apartment housing market. As thousands of unemployed, middle-class tenants left Houston, landlords in the city's western sector restructured apartment operations to rebuild renter populations with new Latino immigrants. Fieldwork in a large apartment complex found that changes made by management to attract Latino immigrants helped these newcomers develop survival strategies. When the recession ended, evolving relations between new immigrants and other tenants helped resist, and cope with, a second restructuring process implemented by apartment management to attract higher-income renters. Throughout Houston's west side, settlement and coping activities of new Latino immigrants have changed the material and symbolic environments.

Houston's economic recession in 1982–1987 contained a dramatic downturn of the city's booming real-estate industry. The sharp decline of manufacturing, construction, and service industries affected all sectors of the city's real-estate market (Feagin, 1988). Apartment capital in the city's west-side, apartment-complex industry was particularly hard hit as thousands of unemployed office workers left the city. Facing the out-migration of middle-income tenants, apartment-complex owners and managers in the west side drastically lowered rents and adopted several other changes to attract new Latino immigrants in order to rebuild their renter populations. In the subsequent economic upturn in the late-eighties, west-side apartment landlords developed a second restructuring process, i.e., the upgrading of apartment complexes to attract higher-income (Anglo) tenants, which reduced the presence of immigrant tenants.

The two processes of apartment restructuring in Houston's west side affected the opportunities for new-immigrant settlement and the development of subsequent relations between new Latino immigrants and established residents. Taking a human-agency perspective (M. P. Smith, 1989) in this paper, we use fieldwork observations to describe (1) how new Latino immigrants used the first apartment restructuring process to develop household survival strategies, and (2) how new Latino immigrants used evolving relations with established residents to cope with measures implemented by landlords in the second apartment restructuring process. While other studies have focused on the ways capitalist actors (bankers, real-estate investors, developers, etc.) influence urban growth (e.g., see Feagin and Parker, 1990; Gottdiener, 1985), we focus on these two developments to illustrate that the actions of more ordinary women and men may also become a medium for urban change.

Our ethnographic setting is Arboleda (pseudonym), a large apartment complex in Houston's west side. As in many other large apartment complexes in the city's west side, Arboleda became a setting where new Latino immigrants, individually and at times collectively with established residents, appropriated, resisted, and accommodated to broad social-structural changes that impeded their tenant-residential community. Through their social actions, i.e., through their "agency," new Latino immigrants modified materially and symbolically many apartment-neighborhood environments in Houston's west side.

Research in Arboleda

The ethnography of social action at Arboleda that we present in this paper is derived from two years of fieldwork at the apartment complex and from our continuing contact with several tenant households at the site. As part of a national study of evolving relations between established residents and new immigrants, in 1988-1989 we observed interaction between Anglo, African-American, and Latino established residents and Mexican and Central American new immigrants at the apartment complex. While our observations covered all areas of the complex (apartment units, patios, swimming pools, tennis courts, parking lots, and a restaurant), we especially focused on intergroup interaction in Building 5 (the back building) of the complex's five apartment buildings. Building 5 contains 132 of the 625 apartment units in the complex and has the most heterogeneous tenant population (Anglos, African-Americans, Mexican-Americans, new immigrants) and the greatest new immigrant concentration in the complex.

To facilitate the fieldwork, Jacqueline Hagan became a tenant in Building 5 several months prior to the study. On a daily basis she interacted with established residents, new immigrants, apartment managers, maintenance workers, and security guards at the complex. She gained acceptance among Latino immigrants in the building by translating their notices, employment forms, and other English-written materials into Spanish and by developing friendships with several immigrant households. Her closest informants in the complex included six new-immigrant and four establish-residents' households in Building 5.

In the first year of fieldwork at Arboleda, we focused on different levels of inter-group relations between established residents and Mexican and Central American newcomers and on the household survival strategies of the immigrants, who were almost entirely undocumented. In the second year, when Arboleda management adopted measures to upgrade the apartment complex to attract higher-income tenants, we shifted our focus to the immigrants' responses to these measures affected and to subsequent intergroup relations among the tenants.

Economic Crisis and Undocumented Latino Immigration

Once viewed as depression-proof, Houston's energy-centered economy entered a dramatic five-year recession in the spring of 1982. When an over-supply of oil in the world market lowered oil prices by 10 percent and, more importantly, the oil-price expectation by 50 percent (B. Smith, 1989), Houston's industrial sector suffered an immediate crash that saw more than 40 percent of the area's manufacturing workforce laid off. The decline of business services and construction in the second phase of the recession (1985-1986) also added to the area's loss of 200,000 jobs. At the height of the area's economic crisis in the summer of 1986, the unemployment rate stood at 13 percent.

The economic crisis severely depressed the real-estate sector which had enjoyed phenomenal expansion in 1975-1982. In this seven-year period, builders doubled the city's office space and added 200,000 units to the area's housing market (B. Smith, 1986). Real-estate development achieved such a high momentum that even after the onset of the recession area builders constructed over 200 office buildings and towers and more than 97,000 housing units (Feagin, 1988; B. Smith 1989). By 1986, however, the recession had clearly enervated the real-estate industry as 485 real-estate firms failed and foreclosures averaged 3,000 per month (Feagin, 1988). In the area's housing market, the number of vacant residential units rose from 86,961 in 1981 to a high of 220,709 in 1985 (B. Smith, 1989).

Out-migration of unemployed workers and overconstruction lowered the area's apartment occupancy rate. The rate plummeted from a high of 99.4 percent in 1982 to a low of 79.8 percent in 1984, rising to 81.5 percent when the economic downturn bottomed-out in 1987 (Bivins, 1991). Many of the apartment vacancies occurred in the city's west and southwest sides, areas of white, middle-class growth where real-estate investors and developers had constructed over a thousand large apartment complexes.

The recession thus threatened to decimate the area's apartment-complex industry. For many west-side apartment landlords desperate to rebuild their tenant populations, a temporary solution soon came in the form of undocumented Latino immigrants.

While Houston has long experienced undocumented Mexican immigration, in the late 1970s this immigration accelerated and was complemented in the early 1980s by undocumented Central American immigration. Fleeing political and economic turmoil in their homelands, the new Central American immigrants entered the city in torrents. In contrast to Mexican immigrants who for decades had settled in west-side immigrant enclaves, the Central American newcomers settled mainly in the city's western half. By the mid-1980s, this part of the city contained the largest numbers of the over 100,000 undocumented Salvadorans, Guatemalans, Hondurans, and Nicaraguans who had settled in the Houston area (Rodriguez and Hagan, 1989).

Central American immigrant settlements in the western half of the city became a major source of low-wage labor for the area's service sector. Many undocumented Central American immigrants found cleaning jobs in restaurants, retail stores, office buildings, and in other business places. Many undocumented Central American immigrant women also found domestic work in middle-class, Anglo homes. The undocumented Central American men who remained unemployed formed street-corner laborer pools as an employment agency of last resort (Rodriguez, 1987).

Large-scale influx of Central Americans and other undocumented Latinos into Houston during the 1980s presented two anomalies: labor immigration in a context of economic decline and, in the case of the city's west side, Latino immigrant settlement in a mainly white, middle-income area several miles removed from established immigrant enclaves. The former anomaly speaks to the ability of undocumented immigrants to develop social strategies for economic survival and to the endurance of the secondary labor market in times of economic decline. The latter anomaly speaks to the effectiveness of apartment-complex restructuring strategies temporarily implemented by landlords to rebuild tenant populations.

Immigrant-Tenant Problems and Intergroup Relations at Arboleda

Arboleda is part of a nationwide, apartment-complex chain headquartered in

Los Angeles. Built in the seventies in Houston's west-side sector of booming white, middle-class neighborhoods and business centers, Arboleda was designed for middle-income, white-collar workers, whose numbers grew with Houston's business expansion. For these tenants, the apartment complex offered maid and laundry services, heated swimming pools and Jacuzzis, tennis courts, and a beauty salon and bar-restaurant in the complex. Monthly rents of $500-$600 and an adults-only rule kept the tenant population young, middle-class and mostly Anglo.

Almost overnight, however, Houston's recession depleted Arboleda's tenant population. The complex's occupancy dropped by over 30 percent as unemployed tenants left the city or sought cheaper housing elsewhere. In the same manner as many other west-side apartment landlords, Arboleda's management responded to the crisis by lowering rents as much as 50 percent for some units and by restructuring its pattern of relationships with tenants to attract arriving Latino immigrants.

The apartment restructuring strategy involved advertising in Spanish, hiring bilingual rental agents and maintenance workers, and printing all apartment notices and bulletins in English and Spanish. Furthermore, Arboleda management developed an amicable, almost sympathetic relationship, with the new Latino immigrant tenants. Management looked the other way when immigrant families moved in with children, which violated the complex's adults-only policy, or when immigrant households expanded beyond the size allowed by rent contracts, which was usually two persons per bedroom. Management also allowed maintenance workers to give discarded apartment furniture to immigrant households. Finally, management ignored several informal business activities that immigrants developed in the apartment complex. The most conspicuous of these activities included an automobile repair shop run by a young Guatemalan on one of the complex's parking areas and the regular assembly of small-truck caravans that transported goods sent by Central American immigrant tenants to families back home. Often the Guatemalan mechanic repaired the battered trucks used for the caravans on the complex grounds.

To maintain and attract more middle-income tenants (which had long been synonymous with white tenants), Arboleda management placed most of its new Latino immigrant renters in the back two apartment buildings, especially in Building 5, away from the visibility of the front entrance. The apartment's rental agents expressed this conscious effort in their comments that the visibility of "those people" (Latino immigrants) would discourage "other people" (Anglos) from moving in. The concern to segregate Latino immigrant tenants in the back of the complex was also demonstrated when Hagan asked to rent an apartment. At first she was shown only apartments in the front three buildings; it was only after her insistence that she was shown an apartment in Building 5.

An alternative census count we conducted in Building 5 in June-July 1990 shows the household composition of the occupied units in the building during the enumeration (Table 1). Homogeneous Latino immigrant households accounted for over two-thirds (68.9 percent) of the 119 occupied apartment units in the building. Anglo, African-American, and Mexican-American households accounted for less than a fifth (16.8 percent) of the households in the building. In terms of total population, Central American and Mexican immigrants accounted for more than three-fourths (76.0 percent) of the 350 tenants in the building. For many of these immigrants Arboleda was their first home in the United States.

Table 1
Arboleda's Building 5 Household Population by Ethnicity and Size

	Cen. Amer.	Mex.	Mex. Ame.	Other Latino[a]	Anglo	African Amer.	African	Other[b]
House-hold Size								
1-2	9	11	4	8	7	9	2	2
3-4	18	16	0	3	0	0	0	9
5-6	12	7	0	1	0	0	0	0
7-8	1	0	0	0	0	0	0	0
n	40	34	4	12	7	9	2	11
% of total	33.6	28.6	3.4	10.1	5.9	7.6	1.7	9.2

a "Other Latino" includes tenants from the Caribbean and South America and ethnically heterogeneous Latino households.
b "Other" includes ethnically mixed households containing Anglos or African Americans.

Immigrant Household Survival Strategies

Arriving in Houston with little or no money and with undocumented status, the Central American and Mexican immigrants in Arboleda organized several household survival strategies common among low-income groups (e.g., see Mullings, 1987; Browning and Rodriguez, 1985). The greater distribution of Central American and Mexican immigrants in larger households (see Table 1) illustrates the strategy to reduce living costs (rent, food, utilities, etc.) by increasing the number of income earners in the household. Many of the Central American and Mexican households with three or more members consisted of workers in their late teens or in their twenties living in one-bedroom apartments.

The Latino immigrant's use of household arrangements as an agency of economic survival substantially altered the apartment complex's household pattern of earlier middle-income tenants. In the alternative enumeration, no Central Americans and less than 10 percent of Mexicans in Building 5 resided in households of single individuals, while this household size predominated among Anglos, African-Americans, and Mexican-Americans in the building. The most complex household arrangement found in the apartment building, i.e., a household composed of a couple with children and related *and* nonrelated individuals, only involved Central Americans and Mexicans. The second most complex level of household arrangement, i.e., a couple with children and related or nonrelated individuals, also only involved Central American and Mexican immigrant tenants.

The apartment household of Pablo and Maria Ixtecoy, who immigrated from the western highlands of Guatemala, illustrates how household-centered social strategies helped undocumented immigrants survive economically in their new environment. After arriving in Houston with little money, Pablo and Maria moved into a Mayan household in a one-bedroom unit in Building 5. When the original members of the household moved out, Pablo and Maria took in four male and one female new Mayan immigrants who were relatives and friends of Pablo. Pablo found cleaning jobs for the four men in a nearby supermarket where he worked. Maria also helped Ana, the new female household member, find part-time, domestic work in the neighborhood where she cleaned homes. Working in the same maintenance crew, Pablo and the four other men did each other's jobs when one of the men was not able to go to work. Maria and Ana also covered for each other when one of them could not go to work. Covering for each other at work was especially important when one of the household members left to visit family back home. When Maria left for three weeks to visit her family in Guatemala, Ana temporarily took over her domestic job and carried out her share of cooking, cleaning, and other household chores in the apartment. By sharing living expenses and covering for each other at work (and at home for Maria and Ana), the household members survived relatively well even as the broader environment suffered through economic decline.

For the new Latino immigrants, complex housing arrangements also provided socio-cultural resources to facilitate their accommodation in U.S. society. Living in households with more experienced immigrants was especially useful to rural-origin newcomers to learn how to enter an urban labor market. Several of the Central American households in Building 5 had members who came from a mainly peasant background and who had never travelled long distances beyond their homes before migrating to the United States. Among the immigrant women, living in complex households also helped them to obtain information on how to use modern home appliances, operate the washers and dryers in the building's laundry room, and how to negotiate through a host of social institutions (e.g., churches, clinics, and schools).

To be sure, the distinction of economic and socio-cultural household agency among immigrants is only an analytical one. In reality, the same process of household formation and maintenance is at once economic, social, and cultural (and political as we occasionally observed among Central Americans in other apartment complexes). For example, the organizing of birthday and wedding celebrations by households involved the economic activity of sharing expenses, such as, the cultural activities of preparing traditional dishes and, among Mayan immigrant women, wearing traditional garments, and the social activities of reuniting relatives, friends, and co-workers for the event.

Evolving Intergroup Relations

The clustering of Latino immigrants in the back two buildings of Arboleda separated these newcomers from the concentration of Anglo and other established residents in the front buildings. Other factors such as ethnicity/race and language differences also formed boundaries between the immigrant and established-resident tenant groups. The passage of the Immigration Reform and Control Act (IRCA) in 1986, however, created documentation needs among undocumented immigrants that brought a number of Latino immigrant and established-resident tenants together in Arboleda.

Many undocumented Latino immigrants in Arboleda applied for legal resident status under IRCA. The legalization program of IRCA required that applicants present documents to establish their personal identification, medical-health condition, U.S. employment history, and to prove that they had resided in the United States since before January 1, 1982. Many of the undocumented immigrants in Arboleda held jobs in the informal labor market where work-related documents such as paycheck stubs and W-2 income tax forms were impossible to obtain. Residential documentation in the form of rent contracts and receipts and utility payments was also difficult to obtain, since many immigrants concealed their presence from apartment managers because they lived in households whose size violated lease agreements. In addition, a number of immigrants resided in apartments where the lease and utilities were still under the names of immigrants who had left the complex. To avoid detection and thus avoid paying apartment and utility deposits, new immigrants had moved into these apartments and continued to pay the rent and utilities in cash under the name of the original tenants.

In the absence of readily available forms of documentation, immigrants relied heavily on affidavits provided by neighbors and co-workers. In over a dozen cases, established residents at Arboleda wrote affidavits stating they had been long-time neighbors and friends of immigrant applicants. Sensing the urgency of the opportunity for immigrants, some established residents even lent money to immigrant neighbors to pay for the legalization application fee. In one case, a Mexican-American tenant in Building 5 not only provided his immigrant neighbor with an affidavit and a loan for the application fee, but also accompanied him to the local office of the Immigration and Naturalization Service (INS) for the final interview to determine legalization. In several other cases, established residents in the complex tutored, free of charge, immigrant neighbors to help them pass the English exam of the legalization program. James, an African-American, for example, tutored Santos, his Guatemalan neighbor, and received Spanish lessons from Santos in return. These types of legalization-related exchanges strengthened relations between established residents and new Latino immigrants and made a number of established residents more sensitive to the needs of their immigrant co-tenants.

Coping with Apartment Changes

As Houston's economy pulled out of the recession in the Spring of 1988, Arboleda's management implemented the first measure to "upgrade" the complex and make it more attractive for potential middle-income tenants. The measure was to enforce the previously ignored adults-only policy, and given the high number of immigrant families with children in the complex, the measure was primarily aimed at the Latino tenants. To search for children among the large number of Latino immigrant households in the complex, management offered $50 to its maintenance and security workers for every apartment unit they found housing small children. An Anglo security guard and a Mexican-American maintenance worker reported several households with children, but two maintenance workers, an African-American and a Mexican-American, opposed the measure and aligned themselves with the immigrant families. The two apartment maintenance workers alerted immigrant families with small children when "management spies" (as they labeled other apartment employees) planned to be in the back apartment buildings.

Despite the efforts of the two sympathetic maintenance workers, management succeeded in evicting over 20 households in less than a month after reenforcing the adults-only policy. The evictions, however, became slower and more difficult for management to carry out when the immigrant families gained the support of other tenants, apartment employees, and in one case of a business employer. The case of Marcelina, a Mexican immigrant tenant with a nine-year old son, illustrates the collective effort to resist the apartment management's quick eviction attempts. After receiving a notice that her family had to move out of the apartment in three days, she stayed at home fearing to leave her son alone. Since her husband was working temporarily in another city, she turned to another tenant, to a Mexican-American maintenance worker, and to her employer (the owner of a nearby restaurant) for help. Together the group approached management and argued her case. Management reconsidered and agreed to give evicted families thirty days to leave the complex. (The Supreme Court later ruled adult-only apartment policies to be illegal.)

In the summer of 1988, Arboleda management implemented a second upgrading measure that created problems for the Latino immigrant tenants in the complex. The measure was the construction of a security steel fence around the complex and around the visitors' parking areas of the back two buildings. Management distributed instructions for operating the fence gates and issued two gate cards per apartment unit. In contrast to the past practice of printing notices in English and Spanish, the instructions for operating the gates were written only in English.

Several Latino immigrants approached Mexican-American apartment employees and bilingual Anglo tenants for assistance in translating the gate instructions into Spanish. Two Anglo tenants met with management and complained that the instructions needed to be translated into Spanish. An apartment manager responded that a bilingual translator was no longer available nor would be hired in the future. When a Mexican-American tenant offered to translate the notice, the apartment manager refused. During a second meeting between tenants and management, the decision was made to hold a meeting with Latino immigrant tenants to explain how to operate the new security fence system. A bilingual Anglo and two Mexican-American tenants conducted the meeting which over 100 immigrant tenants attended.

Issuing only two gate cards per apartment also caused problems for most Latino immigrant households. Two gate cards were simply not enough for immigrant households containing several adult members with different work schedules. The problem of insufficient gate cards was soon overcome through informal tenant strategies. For example, tenants entering or exiting the rear parking areas regularly slowed down at the gate to allow immigrant tenants on foot time to walk through. Parents and friends also asked children to squeeze through the bars of the fence and press the gate switches from the inside. Several months after the installation of the security fence, a group of tenants found that the rear gate switch could be activated by simply raising the gate a few inches off the ground. After this became a regular method of entering and exiting the rear buildings, management responded by having its security guards periodically pass by the gate. The immigrant renters without gate cards and immigrant visitors simply waited for the guards to pass out of sight and then continued to operate the gate with their popular strategies.

Conversations with established residents in the back building indicated they generally supported the immigrants' gate coping strategies because they felt management should have passed out more gate cards to the larger households and because they viewed the security fence as an inconvenience for visitors to the back apartment buildings. Though several established residents in the back buildings knew who were the immigrants that regularly sabotaged the rear gate switch, they never acknowledged this to the security guards who inquired every time the gate had to be repaired. Instead, the established residents took the side of the Latin immigrants.

A third upgrading measure that united established residents and new Latino immigrants in Arboleda involved the apartment's laundry facilities. The washers and dryers in the laundry room in Building 5 usually were in a state of disrepair, causing the building's tenants to use the laundry rooms in the other buildings. When new washers and dryers were installed in the front buildings, established residents in Building 5 complained to management about the deteriorating conditions of the laundry room in their building. Management responded that there was no use in repairing or replacing the washers and driers in Building 5 because the immigrants would only vandalize them again. When management refused to reimburse immigrant tenants for money lost in the broken-down washers and driers in the building, some immigrants responded by jamming washers and driers in the other laundry rooms with foreign coins. After threatening to press charges against anyone caught vandalizing the apartment's laundry equipment, management closed down the laundry room in Building 5. Established-resident tenants in the building discussed the problem with their immigrant neighbors and sympathetic maintenance workers and selected a small group of tenants to confront management. The Anglos in the group threatened to move out of the complex if management did not repair the laundry facilities in their building. After several confrontations, management finally agreed to renovate the laundry facilities in Building 5.

Arboleda management continued to implement upgrading changes in 1990. In the summer of 1990, it started to paint and renovated the front apartment buildings, presumedly leaving the back sections of mainly immigrant renters for last. As part of its restructuring strategy after the 1982–1987 recession, management raised rents in the complex by an average of $100 in just the first half of 1990. Facing higher rents, some Latino immigrant tenants moved to smaller and thus cheaper units in the complex, while other immigrant tenants moved in with other immigrant households in the complex or left the apartment complex for cheaper rents elsewhere in the city.

Our alternative census enumeration in Arboleda's Building 5 in the summer of 1990 indicates that large numbers of Latino immigrants still reside in the complex. Our finding that many of the immigrant tenants in Building 5 were undocumented, and thus new immigrants, indicates that the complex continues to be a viable setting for immigrant survival strategies. Arboleda management's upgrading measures also brought success. In the game of apartment real-estate investment, the real goal of upgrading apartments is not simply to draw higher-income tenants but to use these tenants to make apartments attractive to buyers. Arboleda owners accomplished this goal when they sold the apartment complex in the spring of 1991.

New Latino Immigrant-Related Changes in the West Side

Through their settlement and survival in west-side apartment complexes, Latino immigrants, as well as other new immigrants, have significantly altered the west-side social landscape. Retail centers in the west side now contain a variety of businesses (night clubs, restaurants, supermarkets, etc.) that cater primarily to the area's new immigrant population. Public and other social organizations in the west side have also been significantly affected by the new immigrant settlement. Several public schools, for example, in the 1980s saw their student population change from predominantly Anglo to predominantly Latino-immigrant, creating new pedagogical challenges for administrators and teachers. In places of worship, religious leaders also now experiment with social and language programs to incorporate newcomers into their memberships. Yet, this new urban change has not gone uncontested.

Established-residents groups in several west-side neighborhoods have undertaken actions to limit the changes that new immigrants bring to their areas. In one community, Anglo parents successfully countered a decision to redraw school boundaries which would have created in one school a majority Latino student body from nearby apartment complexes. The parents had the school system implement a student distribution plan that buses the immigrant students to schools with an Anglo student majority. In another community, established residents and apartment owners united to establish a police substation and to have the police department undertake a campaign against vagrants, vandals, and other supposedly criminal persons in the heavily-immigrant apartment complexes in their neighborhood. The "clean up" campaign includes INS raids in the complexes.

In spite of efforts such as these, some of the material and symbolic changes that new Latino immigrants have produced in the west side have gained permanency, especially as in some instances the changes have been incorporated into mainstream institutions. Two cases illustrate this development. One case is an elementary school in an upper middle-class, Anglo neighborhood where the school staff has adopted a *Cinco de Mayo* celebration ("Fiesta Field Day") almost completely without Latino involvement, given the absence of Latino parents in the upper-income neighborhood. While the celebration includes a variety of American games (baseball, three-legged races, dunking booth, etc.), the paintings in the signs and posters used to decorate the event symbolize Latino themes.

The second case involves the opening of a new health clinic in a southwest neighborhood. Since their arrival in large numbers in the west side in the early 1980s, new Latino immigrants had to depend on public health facilities located almost ten miles away. While some immigrants relied on private physicians for medical care, many others unemployed or with no health plans sought medical and health services at public hospitals and clinics (Urrutia-Rojas, 1988). Pregnant immigrant women especially sought prenatal care at public clinics. Occasionally physicians, nurses, and other health professionals offered immigrants free health services in makeshift clinics in the parking lots of churches and apartment complexes in the west side. Prompted by the findings of a health survey among Latino immigrants in a large, apartment district (see Urrutia-Rojas, 1988), in 1990 over a dozen members from Houston public and private community organizations came together forming a task force to locate a health clinic for indigents (mainly new Latino immigrants) in a southwest corridor of the city. After more than a year of lobbying elected officials and established community leaders, the intergroup task force persuaded the City of Houston to contribute $500,000 to a public-private venture to open a health clinic in the southwest corridor. In the clinic's opening day on May 31, 1991, the speeches by the mayor and other public officials indicated that the city's established political structure had finally recognized the new immigrants as part of the west-side community.

Discussion

Economic restructuring has played a central role in the development of capitalist societies (Sassen, 1988; Henderson and Castells, 1987). Previous works have focused on how restructuring impacts the social structure within the manufacturing, primary sector of capital (Beauregard, 1989; Morales, 1983). Our fieldwork in Arboleda shows that restructuring also produces significant changes in the social-structural environment of the real-estate, secondary circuit of capital. Arboleda management's initial restructuring strategy to partially rebuild the renter population with new Latino immigrant tenants became the context for undocumented, immigrant-survival strategies, and evolving intergroup relations. These developments later became sources of individual and collective intergroup resistance against upgrading measures adopted by management as a second restructuring strategy, aimed this time to attract higher-income tenants.

Facing a variety of constraints related to their undocumented and new immigrant status and to the decline of the city's economic environment, the Latino newcomers at Arboleda developed household social strategies to appropriate living space within the complex. By letting relatives, friends, and co-workers move into their households, the immigrants enhanced the apartments' use-value while their exchange value (rent) remained unchanged. But the undocumented Latino immigrants appropriated more than apartment space; they also appropriated the apartment environment in the back two buildings and through social actions, such as their informal business activities, reconstituted the symbolic dimension of the buildings' social space. The buildings, which once symbolized the affluent life styles of young, middle-income professionals, now represented the new Latino immigrant community experience in Houston.

Appropriation of apartment space and building environment constituted but one "aggravation" in the apartment complex as a setting of capitalist space (see Lefebvre, 1979). The struggles over the rear gate and the laundry facilities in Building 5 constituted two more. To an extent, the rear gate represented managements' attempt to reclaim the environment of the rear two buildings, to bring it "under control." But what management saw as endangered profit-making space, the Latino immigrants saw as community space, *their* community space. In addition to causing problems for households who needed more than two gate cards, the security fence significantly restricted the daily visits by relatives and friends coming from surrounding apartment complexes. That is, it restricted an important social resource for community nurturing. The immigrants' regular sabotaging of the rear gate switch thus represented attempts to maintain control of access to their community space.

In a similar way, we believe, the struggles over the laundry facilities in Building 5 represented a community-related issue but at a broader level, since it drew the active involvement of several established-resident tenants in the building. The laundry room in Building 5 was more than just a shared physical space where tenants came together to wash and dry their clothes. Over the course of our fieldwork, the laundry room became a common *social space* where different groups of women (Anglo, African-American, Latina) chatted, exchanged stories, and looked after each others washing load or small children if one had to leave the laundry room momentarily. Moreover, the laundry room had helped to promote a degree of community solidarity as the immigrants who "fixed the driers to work for free" taught their established-resident neighbors how to do the same. The whole laundry room episode demonstrated the significance that common space can have in the formation of intergroup solidarity.

Our description of resistance to upgrading measures at Arboleda should not be taken to mean that the complex has turned into a hostile environment where management and tenants daily confront each other. Arboleda is generally a tranquil setting where immigrants and other tenants in the back section pursue household and community activities much like residents in other working-class neighborhoods. What has changed at Arboleda, and is directly related to the immigrants' presence, is that in contrast to earlier days some issues now thrust the complex's back section into contested terrain. Management can no longer assume that its apartment policies will be automatically accepted in all sections of the complex.

As we have described above, new Latino immigration in the 1980's has significantly affected the social environment of Houston's west side. The change that this immigration has produced is greater than the emergence of Latino ethnic enterprises and the penetration of new Latinos into mainstream institutions (educational, health, religious, etc.) in the area. The immigration of Latinos, and other populations, affects the very social structure of the west side. Immigration has deepened the infusion of ethnic/racial and class dimensions into the social-structural foundation of the area, creating new possibilities for contention in the area's future growth. What this amounts to is that settings beyond apartment complexes will also become contested terrain in the west side, especially as the large number of legalized immigrants acquire more experience in the city's political-economic arenas.

Conclusion

The Arboleda immigrant experience, as well as the greater west-side immigrant experience in Houston, demonstrates the relationship between macro-structural change (Houston's recession and later upswing) and the everyday actions of women and men of appropriating, resisting, or accommodating in order to survive in constraining social structures. These social actions accomplish more than economic survival—they change materially and symbolically the urban environment. Thus, social actions of ordinary women and men undertaken in response to structural conditions become an agency for urban change. In this vein of thought, people are not simply objects of impersonal structural forces but are historical actors in the production and transformation of urban space.

Acknowledgements

We are thankful to Robert A. Beauregard, Joe R. Feagin, Mark Gottdiener, and Robert Parker for their comments on an earlier version of this paper. We are also thankful to Robert L. Bach for the many discussions we had with him on new evolving intergroup relations. Finally, we are especially thankful to the tenants and staff at Arboleda who shared their stories and lives with us. The Changing Relations Project (Ford Foundation), the Research Methods Section of the U.S. Bureau of the Census, and the College of Social Science at the University of Houston provided support for the research presented in this paper.

References

Beauregard, Rogert A. (Ed.) (1989) *Economic Restructuring and Political Response.* Newbury Park, CA: Sage.

Bivens, Ralph (1991) Apartment rents up 17%, but rise is expected to ease. *Houston Chronicle*, April 3, 1991, Section A, page 1.

Browning, Harley L., and Nestor Rodriguez (1985) The Migration of Mexican Indocumentados as a Settlement Process: Implications for Work. In George J. Borgas and Marta Tienda (Eds.), *Hispanics in the U.S. Economy*, 277-298. New York: Academic Press.

Feagin, Joe R. (1988) *Free Enterprise City: Houston in Political and Economic Perspective.* New Brunswick, NJ: Rutgers University Press.

Feagin, Joe R., and Robert Parker (1990) *Building American Cities: The Urban Real Estate Game.* Engelwood Cliffs, NJ: Prentice Hall.

Gottdiener, M. (1985) *The Social Production of Urban Space.* Austin, TX: University of Texas Press.

Henderson, Jeffery, and Manuel Castells (1987) *Global Restructuring and Territorial*

Development. Newbury Park, CA: Sage.

Lefebvre, Henri (1979) Space: Social Product and Use Value. In J. W. Freiberg (Ed.), *Critical Sociology: European Perspectives*, 285-295. New York: Irvington Publishers.

Morales, Rebecca (1983) Transnational Labor: Undocumented Workers in the Los Angeles Automobile Industry, *International Migration Review*, 17, 570-596.

Mullings, Leith (Ed.) (1987) *Cities of the United States*. New York: Columbia University Press.

Rodriguez, Nestor P. (1987) Undocumented Central Americans in Houston: Diverse Populations, *International Migration Review*, 21, 4-26.

Rodriguez, Nestor P., and Jacqueline Hagan (1989) Undocumented Central American Migration to Houston in the 1980s, *La Raza Studies*, 2, 1-3.

Sassen, Saskia (1988) *The Mobility of Labor and Capital: A Study in International Investment and Labor Flow*. Cambridge: Cambridge University Press.

Smith, Michael Peter (1989) Urbanism: Medium or Outcome of Human Agency?, *Urban Affairs Quarterly*, 24, 353-357.

Smith, Barton (1986) *Handbook on the Houston Economy*. Houston: Center for Public Policy, University of Houston.

Urrutia-Rojas, Ximena (1988) Health Care Needs and Utilization among Hispanic Immigrants and Refugees in Southwest Houston. Master's Thesis, The University of Texas Health Science Center at Houston, Houston, TX.

FROM DUALISM TO TERRITORIAL PROBLEMATIC IN ITALY: A RESTRUCTURING OF INDUSTRY AND THEORY

Marco Cenzatti

University of California, Los Angeles

This paper traces the evolution of the literature analyzing the geographical and structural changes of the Italian economy over the last two decades. After the economic crisis of the early 1970s, Italy's recovery was led by the unexpected growth of small industries in the central regions of the country. It is argued that, in parallel to this shift, established explanatory models assuming a universal dynamic of development lost their supremacy and a new theoretical framework, emphasizing the influence of local conditions in shaping the restructuring process, has now become dominant. This new analytical framework shares several features with the American and British debates over "flexible production" and "locality studies." The paper concludes by pointing out that the new approach, by progressively loosing sight of any general dynamic of the Italian economy, can lead to a balkanized picture of the country.

Over the last fifteen years, the Italian industrial structure underwent a series of unforeseen changes. Large industry in the "industrial triangle" (Milan-Turin-Genoa), although unable after the 1969-73 crisis[1] to continue its excellent performance of the 1950s and 1960s, remains the backbone of the economy, while the South is still lagging behind. However, since 1970, significant industrial growth took place in the Northeast and Center of the country in the form of a myriad of small firms. A "Third Italy," located geographically and economically between the North and the South, began to emerge. At first, the economic literature reacted by downplaying this phenomenon, calling it "conjunctural." As soon as the economic crisis was over, it was argued, small industry would either go back to its naturally subordinate relationship with large firms, or it would itself grow into large industry. However, by the mid-1970s, since this did not occur, a new body of literature started to appear, attempting to explain this development as an important structural reorganization of production.

Until the 1970s, the industrial development of the country had been based on, and analyzed as, a series of polarizations: between the industrial Northwest and

and analyzed as, a series of polarizations: between the industrial Northwest and the underdeveloped South; between modern and traditional, or backward, economic sectors; between the primary labor market (with stable and well-paid employment) and the secondary one (with seasonal and part-time employment, low wages, poor working conditions). The question common to all analyses was how to expand the modern model of Northwestern industrialization to the entire country. To be sure, answers changed according to the political perspective of the analysis. For studies rooted in political economy, the elimination of backwardness was an unattainable result since these dichotomies were part of the unevenness which had marked (Italian) capitalism from its birth and continued to shape its growth. Mainstream analyses, on the other hand, proposed policy after policy to correct the disequilibriums. Regardless of their political orientation, all analyses shared the assumption that there was no middle-ground between the two poles of the dichotomy: either "modern" or doomed to stagnation. Unexpectedly, however, much new development after 1970 took place exactly in that middle-ground. The Central regions, where most of the new economic growth was concentrated, had been largely ignored in the economic literature of the previous decades, and the industry responsible for that growth was not the modern, large industry of the Northwest but small enterprises that grew out of the informal economy and the long-standing artisanal activities of the area. In the previous decades, both of these factors were typically seen as inefficient distortions of the economic structure.

By the early 1980s, as the economy of the Third Italy kept growing,[2] research focusing on the Third Italy not only documented a critical change in the Italian industrial structure, but also rejected established explanatory frameworks which couldn't fully comprehend this phenomenon. Instead, an alternative perspective began developing, the "Territorial Problematic." This offers two complementary features which separate it from the previously dominant approaches. The new framework emphasizes the importance of specific socio-economic characteristics of individual geographical areas. This is seen as a factor which not only allows but shapes the new forms of industrialization. Thus, in the Third Italy, the new industrialization and its particular characteristics are not seen as dictated by external circumstances—such as, the influence of Northwestern industry—but rather as a form of *endogenous development*, which depends on the particular political, social, and economic make-up of the region. Second, this framework also identifies the development of small industry and its spatial expression—the *fabbrica diffusa, diffused industrialization*—as a fundamental element of a new manufacturing organization. Small firms do not necessarily evolve into large ones—as predicted by traditional models of industrial growth—but can exist as an autonomous form of development where economic growth does not result in growth in the size of firms (and reduction of their number) but in an increased number of small firms.

This review essay offers two interwoven themes. First, it provides sources for a study of the "Italian case." Second, it highlights the theoretical evolution and implications of the new problematic. This second theme should be of particular interest to Anglo-American readers since a similar shift has occurred in the discussions of industrial restructuring in the U.S. and Britain. In fact, the "locality studies" which have developed out of the CURS initiative[3] echo the endogenous development view with their calls for more analytical attention to local cultures, political organizations, family structures, and social relations of particular areas. In short, both "locality" and "endogenous" development studies give a privileged role to the differentiation and particularity of individual places in determining their own economic pathway.

The parallel between "diffused industrialization" and the "flexible specialization" thesis which grew out of Piore and Sabel's work[4] is even more obvious. For supporters of the "flexible specialization" thesis, the Third Italy has become a standard example to show that mass production, with its attributes of standardized and ever-increasing output, internal economies of scale, use of single-purpose machinery, etc., is not the only means by which industrialization can progress. A system of small firms, *á la* Third Italy, based on the use of multi-purpose machines, small production batches, and external economies of agglomeration can be equally successful, they argue, since it offers the ability to modify output and adjust to demand change that cannot be matched by standardized production. The point, made explicit by the "flexible specialization" thesis but already implicit in the *fabbrica diffusa* explanations, is that the "technological paradigm" of mass production has no inherent superiority over alternatives such as flexible specialization. Rather, the dominance of a paradigm is linked to the social conditions in which it evolves: "the success of mass production . . . [is rooted] in the politically defined interests of producers and consumers—rather than in the logic of industrial efficiency" (Piore and Sabel, 1984, p. 21). If alternative forms of industrial organization are available, their success depends on the social conditions in which they are embedded. In fact, the "flexible specialization" school carries the point even further by postulating a change, after the 1973 economic crisis, in the social conditions which underlay the development of mass production. The success of the industrialization of the Third Italy, Southern Germany, and even Japan are signs that we are passing through a "divide" where changing global, social conditions make flexible specialization a viable alternative to mass production. Here the "flexible specialization" and *fabbrica diffusa* approach converge with the endogenous development thesis and call for an understanding of the social and spatial milieu in which industrialization is taking place, rather than relying on "ironclad laws" of capitalist development.

At a more theoretical level, there is a final parallel to be drawn between the Italian and American studies. In the last several years, following the influence of thinkers such as Foucault, Lyotard, Derrida, and Vattimo, a debate has flourished in the U.S. around poststructuralism and the "death of Grand Theory" in social sciences.[5] One general feature of poststructuralism, regardless of the differences between its authors, is the rejection of the modernist attempt to encapsulate the entire social reality into hierarchical structures and its history into a linear evolution. Poststructuralism emphasizes the importance of abandoning "totalizations," broadening the focus, loosening the hierarchy, and paying due attention to the social actors, places, and phenomena which the modernist discourse, in its attempt to outline a unilinear direction of progress, marginalized. By contrast, the postmodernist discourse has no privileged subjects or centers. In consequence, history too breaks down into a kaleidoscope of micro-histories, or "genealogies" as Foucault has it, limited to the specific objects of inquiry not as part of an universal design.

Neither Territorial Problematic nor Flexible Specialization authors have entered directly into the poststructuralism debate. It is possible, however, to recognize in both schools several features that echo postmodernist views. To begin with, just as poststructuralism denounces the totalizing historical explanations of modernism, both schools explicitly reject the traditional belief (the metanarrative, a postmodernist would say) that firms begin small and, unless limited to niche markets or part of an underdeveloped economy, must grow to succeed. Furthermore, since there is no determinism shaping the industrial organization, then other factors must be responsible for the direction of development, and since the growth of the Third Italy has not occurred everywhere, these factors must be spatially specific. Thus, the Territorial Problematic and the Flexible Specialization schools, in order to understand the causes of the development of a specific area, must, in an almost Foucaultian archeology, dig into the micro-history of the region to find the endogenous causes that shape its growth. Yet, like Foucault, who moved from archeology to genealogy, and like Derrida, who speaks of "traces" of the past in the present, for these schools the influence of the past is not limited to creating the conditions for the birth of the new industries but continues to assert its presence in the way the system of firms grows and works. Thus, political organizations, cultural customs, and craft traditions form the "industrial atmosphere" of the area and the continuing presence of these past traditions allows the Third Italy to grow.

The rejection of metanarratives has another consequence for both schools. The progressive abandonment, in the Italian studies, of the "totalizing" dualisms of the previous problematics has not only eliminated the view of a monolithic (if polarized) Italy, it has also eliminated the relevance of the factors that were traditionally—particularly from a politically economic perspective—central to the analyses: exploitation of labor, uneven development, capital competition. As a result, the Territorial Problematic is more apt than other views to detect the locally specific factors promoting industrialization. But, at the same time, it is largely unable to explain *why* those factors have become important over the last two decades since in most areas of the Third Italy the presence of craft tradition, cultural customs, etc., can be traced back in most cases to the turn of the century. Similarly, the Flexible Specialization school's interest is on the possibility of alternative, non-technologically-determined forms of industrialization with the reasons for the "industrial divide" as a secondary concern. When reasons for this shift are mentioned, they tend to be limited to changes in consumer markets.[6] In other words, just as the question central to Foucault's thinking was "how" certain phenomena took place and shape rather than "why," the focus of the Territorial Problematic (and the Flexible Specialization school) is on "how" new forms of industrialization are taking place rather than "why" industrial districts and other flexible production systems are becoming so important.

This shift from "why" to "how" provides these approaches with a new sensitivity to the local conditions that allow industrial growth to occur, but at the same time, poses the danger of an understanding of industrialization as a "quilt" of specific cases that denies the existence of more global dynamics of capitalist development.

Pre-Crisis Approaches

Each of the pre-crisis problematics (Model of Development, North-South, Labor Market) focused on a specific set of elements in charting a path through the obstacles of Italian post-war economic development.[7] The Model of Development approach was based on economistic analyses in which a single economic variable was identified as the motor of development (for example, patterns of internal consumption, sectorial differentiations of investment, leading role of exports, international competitiveness based on cheap labor, etc.). These analyses presented dualistic models in which the leading role of a sector, a market, or a type of consumption, was coupled with the lack of development or even active underdevelopment of complementary sectors, markets, etc. Thus, for example, the growth of the export market was paralleled by a weak internal market, the low cost of labor by a delay in the introduction of new technologies, and the development of modern and internationally competitive sectors was matched by backward traditional sectors. Up to the early 1970s, this approach evolved alongside changes in the Italian economy. At first, this disequilibrium between variables was seen as a problem needing correction, then explained both as a fundamental component of Italian development and as a potential limit to growth. More recently, this disequilibrium was identified as the cause of the economic crisis of the 1970s.

The North-South Polarization spatialized this economic dualism by geographically locating the dynamic socio-economic elements in the Northwest and the backward sectors in the South. This approach was strongly influenced by international discussions on underdevelopment and, by the end of the 1960s, most studies shifted from positions inspired by Rostow's "Modernization Theory" to "Dependency School" approaches.[8] Like the Model of Development, the North-South problematic changed over the years in response to the changes of the Italian economy: shifting from confidence in the South's ability to catch up in the 1950s, to expressing doubt during the 1960s, and finally, finding the cause of the 1973 crisis in an irresolvable geographical dualism.

In contrast to the previous two, the Labor Market problematic developed out of the crisis. Rather than explaining the development of the 1950s and 1960s, it originated as an interpretation of the "limits to growth" of the early 1970s. Its central element was the division of the laborforce into three labor markets—central, peripheral, and marginal—increasingly closed off from one other. In the central segment, this resulted in a situation of artificially full employment with high wages, unionization, and employment security. The marginal and the peripheral labor markets, by contrast, showed increasingly high rates of low paying, temporary, and part-time employment, as well as hidden unemployment. According to this view, central industry's inability to tap the labor reserves in the latter two markets explained the economic downturn.

These three problematics offer three distinct perspectives (economic, spatial, and labor) which continue to be fundamental in the subsequent literature and supply complementary analyses of the crisis. They remained, however, unable to identify the avenues open to restructuring as a solution to the crisis.

North-South Polarization

The North-South model is obviously based on the geographical dualism between the industrialized North and the underdeveloped South. The dualism, however, is not a simple description of two different realities, as in classical *Meridionalismo,* where the South was considered a yet undeveloped region needing state help to "take off." On the contrary, the North-South dualism was based on the assumption that the under-development of one region was structurally necessary for the development of the other. Although this interpretation had been touched on in specialized literature since Gramsci's analysis, in the early 1960s it was applied to specific aspects of dependency, such as, agricultural and industrial development, or state policies. The argument recognized that the social and economic changes of the South—with particular emphasis given to state intervention—were not aimed at developing the region but actually were intended to avoid conflicts which might hamper growth in the North. These changes were not only useful for but directly geared to the economic development of Northern industry.

Thus, for example, Mottura and Pugliese (1971) pointed out that the goal of the 1950 land reform was not to rationalize agricultural production in the Mezzogiorno since the subdivision of large land holdings and the redistribution of land ownership in small lots was actually an obstacle to mechanization and intensive agriculture. Its purpose was to re-establish social peace in the region in response to the peasant upheavals of the period. Del Monte and Giannola (1978) recognized a similar function of social control in the hypertrophic growth, in more recent years, of the tertiary sector in the South. The state-guided industrialization of the South did not generate local development either. For Giannola (1977), subsidies to private industry that were intended to stimulate local industry worked to the advantage of Northern, large, industrial complexes by allowing them to open dependent plants in the South. New industry not only did not bring benefits to the South but actually disrupted the preexisting labor market (via wage increases and competition over skilled manpower) which created further obstacles for local small- and medium-sized industry. Southern underdevelopment was not only caused by the North but it also was necessary for the development of the North itself, as the subsidized growth of heavy industry in the South furthered the growth of the existing intermediate industry in the North. Paci (1970) identified a similar mechanism in labor migrating from the South to the "industrial triangle." In his view, the role of internal migration was not simply to meet excess labor demand from the North (as classical *meridionalismo* assumed) but acted as a process of laborforce substitution to decrease the cost of labor. This process of importing unemployment from the South resulted in the recreation of a miniature North-South polarization in the North itself. Thus, polarization was not simply a given condition with which the economy had to deal but was recreated by the working of the economy itself and was fundamental to the Italian process of accumulation.

Other studies stressed other aspects of this dependency, such as, the role of the South as a reservoir of conservative votes (Graziano, 1973). The element that unified all these positions was not only the identification of an explicit process organizing Southern underdevelopment but also (and this was the hegemonic character of the problematic) the increasingly explicit assumption that the process of accumulation in Italy should be understood as grounded in the articulation of these two territorial sub-systems.

Model of Development

Dualism was also at the base of the Economic Model of Development approach. In this case, the elements of the dichotomy were different economic subjects, but, as in the passage from classical *meridionalismo* to the dependency view, there was an increasing certitude that economic dualism was not an accident that could be eliminated but the basis of Italian development. The evolution of the Model of Development can be seen in two phases.

1) *The period 1950-60.* These were the years of the economic boom. The low cost of labor and Italy's increased international competitiveness allowed the growth of a system which apparently supported the neoclassical hypothesis of the natural workings of the model. If contradictory elements appeared, they were justified as "rigidities," obstacles to be overcome. The social conflicts of the period (such as, the peasant upheavals in the South), even if analyzed from opposite political positions with opposite conclusions, were still seen as obstacles to overcome while moving towards equilibrium. The question of how to overcome them was where the different political positions had a bearing.

On the right, Vera Lutz (1958; 1962) identified in the Italian model a dualism between well-paid workers employed in the large industry and workers who, although performing the same tasks (or able to do so), received lower wages working for small-sized firms. From this bifurcation other dualisms derived: since mechanization increased with the rate of output, the first group was more productive; since some goods could be profitably produced only in large quantities, sectorial differentiations also appeared; and since access to credit was more difficult for small firms, capital formation was also uneven. Lutz' conclusion was that union activity, which protected labor primarily in the first group, created a small labor aristocracy at the expense of other workers, actually distorting the overall development of the country which would have been better off left to the forces of the free market. The more progressive Saraceno (1963) identified another dualism, this time between industry and agriculture. In his view, the wage gap resulted from the higher productivity of industrial-over-agricultural labor, but, unlike Lutz' position, his proposed solution was to step up state intervention and devolve as much national income as possible to capital formation and modernization in agriculture.

In these two examples, as well as in other studies in this problematic, the Southern question was not ignored, but, as Saraceno put it, seen as "the largest territorial expression of a more comprehensive disequilibrium." For the Model of Development, geographical unevenness was a result of economic unevenness rather than its cause, as the North-South approach maintained.

2) *The period 1960-70.* The social conflicts of 1960-62 brought the "economic miracle" of the previous decade to a sudden halt. In the following years, studies identified two interwoven elements as fundamental in both the economic miracle and the succeeding economic crisis: 1) the importance of the production of durable and luxury goods for the international market, while production of necessary goods for internal consumption was systematically lagging behind; and 2) Italy's competitive position in the international market which was based on the low cost of domestic labor which, in turn, required a depressed internal market.

Napoleoni (1964), recognizing that the Italian economy depended on production for the international market, pointed out that this model of development, although successful in the previous decade, brought with it elements of potential crisis since it neglected investment for necessary goods and workers' demands for better working and living conditions that could easily break the mechanism of accumulation. Furthermore, as Graziani (1968, 1972) noted, the comparative advantage of Italian industry during the 1950s was based both on the low cost of labor and weak international competition in European markets. As other countries entered the market, the Italian advantage decreased. The development of internal markets to compensate for the declining international competitiveness, however, was limited by the continuing low cost of labor which translated into low internal demand.

The economic recovery of the second half of the 1960s did not change the structure of the economy. According to Sylos Labini (1972a, 1972b), the potential for a new crisis remained since the recovery of profitability following the 1959-62 labor conflicts was achieved without investments in new technology but by neutralizing the gains obtained by the workers in the previous years. In the short run, this allowed for recovery, but it also left the economic system vulnerable to new conflicts.

During this period, the theoretical viewpoint evolved in a direction parallel to that of the North-South debate. The assumed "rigidities" were now seen as structural contradictions which were paradoxically functional to accumulation. Thus, the pairing of a relative technological backwardness with specialization in labor-intensive sectors, the growth of production for international markets along with lack of investment for internal consumption, and polarized income distribution were distortions that played a double role. At the same time that they promoted and shaped the "economic miracle" of the previous decade, they also established the limits of the miracle itself.

Changing Reality and Changing Models

By the 1970s, the mounting evidence of the new type of growth occurring in the Third Italy was reflected in attempts to adjust both problematics to the new reality. In the process, both approaches lost their ability to explain the entire picture.[9]

From the North-South approach, a more faceted view appeared in which different regions played different roles (in time, as well as space) in the national economy. Thus, Secchi (1974; 1977) rejected many aspects of both the dualist and the internal colonialism theses and maintained that:

> "*regional inequalities affected* the modality and the intensity of the utilization of the labour force, and, therefore, *the direction and intensity of the technical progress* during the different phases of the process of Italian development . . . [T]he existence and growth of regional inequalities made the Italian economic system more flexible in terms of labor supply than it would have been in a better balanced regional situation . . ." (1977, p. 36) [emphasis mine]

Secchi's argument was important not only because it broke down the North-South polarity into a more comprehensive articulation of variable regional inequalities but also because he identified the active role played by spatial differentiation in national economic development. It was no longer a question of the center guiding the process of development (and the periphery suffering the consequences) but of development itself being the outcome of the changing relationships between regional spaces. In a sense, Secchi is no longer in the simple North-South problematic but already moving towards the new debate on the Third Italy. Yet, his insights into the interplay between different regions in determining the direction and form of development have been generally ignored by the Territorial Problematic which focuses on the internal characteristics of each region.

In a similar fashion the Model of Development approach was put off balance not by the crisis, which it foresaw, but by the way in which the crisis was overcome. The most representative work of the period is Salvati's (1972a; 1972b). His "precocious maturity" thesis synthesized the views of the leading Italian economists of the time (Fuà, Graziani, Sylos Labini, Lombardini, Spaventa, in addition to himself). Salvati pointed out that a major cause of the stagnation afflicting the Italian economy from the end of the 1960s onward was Northern industry's inability to tap the large reserve of labor still available in the South as the labor market in the North grew increasingly tight. Among several reasons for the appearance of this bottleneck (which ranged from the marginally improved agricultural situation after the land reforms, to the increasing cost of living in the North, to better wages abroad which favored international-over-internal migration), Salvati gave particular importance to the "social preservation of inefficient, archaic small industries" due to the political interests of the ruling parties. The result of the "seal" between the two labor markets was, by the late 1960s, a situation of artificially full employment despite the presence of large reserves of labor "locked" in areas, sectors, and layers of population which did not act as part of the laborforce because capital couldn't use them. Salvati (1975) concluded by depicting a stalemate in which the political forces that could induce change paralyzed one another with no hope for reforms.

The Labor Market Problematic

The same phenomenon of closure between labor markets marked not only the pessimistic conclusions of the Model of Development approach but also gave rise to the Labor Market approach as an independent problematic. While, until the 1970s, labor market issues were either part of the *Questione Meridionale* or included in the Model of Development approach, a specific event sparked the evolution of labor market studies into an independent approach, developing a new direction.

Throughout the 1960s, Italian economic development was characterized by a parallel fall in the rate of employment and unemployment.[10] An influential article by De Meo (1969) explained this phenomenon as a consequence of the level of prosperity reached by the Italian system (later schooling, early retirement, higher income which relieved the family from the need for female employment). This thesis implicitly maintained the traditional interpretation that a decrease in the rate of unemployment led to a rigid supply of labor which, in turn, strengthened the working class and its demands. The volley of criticisms that met De Meo's thesis was in part focused on the inadequacy of the statistical categories used (such as, the definition of workforce and unemployment).[11] The implications of these criticisms, however, went well beyond the statistical data. In fact, the rejection of De Meo's position reversed the question: why did the workers' struggles of 1969-73 reach and maintain such a high intensity under conditions of high unemployment when those conditions should have led, according to theory, to workers' weakness? This question became the fundamental focus of the problematic.

The " precocious maturity" thesis already supplied a partial answer. Sylos Labini (1974) proposed an analysis of Italian development based on two complementary elements: the late-comer character of Italian capitalism and, following from it, the presence of a large middle-class inherited from its pre-capitalist social organization. Although this class was not "efficient" from an economic standpoint, it did not collapse into one of the two classes of the capitalist mode of production but found its own position between capital and labor in two ways: 1) as a traditional middle-class, composed of small land owners whose number was decreasing and artisans who were economically surviving by changing from independent and competive to satellites of modern industry; and 2) as a non-productive middle-class, composed of small merchants and state bureaucrats who survived as the result of their stabilizing function over the social and political structure. Around these two social strata a precarious proletariat formed, working in small shops or in the lower level of state offices. In other words, Sylos Labini underscored that this archaic and inefficient social division of labor corresponded to Salvati's "inefficient and archaic firms," and that the "seal" between the modern (proletarianized) and the inefficient (inherited) segments of the labor market were the cause of "artificial" strength of workers' organizations in the modern sectors.

A more complete answer developed out of the debate sparked by Sylos Labini's essay.[12] In fact, although his interpretation explained why a portion of the workforce was unavailable to "modern" sectors of the economy, it left largely unexplained why this group was actually expanding. His critics contended that the inefficient economic sectors and labor segments were not just inherited from the past but continually re-created by the working of the Italian economy (Meldolesi, 1972; Paci, 1973, 75, 78; De Cecco, 1973; Mantovani, 1973). Paci described the mechanisms by which the labor market, after the 1960-62 economic crisis, actually expelled the weak and unstable segments of the workforce (women, the young, the relatively old).[13] In his analysis, the labor market was divided into three segments: the marginal labor market, formed by the latent unemployment in agriculture and in other activities and readily attracted into the central segment to increase the supply of labor for modern industry; the central market, composed of workers either employed in modern industry, or between jobs, or actively looking for a job; and the peripheral labor market, characterized by insecure employment, home work, seasonal work, etc., and constituted by workers coming from the other two markets—either expelled from the central segment or attracted from the marginal one without being able to actually become part of the central labor market. This last segment was tightly linked not only to the existence but to the development of small and artisanal production units.

In these studies the way out of the economic crisis of the 1970s began to appear. If Italian industry was unable to attract the "peripheral" workers, the peripheral labor market could attract the industry, as far as the industry could restructure and adjust to the characteristics of peripheral labor. Salvati's "archaic" industries were not doomed to remain archaic forever.

Decentralization of Production

By the mid-1970s, while the North-South and Model of Development problematics were falling into the background and the Labor Market approach was gaining momentum, another set of studies was calling attention to, and proposing explanations for, the new forms of geographical and sectorial decentralization of production then taking place. Like the Labor Market problematic, these studies emphasized the segmentation of the labor market and its influence on the growth of "peripheral" economic activities. Yet, instead of focusing on the labor market itself, these studies turned their attention to the changes taking place in the Italian industrial structure. At first, they highlighted phenomena such as the increasing importance of the underground economy and the multi-plant firm which still depended upon the decisions and restructuring of large enterprises. Increasingly, however, attention shifted to the emergence of small- and medium-sized firms as an independent theoretical subject.

The Underground Economy

The term "underground economy" was coined in the early 1970s and included activities such as "black work," part-time and double employment, and, in many cases, sub-contracting and artisanal forms of work. As Gallino (1979) later noted, the common feature of these activities was that they could not be gauged by the models used to analyze the "formal" economy and were outside the area of intervention of institutional agencies (government, unions, parties). In studies on the subject, there was a basic agreement on the importance of the phenomenon in explaining both the fall in the rate of activity pointed out by De Meo[14] and the slow growth of large industry even during the economic recovery after 1973.

For Garavini (1973) the underground economy, and home work in particular, was a direct consequence of the blocked accumulation of the late 1960s since it required very low capital investment, allowed the use of a very flexible laborforce, avoided labor conflicts, and, most important, paid lower wages (around 50-70 percent of the factory wage for the same work). Avoiding health and retirement benefits, not having to account for working conditions, and tax evasion offered further savings on labor costs. In brief, home work (organized by a "jobber" who supplied the home workers with the raw material, gave the order, and collected the product for a firm) was not just the residue of a backward industrial structure but a department of production outside the factory and outside the conditions of artificially full employment of the central segment of the labor market.

The negative features identified in the underground economy weren't limited to the super-exploitation of labor but included its inefficient organization. For Gallino, "Our society, through the invisible economy, has built a system in which, by working twelve, fourteen, or eighteen hours a day, we can do badly what we could do well in eight." In other words, although Gallino identified the importance of the underground economy, he still saw it as a residual category incapable of autonomous growth (just as labor market studies considered marginal labor as a residual category). Small industry, insofar as it grew out of this invisible economy, was still based on backward technology and super-exploitation and was, in the long run, unable to lead anywhere.

Two changes were necessary for the assessment of the underground economy to shift from a depiction as a temporary and negative palliative to being viewed as the seed of a new form of development. First, the underground economy had to start appearing "above ground." This happened not only through a relative increase in output and in the size of the units of production which, in many cases, became artisanal laboratories or family run firms but also through the availability of more precise data gathered in specific case studies, or by unions and regional planning agencies. Second, new analyses increasingly recognized the dynamic character of the new firms and questioned their relationship to the "official" industry in terms of efficiency, sectorial development, and technological change. As a result, Garavini and Gallino's assumption that underground economy was an expanding but inefficient form of growth came into question.

By 1980, Cantelli had already identified specific sectors of light industry (leather and footwear, clothing, furniture) which, beginning in the second half of the 1970s, took a more central role in the economy of the country. In these sectors, the number of plants increased considerably while the average size of the plant decreased. Although he still referred to the phenomenon as *Economia Sommersa,* his study had already moved onto the subject of the small industry.

Multi-Plants, Sectorial Studies, Technological Changes, and Location

As an alternative to the view of peripheral development as a temporary phenomenon, other authors saw it as part of a more coherent restructuring process implemented by large industry via the use of branch-plants, sub-contracting, and Just-In-Time production. The privileged object of study in this area was and is FIAT.[15] Not only is FIAT the major Italian corporation with the largest impact on the national economy but in the last twenty years it has also undergone a number of changes which well represent all the major aspects of industrial restructuring: it has decentralized production by opening new plants in the Third World and in Southern Italy; it has widely used different forms of sub-contracting; and it has reorganized the production processes by means of "work islands"as well as by robotization.

Libertini (1975) used FIAT to exemplify the influence of large firms on the level of employment in small- and medium-sized industry. In the early 1960s, FIAT relied heavily on outside firms for component production (Borletti, Marelli, Vernici, etc.). In this period, local employment in small and medium industry increased by 46 percent. Following the 1962 recession, FIAT initiated a national and international process of "integrated decentralization," i.e., decentralization of its own large plants with less input from outside suppliers. In Piedmont, small and medium industry employment decreased by ten points in the following years. However, after the *autunno caldo* of 1969, the increasing rigidities of the labor market and the rising cost of labor led FIAT to rely on independent firms for the production of labor intensive components, leading to a new increase of employment in the small and medium industry of the region.

While Libertini linked changes in small and medium industry to FIAT's organizational and technological changes, Amin (1982, 1985) added geographical decentralization to the picture. In the 1970's, FIAT opened a number of branch plants in Central and Southern Italy (Sulmona, Cassino, Termoli, Bari, Termoli Imerese). An important reason for the new locations was FIAT's introduction of new, capital intensive, production processes (particularly in assembly work) so that the new plants: "were only marginally dependent upon a skilled labor market, and therefore could be located in depressed rural areas of the South which offered an abundant supply of semi-skilled and unskilled labor" (1985, p.189).

Although these plants did create a new network of suppliers in the region (453 firms by 1980), they had a limited effect on the regional economy:

> "Most of the locally owned firms which have arisen as a result of the FIAT investments are small family enterprises or businesses that are peripheral (in terms of value of trade) suppliers of FIAT. Moreover, they are highly dependent on FIAT and have limited prospects of expansion." (ibid.)

In these analyses, the growth of small industry was seen as depending on the reorganization of large industry. Libertini and Amin's position, in common with the *economia sommersa* approach, was that small industry suffered from low productivity and could grow only when other economic actors, namely, large firms, could use its growth for their own advantage. For small-size industry to become an independent object of analysis, it was necessary to see its development as independently provoked. This process of "uncoupling" the development of small industry from dynamics dictated by large corporations appeared in yet another strand of literature which began to question the technical superiority of large scale production.

One of these writers, Brusco (1975a, 1975b), pointed out that, after the passage from the steam to the electric engine, technical economies of scale no longer needed to be gauged on the whole production process but on its individual phases. Thus, the comparative advantage of lower labor costs in small industry, together with the decreasing importance of economies of scale (as far as small industry performed a complete phase of production), in many cases countered the advantages historically connected with integrated production. Furthermore, as Caselli (1974a, 1974b) maintained, in the Italian case, and for specific types of production, decentralization offered advantages, such as, access to cheaper labor, avoidance of limiting regulations, etc., which offset the savings attainable by vertical integration even without challenging the general importance of economies of scale.

Other studies pushed the argument further by maintaining that the changes in progress were neither a result of technological advancements nor the outcome of large corporations' decisions but that both small and large firms were equally and directly responding to the new social conditions of the country and to the obstacles to accumulation which appeared in the early 1970s. Restructuring was a social process leading to a re-definition of the boundaries between central (large industry - monopoly capital) and peripheral capital (small industry - competitive capital) (Rullani, 1974). It also represented another episode of class struggle in which capital selectively used new technologies, disinvestment from particular phases of production by large industry, and "peripheral development" in order to regain control over the working class lost with the 1969 autunno caldo (Masiero, 1975).

Along with these attempts to explain the general dynamics of the restructuring, the 1970s also saw the development of a large body of empirical case studies. While most theoretical questions and interpretations were the same as in the general works outlined above, these researches highlighted three new elements. In the first place, as Cantelli (1980) pointed out, the growth of small industry took place in those sectors (textile, apparel, leather, metal-mechanic) where large industry was actually absent. Second, in those sectors small-firm production was expanding from the production of consumer goods to the production of means of production. For example, in the Prato area (near Florence), the textile industry moved into the production of looms and textile machinery (Becattini, 1975). Third, these studies identified specific geographical areas specializing in well-determined sectors. Some areas of Emilia-Romagna were predominantly devoted to mechanical industry (Bologna, Modena), others to apparel and furniture (Forlí), or to the ceramic industry (Sassuolo). In Tuscany, areas specialized in textile production (Prato), in footwear (Lucca and Pisa), and in leather products (Valdarno). The main production of the Marche was footwear (Pesaro and Macerata), musical instruments (Castelfidardo), and furniture. In Veneto, the area around Verona was the center for small metal-mechanic firms and the province of Vicenza specialized in textiles, apparel, and textile machinery. From this mosaic of individual cases, the shape of the Third Italy began to appear.

Small and Medium Industry

The long turning point that led from the view of the development of small industry as peripheral and dependent on the decisions of "central" industry to the view of small industry as a legitimate and independent economic agent had already started in the works of Brusco, Masiero, and others. It also was evident in the conferences and debates that appeared in the mid-1970s. Specialized journals (like, *Inchiesta, Quaderni del Territorio, Quaderni Piacentini, Economia e Politica Industriale*) together with studies financed by research institutes (Fondazione Agnelli, Fondazione Feltrinelli, Istituto Gramsci) or by the Trade Unions (Federazione Lavoratori Metalmeccanici) become major arenas of discussion.

As part of these debates, Frey's studies (1973, 1974b, 1975) moved a step further in defining the small industry as an independent subject. Frey identified several factors basic to the development of the small industry. Among them: 1) the search for flexibility in order to quickly adjust production to variable demand; 2) the use of small firms for testing the introduction of new products and techniques of production which could then be mass produced by large firms after their market ability was proved; 3) the possibility of externalizing (or at least postponing) cost increases in raw materials; 4) the reduction of permanent employment; 5) the advantage of lower investment in fixed capital; 6) the ability to increase the range of products offered on the market without increasing the internal size of the firm.16 Similarly, Paci (1975), pursuing his studies on the absorption, expulsion, and reproduction of the laborforce, identified five overlapping types of small industry: 1) the *sponge-firm*, with functions of non-selective absorption of the workforce; 2) the *reservoir-firm*, which absorbed labor as a first step in the industrialization process, expelling it as soon as development took off; 3) the *shock absorber-firm*, which absorbed workers in periods of crisis and released them in phases of recovery; 4) the *lung-firm*, in which employment increased during expansive economic phases; 5) the *gear-firm*, which resulted from the decentralization of some phases of production and was an integral part of the circuit of central capital.

While it is obvious that in this list the real subject of the dynamic was still large industry now reaping the fruits of decentralization, two important points emerge from Frey's and Paci's analysis. First, the decentralization of production was not limited to the opening of new plants by large firms where labor was cheaper. If small firms were merely plants of large firms, the advantages offered by the factors identified by Frey and Paci would be very limited. Secondly, as Paci and others (Cacciari, 1975; Becattini, 1978) note, a number of social elements, ranging from the agricultural background of the area to the family structure, enter the picture as preconditions necessary for the development of small firms by offering additional means of subsistence to complement low wages and insecure employment.

For Varaldo (1979), the type of decentralization identified by Paci and Frey, although only indirectly depending upon the presence of large firms, was still not the whole picture; entire sectors were characterized by the presence of small-size industries without the domination of large industry. In this case, as in Brusco's analysis, the specialization of each production unit in only one specific phase of production could guarantee the realization of adequate economies of scale. Furthermore, in these sectors, firms were mostly owned by local entrepreneurs and were family run. Their small size fitted well with the limited economic and organizational resources available. Often the introduction of innovations, matched by the limited resources and inexperience with new techniques, forced small- and medium-sized industries to resort to external specialized producers, further increasing the decentralization process. In Varaldo's work, small industry took on a life of its own.

Synthesis

Bagnasco and Messori's article was probably the first comprehensive attempt to synthesize the theme of decentralization by bringing together several of the strands that have appeared so far. The authors saw three logics determining the growth of the small industry. *The residual logic* went back to the uneven sectorial development of Italy and the small industry that fell in this category belonged to the "inefficient," backward sectors of the economy that were still structurally necessary for capital accumulation either economically for production for local or segmented markets, or politically as a form of political control. (See, Salvati).

The second type of small industry responded to *the logic of the international division of labor* and to the dependent role played by the Italian economy in the world market. Because of this position, the central portion of the economy (i.e., sectors linked to the international market with high capital intensity, high technology, and control over the "strategic parts of the production process") had little room for independent growth. According to the same logic, however, sectors of the economy with low capital intensity (mostly traditional sectors) and sectors with a relatively new technology but still in an interstitial position (producing for structurally small markets) could grow freely since their ties with the international division of labor were weaker.

The third kind of industry responded to a *logic of diffusion* representing capital's response to the political conflicts of 1969-73 using decentralization to eliminate the rigidities that the unions had been able to impose. The authors were careful not to create three Procrustean beds in which each individual firm should fit ("a real firm will be at the crossroads of more than one logic"). However, in general terms, decentralization of production could be defined as "the political strategy that, in responding to the 1969-70 conflicts, is articulated by the concrete structure of the social formation determined by the international division of labor and shaped by the internal inherited characteristics of the country" (p. 78). This implied a change in the understanding of decentralization, now depicted as central capital dominating peripheral rather than large industry dominating small. In turn, Italian central capital occupied an intermediate position in the international circuit of capital. Bagnasco and Messori thus substituted a hierarchy among capitals for the large-small industry hierarchy. Decentralization, far from becoming an independent object of analysis, became linked to the response of Italian central capital to class struggle, a response that, in turn, had to fit in with the dictates of international capital.

Ferrero (1979) pushed the argument even further, denying the theoretical validity of the distinction between the two types of industry. In an introductory essay supplying the framework for the case studies of his book, he questioned the very validity of small industry as a theoretical construct. He argued that small industry could not be objectively defined on any ground. Technologically, small industry ranged from artisanal enterprises, to departments of production expelled by large firms to decrease labor costs in a number of ways (by avoiding unionization or evading costly precautions required for toxic operations, etc.), to high-tech production in activities where large industry was not interested to commit itself to innovation. In relation to the market, small firms could produce for a local market, or as suppliers of large firms, or could turn independently and directly to the international market. In terms of goods produced, the only condition was that their quality and price was competitive with the production of larger firms. Employment was the element usually considered for defining small industry. However, this too was meaningless unless connected to the amount of output, which led back to the question of the technology used.

In Bagnasco and Messori's view, decentralization was a phenomenon which could not be isolated from a larger process of restructuring. For Ferrero, the very concept of small firm was questionable. Ironically, the attempt to understand the development of small firms *per se*, rather than as an induced phenomenon, had a long and difficult incubation, but when the different elements eventually came together, they did so only to deny the possibility of such a study within the framework of the decentralization of production approach.

Territorial Problematic:
Endogenous Development and *Fabbrica Diffusa*

The theme of decentralization of production was unable to produce a conceptual shift in the understanding of the new form of industrialization. However, it brought to the forefront a number of topics (the importance of small industry in connection to the whole economic system rather than to large industry, the fragmentation of labor markets, sectorial differentiation and new technological possibilities, and the social characteristics of geographical areas) that, organized differently, became central to the new problematic. Furthermore, due to the lack of reliable data on home work, sub-contracting, and on small firms in general, researchers turned their attention to the study of these issues in empirical case studies. By simply "mapping" these cases, it became clear that the bulk of the studies and the phenomenon itself delineated a specific area of the country.

Bagnasco's *Tre Italie* (1977) was the first study that joined the geographical area emerging from the case studies with the organizational characteristics of the new type of industrial development.[17] Bagnasco maintained a connection between the North-South problematic and the new "territorialism." In fact, starting from the traditional polarity of the North as locus of central capital and the South as the marginal pole, he identified the Third Italy as a geographical area of peripheral economy, dependent from the center of the system and substantially similar to Wallerstein's semi-periphery.[18] Extending from his earlier article with Messori, Bagnasco distinguished between the small firms of the South, producing for local consumption (corresponding to Paci's "sponge-firm"), and the small firms of the Northwest, which produced directly for large enterprises ("gear-firms"). The peripheral industry of the Northeast-Center was based on traditional and interstitial production determined by the international division of labor and by the process of diffusion as defined in the article with Messori. However, and here are the seeds of the new problematic, his interpretation of the Third Italy went beyond the concept of decentralization as an induced phenomenon; it pointed at the new form of industrialization no longer from a industrial location perspective (i.e., industry "going" to new areas) but from a territorial perspective where the subject was the area rather than the firm; it proposed a link between sectors and areas and, in doing so, it emphasized the importance of the pre-existing tradition in the developing sectors.

If Bagnasco's book signals the opening of the new problematic, Fuá and Zacchia's *Industrializzazione senza Fratture* (1983) represents the drastic change that had taken place by the early 1980s in the perception of the role of small industry. Fuá identifies a number of substantially similar elements shared by the regions of the Third Italy (or NEC, North, East, Center, as he calls it). They include: the diffusion of small and medium towns in the whole area; a good road network in the countryside; a large rural population closely tied to the urban areas;[19] a tradition of independent work (e.g., small farmers or artisans); and some type of "solidarity" among the population (e.g., the enlarged family, a sense of community, political uniformity, or diffused union membership). These elements function as pre-conditions necessary for diffused industrialization to occur and are common to all the NEC regions.

The entire NEC also shares the reasons that made endogenous development viable. The most important factor is lower labor costs which come from two sources. First, in family run companies, family members are willing to work long hours for their direct stake in the firm. Secondly, wage-workers are willing to accept wages lower than in areas of older industrialization since they can count on a lower cost of living and on family support in the form of free rent and/or participation in the agricultural activities and in the small farm often owned by the family. An additional factor is the generally weak class polarization in the NEC. Workers are not completely proletarianized, on the one hand, since they can still count on their family's piece of land, or shop, or at least house. On the other hand, entrepreneurs are not members of "higher social strata." The first generation of investors was local and the new arrivals are, by and large, workers who started their own activity after years of dependent work where they developed the necessary knowledge and contacts.[20]

Several catalysts facilitated the industrialization even further. In addition to the branch plants and/or putting out strategies implemented by large firms, Fuá identified the decreasing employment in local agriculture and the return (from Northwestern Italy or Northern Europe) of emigrants bringing with them skills and enough capital to start their own small business. In still other cases, the triggering factor was the accumulation of local capital and the search for new possibilities for investment (as with revenues from tourism and agricultural cooperatives in Emilia-Romagna). Finally, endogenous development began in sectors for which the small size was not an handicap and which were related to, if not a direct extension of, artisanal activities typical to the area (cf., Cantelli, 1980).

If the endogenous characteristics of the regions are sufficient to explain the origin of the new industrial organization, a second set of reasons is necessary to explain its success. In fact, Fuá in his previous work (1976, 1980) still held to the notion that large industry was the motor of industrialization and small industry was just a stepping stone in industrial development. Firms started small and over time they either grew large or failed. He still maintains, as he did in his earlier work, that the late industrialization of the country is the cause of the particularly large number of small firms. Now, however, rather than seeing this as an obstacle or a phase, he characterizes this inheritance from the past as a hope and a possibility for new development.

Some of the reasons for the success of small firms, such as, the introduction of new technology and access to cheaper and more docile labor via sub-contracting and branch plants, have already been pointed out. However, the factor that provoked Fuá's change of perspective lies in the flexibility typical of small firms. Large firms, with their single purpose machinery, rigid laborforce, and standardized output, cannot react rapidly to increasing fragmentation and differentiation of demand. In contrast, not only can small firms achieve rapid production changes without costly retooling due to the use of general-purpose machines, but, above all, they have much more latitude in hiring, firing, or changing job requirements, and therefore they can respond more quickly to market changes.[21]

Furthermore, in the Territorial Problematic, the flexibility of the individual firm becomes secondary to the flexibility of the system. Individual (small) firms may even be rigid (i.e., specialized in the production of a limited number of goods with no resources to differentiate production), while the territorial system of production is still flexible. In fact, the flexibility results from the large number of firms that continuously enter (and exit) the system and from the relations between firms rather than from the internal structure of the individual firm. The system can change the characteristics of its output by reorganizing the network of suppliers and part-producers, while large industry, to obtain the same result, has to undertake several economically and socially costly internal transformations. Output increases can be achieved by increasing the number of sub-contractors, while decline in demand can be countered by reducing their number and distributing the impact of the downturn over the entire system.[22] Finally, the small firm system has a low capital-entry cost and therefore a large number of entrepreneurs could enter the system at any moment. Thus, the continuous appearance of newcomers with new ideas and a continuous flux of small innovations counters the most negative element of the model, i.e., the lack of investment for research and development (see also note 23).

According to Fuá, the development of the *fabbrica diffusa* took place in two phases. In the first period, the new firm was unable to be fully competitive on the market but could make up for its weakness by resorting to cheap labor and avoiding state regulations. In the second phase, the supply of labor decreases while unionization and state control over the conditions of production increase. To remain competitive, firms increase their productivity by specializing in high quality or small series production (e.g., fashion) or even custom-made production (e.g., industrial robots) and by increasing their integration into a system of small enterprises. The form of this system of small firms varies from area to area, but the presence of interconnections is universal. In Emilia-Romagna, for example, artisanal associations have developed into regional associations offering financial services to small firms, seeking new outlets for their products, providing technical assistance, and finding new financing by dealing with banks on behalf of the individual firm (Brusco, 1983). In Tuscany, purchasing offices play an important role by gauging demand, suggesting output adjustments to producers, and by supplying financing and quality control for the products (Becattini, et al., 1983).

The two elements of the new problematic appear most clearly here in the evolution and final viability of the system of small firms. The system of firms, the *fabbrica diffusa*, shows that this form of development can successfully replace the usual pattern of growth from small to large. A number of researchers (cf., Becattini, 1979, 1987) have drawn attention to the presence of economies external to the individual firm, but internal to the system, which can be achieved by clustering complementary activities in the same geographical area. They have also noted, however, that these systems did not develop in a vacuum but grew out of the "industrial atmosphere" which in turn derives from the particular socio-cultural environment of the region.

Becattini's argument is relevant beyond the Italian case. He notices that the main attributes of industrialization in the Third Italy are similar to the ones identified by Alfred Marshall in the "industrial districts" of Victorian England. For Marshall, the industrial city is characterized by spatial density and differentiation of economic activities. By contrast, industrialization in a district—as in the Third Italy—is more diffused across the area and more concentrated around activities of a specific sector. Over time, however, an increasing number of complementary activities—such as the production of looms in Prato or the expansion of financial services in Emilia-Romagna—will grow, moving beyond the original specialization. The most important characteristic of Marshall's industrial district which helps to explain the success of the *fabbrica diffusa* is the presence in the district of economies of aggregation. That is to say, the spatial proximity of a number of small firms allows savings unavailable where production was carried out in large plants or by small firms distant from one another. Among these advantages, Bellandi (1982) mentions easy personal contacts between suppliers and customers, the availability of timely part-supply, the need for lower inventory, ease in changing part-orders for non-standardized production, and even easier introduction of technological innovations.[23]

The Territorial Problematic does not claim the superiority of the industrial district over the more typical organization of mass production. It claims, however, that under certain circumstances the system of small firms is a viable alternative. Thus, the process of industrial restructuring is not seen as an abstract search for economic efficiency which leads to the same technical and organizational results across the globe. Instead, *the very reorganization of production depends on the social characteristics of the area where production takes place.*

Conclusions

Each of the pre-crisis problematics offered a different perspective of Italian socio-economic system by portraying a single aspect of the system as dominant and interpreting all other aspects as correctives to this basic dynamic. Yet, they all shared the assumption that it was possible to outline a unitary dynamic responsible for the major characteristics and the changes of the industrial structure over time. The turning point in the development of the Territorial Problematic occurred by abandoning the search for a cohesive model of development for the entire social formation and emphasizing social and spatial diversity. It replaced the unique technological trajectory implied by the Model of Development paradigm with a multiplicity of possibilities depending on local conditions, broke down the North-South polarity into a mosaic of different local spaces, and differentiated and located labor markets in space. In addition to the importance that the new problematic attributes to the political, social, and spatial characteristics of individual areas, however, there is a second consideration to keep in mind in this break from the previous approaches; that is, the new problematic evolved in parallel to, if not as a consequence of, a change in the industrial organization of the country. The attention to this linkage between the new explanatory model and a changing reality has been progressively disappearing from the new studies.

Attempts at incorporating in the framework explanations for the reasons of the success of the new round of industrialization (i.e., to explain "why" the Third Italy has suddenly blossomed) remain on the margin of the framework itself with reference to the flexibility of the system, low capital-entry costs, etc. In fact, the weakness of these explanations is that, since the authors of the Territorial Problematic point out that flexibility is not a consequence of technological innovations, all these factors have been available also in the pre-crisis years without triggering new growth. Ultimately, like in Piore and Sabel's "industrial divide," the only remaining reason for the shift is an off-hand reference to changes in consumer markets demanding flexibility.

A recent study carried out by CENSIS (1988) well illustrates the vanishing concern for locating the growth of the Third Italy into a broader context. Instead of dealing with any single area, the study includes the whole country. It is, however, a summary of separate area-studies, describing the national economic and social situation by adding up individual cases. The unit of analysis of the study is the individual municipality (more than 8,000 in Italy) over the time-period of three censuses (1951–81). The individual cases are then aggregated to identify areas with comparable social and economic characteristics and with a similar evolution over time. This leads a picture of Italy as a mosaic of areas with different attributes. The researchers at CENSIS consciously reject any hierarchical reading of this picture. Thus, they point out that while in the Northeast and Center endogenous development has succeeded, the South did not experience a similar form of development. However, they also warn not to fall back in the North-South dualism to explain the differences in the recent evolution of the two regions. For CENSIS, to force an interpretation of the system into the "monolithic schemas of the North-South polarization" would mean to totally miss the positive aspects of the restructuring. Therefore, the reasons for the Southern lack of success should be found by identifying elements missing or not functioning at the local level.

The CENSIS study shows that the new approach can be as totalizing as the previous "monolithic schemas," this time by rejecting any comprehensive reading of the Italian social formation, and thus, limiting the theoretical horizon to an empiricist view composed solely by case studies. The Territorial Problematic makes a convincing case for rejecting preconceived totalizations and for emphasizing spatial differentiation. However, its evolution also indicates a danger inherent to the new approach: the possibility of a "negative" totalization which, in a sort of zerosum game, privileges the local, but does not leave any room for the study of macro-dynamics. To paraphrase Marshall Berman, capitalism melts into air.

Notes

1. Although interwoven with the international economic crisis of the first half of the 1970s, the Italian crisis is clearly rooted in the national internal dynamics. The first warnings occurred in 1962, with workers' unrest leading to generalized wage increases. The resulting downturn of the economy was quickly overcome via increased inflation and higher pace of work, which re-established the margins of profitability without requiring large new capital investments. For capital, the 1969–73 conflicts were more difficult to overcome since workers' demands were not limited to better wages but included various forms of control over the production process (such as, limiting the use of overtime and the movements of workers between departments or imposing the union's control over the pace of work and working conditions).

2. The decade between 1961 and 1971 already hinted at the growing importance of the Central regions of the country. Overall, manufacturing employment grew from 4,495,563 to 5,301,801 (+17.9%) units. Most of the growth was already concentrated in the Third Italy, with an increase in the Northwest of 239,305 units (10.3%), in the Third Italy of 405,908 (29.2%), and in the South of 161,025 (20.2%).

   In the following decade this growth became even more evident. While national manufacturing employment grew by 15%, employment in the Northwest remained basically unchanged (+34,837), while the Third Italy added over 465,000 new jobs (+33%).

   The other feature of the period is the growing importance of the small- and medium-sized industry. From 1961 to 1971 large industry (over 500 employees) added 255,887 jobs (+26.5%), while in the following years it lost 162,048 jobs. By contrast, firms employing between 10 and 50 workers grew by 31.4% (+266,226 jobs) and by 38.6% during the two decades respectively (See Becattini, 1987, pp. 15-16).

3. See J. Urry (1981) "Localities, Regions, and Social Class," *International Journal of Urban and Regional Research*, Vol. 5, No. 4, pp. 455-73; M. Savage, J. Barlow, S. Duncan, and P. Saunders (1987), "Locality Research: the Sussex Programme on Economic Restructuring, Social Change, and the Locality," *The Quarterly Journal of Social Affairs*, Vol. 3, No. 1, pp. 27-51. For a discussion on the "empirical turn" of locality research, see the debate in *Antipode* (1987, Vol. 19): N. Smith, "Dangers of the Empirical Turn: Some Comments on the CURS Initiative," pp. 59-68; P. Cooke, "Clinical Interference and Geographical Theory," pp. 69-78; N. Gregson, "The CURS Initiative: Some Further Comments," pp. 364-70.

4. M. J. Piore and C. Sabel (1984) *The Second Industrial Divide*, New York: Basic Books. See also A. J. Scott (1988) *New Industrial Spaces*, London: Pion; M. Storper and R. Walker (1989) *The Capitalist Imperative*, New York: Basil Blackwell; P. Hirst and J. Zeitlin (1989) "Flexible Specialization and the Competitive Failure of UK Manufacturing," *Political Quarterly*, Vol. 60, No. 3, pp. 164-78.

5. See, for example: the debate between Jameson (1984, "Postmodernism, or the Cultural Logic of Late Capitalism," *New Left Review*, No. 146, pp. 53-92), Latimer (1984, "Jameson and Post-Modernism," *New Left Review*, No. 148, pp. 116-127), Davis (1985, "Urban Renaissance and the Spirit of Postmodernism," *New Left Review*, No. 151, pp. 106-114), and Preziosi (1988, "La Vi(ll)e en Rose: Reading Jameson Mapping Space," *Strategies*, No. 1, p. 82-99); "Reconsidering Social Theory: a Debate" in *Environment and Planning D: Society and Space*, 1987, Vol. 5, pp. 367-427; Harvey (1989, *The Condition of Postmodernity*, Oxford: Basil Blackwell) and Soja (1989, Postmodern Geographies, London: Verso Books).

6. For a critique of this position see K. Williams, T. Cutler, J. Williams, and C. Haslam, 1987, "The End of Mass Production: Review of Piore and Sabel's *The Second Industrial Divide*." *Economy and Society*, 16, pp. 405-439).

7. The distinction between these three approaches derives from a famous article by Bagnasco and Messori (1976). For a detailed history of the Southern question in its economic, social, and political aspects see Villari (1961; 1978): a very complete anthology published and improved several times over the years that covers the evolution and the social and economic aspects of the *questione meridionale* through the writings of authors from different political perspectives (from

Gramsci, Labriola, and Amendola to Sturzo, Sonnino, Nitti, and Rossi Doria). For more recent developments of the debate, see Indovina (1978), Accornero and Andriani (1979), and Villani and Marrone (1981). For a complete account of the Model of Development approach, see the anthology edited by A. Graziani (1975, 1979). For the Labor Market approach, the various positions and a complete bibliography are presented in M. Paci (Ed., 1978).

8. It should be noted that the various problematics are characterized by the preeminence given to a particular set of factors but not by a common political perspective. For example, the Model of Development includes clearly neoclassical studies, such as V. Lutz' works and leftist interpretations, as A. Graziani's. The North-South problematic ranges from classical *meridionalismo* to Gramsci and Togliatti.

9. This does not mean that these approaches actually disappeared. In particular, the North-South perspective is still alive and well but limited to studies dealing with the South. It has lost its hegemonic character as explanation of the whole Italian economic development.

10. The rate of activity (i.e., the ratio of laborforce, which includes employed and unemployed, to population) fell from 43.8 in 1959, to 40.3 in 1963, to 37.4 in 1968. This fall of the rate of activity didn't occur in any other industrialized country.

11. For example, La Malfa and Vinci (1970) proposed the opposing thesis of the "discouraged worker" who didn't look any longer for employment knowing that there wasn't any. By introducing this thesis in Italy, they denied the significance of the rate of unemployment that De Meo took as the basis of his analysis.

12. Among the many contributions: Maitan (1975); Ricolfi (1975); Sylos Labini (1975).

13. This tendency is illustrated by FIAT policy of the period to hire male workers, in their thirties, with families, and with secondary schooling as more reliable and submissive employees.

14. The official rate of employment for 1979 was about 34 percent. According to Gallino, "underground" activities would raise that percentage by 15 to 18 points.

15. See Trentin (1978) and the entire book *FIAT e lo Stato* where Trentin's article is published; Turani (1978); Comito, (1982). For studies of other corporations (Olivetti, Zanussi, Italsider) see Focellini (1978).

16. On the basis of his empirical research in the textile and apparel sectors, Frey also pointed out the preconditions that could make the phenomenon possible in areas other than the Third Italy: a) the pre-existence of small production units; b) production of goods of quality comparable to the ones of large industry; c)

the presence of large laborpools ready for industrial employment; and d) economic and socio-cultural differences that influenced the bargaining power of the workers. Frey recognized that at the origin of the small industry was home work and the underground economy. However, black work was a phenomenon that interested all Italian regions. The fact that in the South, where it actually was more prevalent, it had not developed into into "legitimate" industry as it did in the North-East and Center, should have led to the question of the different role of the South versus the North-East-Center. Yet, Frey limited himself to predict that small industry will develop also in the South.

17. Just one year earlier, in the article mentioned in the previous pages, Bagnasco and Messori did not make any reference to the spatial dimension of the decentralization process.

18. Wallerstein's and Bagnasco's terminologies can be confusing. Wallerstein's "periphery "corresponds to Bagnasco's (and Paci's) "marginal" areas. The "peripheral" areas of the Italian studies correspond to Wallerstein's "semi-periphery."

19. For characteristics of the urban system in the Third Italy and its changes in parallel with the development endogenous industrialization, see Innocenti (1985).

20. Piore and Sabel (1983) exemplify the weak class polarization even in the case of Emilia-Romagna, a region highly politicized and with a long-standing communist tradition. They point out that often entrepreneurs were union members before starting their own firm and maintained their membership even afterwards. The unusual case of entrepreneurs and workers belonging to the same union actually facilitates the solution of work disputes.

21. Brusco (1982, 1983) in the case of Emilia-Romagna, identifies two mechanisms of laborforce flexibility based on two two types of labor markets. In the first type, labor-management relations are regulated by the strong presence of the unions in the region (50% of manufacturing firms with more than 30 employees are organized). In this case, the weak class polarization between management and labor, noticed by Piore and Sabel, makes both parties "reasonable" in order to reach quickly an agreement over production changes. In the other case, flexibility of labor is achieved with the use of "external," non-unionized labor ranging from home work, to students, moonlighters, or pensioners working part time to workers registered as independent artisans although actually working for only one firm. In this second case, a firm can increase overtime or employment or fire workers without having to deal with the constraints of labor legislation.

22. In Brusco's two-tier system, firms in the first (unionized) tier minimize dismissals by passing them on to second tier firms (sub-contractors) where the loss

of jobs is more readily accepted.

23. Bellandi recognizes that limited resources can be a limit to the introduction of innovation in small firms. In a district, however, innovation can be supported by contacts and cooperation among firms. A specialized producer can tailor investment and direction of research for innovation by contacts with potential costumers in the area. The producer can even find financial and technical support for the research and development from firms which are interested in the use of the new equipment but don't have the means or the size to individually pursue its development (See also Piore and Sabel, 1983).

References

Pre-Crisis Approaches

North-South Dichotomy

Andriani, S. (1979). "I Nuovi Termini della Questione Meridionale." In Accomero A. and S. Andriani (Eds.), *Gli Anni '70 nel Mezzogiorno*. Bari: De Donato.

Del Monte, A. and A. Giannola (1978). *Il Mezzogiorno nell' Economia Italiana*. Bologna: Il Mulino.

Donolo, C. (1975). " Crisi Organica e Questione Meridionale." *Quaderni Piacentini*, 55, pp. 49-68.

Graziano, L. (1973). "Rapporti Clientelari nell' Italia Meridionale." In Farneti P. (Ed.) *Il Sistema Politico Italiano*. Bologna: Il Mulino.

Indovina, F. (Ed., 1978) *Mezzogiorno e Crisi*. Milan: Franco Angeli.

Mottura, G. and E. Pugliese (1971). "Agricultura Capitalista e Funzione dell' Inchiesta." *Inchiesta*, 3, pp. 3-18.

Paci, M. (1970). "Migrazioni Interne e Mercato Capitalistico del Lavoro." *Problemi del Socialismo*, 48, pp. 671-687.

Secchi, B. (1974). *Squilibri Regionali e Sviluppo Economico*. Venice: Marsilio.

Secchi, B. (1977). "Central and Peripheral Regions in a Process of Economic Development: The Italian Case." In Massey D. and P.W.J. Batey (Eds.) *Alternative Frameworks of Analysis*. London: Pion.

Villani, P. and N. Marrone (1981). *Riforma Agraria e Questione Meridionale*. Antologia Critica 1943-1980. Bari: De Donato.

Villari, R. (Ed., 1961; 1978). *Il Sud nella Storia d' Italia*. Bari: Laterza.

Model of Development

D'Antonio, M. (1973). *Sviluppo e Crisi del Capitalismo Italiano*. Bari: De Donato.

Fuá, G. (1976). *Occupazione e Capacitá Produttive: La Realtá Italiana*. Bologna:

Il Mulino.

Fuá, G. (1980). *Problemi dello Sviluppo Tardivo in Europa*. Bologna: Il Mulino.

Graziani, A. (1968). *Lo Sviluppo di un' Economia Aperta*. Naples: ESI.

Graziani, A. (Ed., 1972; 1979). *L' Economia Italiana dal 1945 ad Oggi*. Bologna: Il Mulino.

Graziani, A. (Ed., 1975). *Crisi e Ristrutturazione nell' Economia Italiana*. Turin: Einaudi.

Lutz, V. (1958). "Il processo di Sviluppo in un Sistema Economico Dualistico." *Moneta e Credito*, 44, pp. 459-506.

Lutz, V. (1962). Italy. *A Study in Economic Development*. London: Oxford University Press.

Napoleoni, C. (1964). "Note sulla Congiuntura Economica Italiana." *La Rivista Trimestrale*, 19, pp. 117-125.

Salvati, M. (1972a). "Impasse for Italian Capitalism." *New Left Review*, 76, pp. 3-33.

Salvati, M. (1972b). "L' Origine della Crisi in Corso. " *Quaderni Piacentini*, 46, pp. 2-30.

Salvati, M. (1974). "Subordinazione e Autonomia delle Piccole Imprese: Valutazione Politica o Economica?" *Economia Politica e Industriale*, 7-8, pp. 4-15.

Salvati, M. (1975). *Il Sistema Economico Italiano: Analisi di una Crisi*. Bologna: Il Mulino.

Saraceno, P. (1963). "La Mancata Unificazione Economica a Cento Anni dall' Unificazione Politica." In Saraceno P., *L' Italia verso la Piena Occupazione*. Milan: Feltrinelli.

Spaventa, L. (1959). "Dualism in Economic Growth." Banca Nazionale del Lavoro *Quarterly Review*, 51, pp. 386-420.

Sylos Labini, P. (1967). "Distribution and Investment in Italy 1951-66: an Interpretation." Banca Nazionale del Lavoro *Quarterly Review*, 83, pp. 316-375.

Sylos Labini, P. (1972a). "Sviluppo Economico e Classi Sociali in Italia." *Quaderni di Sociologia*, 4, pp. 371-443.

Sylos Labini, P. (1972b). Sindacati, Inflazione e Produttivitá. Bari: Laterza.

Labor Market

Calzabini, P. (1973). "Problemi per Un' Analisi delle Classi Sociali in Italia." *Inchiesta*, 11, pp. 14-27.

Cassetti, M., L.Frey and R.Livraghi (1975). *Le Ricerche sul Mercato del Lavoro in Italia*. Milan: F.Angeli.

De Cecco, M. (1973). "Un' Interpretazione Ricardiana della Forza Lavoro in Italia nel Decennio 1958-68." In P. Leon and M. Marocchi (Eds.) *Sviluppo Economico e Forza Lavoro*. Venice: Marsilio.

De Meo, G. (1969). "Evoluzione Storica e Recenti Tendenze delle Forze di Lavoro in Italia." *Giornale degli Economisti e Annali di Economia*, XXXXVIII, 7-8, pp. 409-428.

La Malfa, G. and S. Vinci (1970). "Il Saggio di Partecipazione delle Forze di Lavoro in Italia." *L' Industria*, 4, pp. 443-469.

Maitan, L. (1975). *Dinamica delle Classi Sociali in Italia. Una Critica Marxista al Saggio di Sylos Labini*. Rome: Savelli.

Mantovani, E. (1973). "Mercato del Lavoro, Accumulazione e Sovrapopolazione Relativa." *Inchiesta*, 9, pp. 65-77.

Meldolesi, L. (1972). *Disoccupazione ed Esercito Industriale di Riserva*. Bari: Laterza.

Paci, M. (1973). *Mercato del Lavoro e Classi Sociali in Italia*. Bologna: Il Mulino.

Paci, M. (1975). "Crisi, Ristrutturazione e Piccola Impresa." *Inchiesta*, 20, pp. 3-8.

Paci, M. (Ed., 1978). *Capitalismo e Classi Sociali in Italia*. Bologna: Il Mulino.

Paci, M. (1979). "Class Structure of Italian Society." *European Journal of Sociology*, 1, pp. 40-58.

Pazzagli, C. (1975). "Classi Sociali e Ricerca Storica (A Proposito del 'Saggio' di Sylos Labini)." *Studi Storici*, 3, pp. 710-732.

Ricolfi, L. (1975). "A Proposito del Saggio di Sylos Labini. La Base Statistica." *Quaderni Piacentini*, 37, pp. 60-76.

Sylos Labini, P. (1974). *Saggio sulle Classi Sociali*. Bari: Laterza.

Sylos Labini, P. (1975). "Le Classi Sociali, la Repplica di Sylos Labini." *Rinascita*, 26.

Vinci, S. (1974). *Il Mercato del Lavoro in Italia*. Milan: F. Angeli.

Decentralization of Production

The Underground Economy

Cantelli, P. (1980). *L' Economia Sommersa*. Rome: Editori Riuniti.

Alessandrini, P. (Ed., 1978) *Lavoro Regolare e Lavoro Nero*. Bologna: Il Mulino.

Centro Studi Investimenti Sociali (1979a). "Il Territorio dell' Economia Sommersa." *Quindicinale di Note e Commenti*, 323, pp. 875-883.

Centro Studi Investimenti Sociali (1979b). "I Nodi dell' Economia Sommersa." *Quindicinale di Note e Commenti*, 323, pp. 884-904.

Contini, B. (1979). *Lo Sviluppo di un' Economia Parallela*. Milan: Feltrinelli.

Del Giudice, G. and G. Pezzioli (1976). *Ristrutturazione Produttiva e Lavoro a Domicilio*. Verona: Bertani.

De Marco, M. and M. Talamo (1976). *Lavoro Nero - Decentramento Produttivo e Lavoro a Domicilio*. Milan: Mazzotta.

Gallino, L. (1979). "L' Economia Invisibile." In Ferrero, F. and S. Scamuzzi (Eds.) Op. Cit.

Garavini, S. (1975). "Il Lavoro a Domicilio." In Pallante, M. and P. Pallante (Eds.) *L' Italia Contemporanea*, Vol. 2. Bologna: Zanichelli.

Quaderni di Rassegna Sindacale (1973). *Il Lavoro a Domicilio*, 44-45, Monographic issue.

Tesini, A. et Al.(1974). *Occupazione, Lavoro Precario, Piccola e Media Impresa*. Rome: Coines.

Multi-plants, Sectoral Studies, Technological Changes and Location

Amin, A. (1982). "La Ristrutturazione alla FIAT e il Decentramento Produttivo nel Mezzogiorno." *Archivio di Studi Urbani e Regionali*, 13-14, pp. 47-88.

Amin, A. (1985). "Restructuring in Fiat and the Decentralization of Production into Southern Italy." In Hudson R. and J. Lewis (Eds.) *Uneven Development in Southern Europe*. London: Methuen.

Brusco, S. (1975a). "Economia di Scala a Livello Tecnologico nelle Piccole Imprese." In Graziani, A. (Ed.) *Crisi e Ristrutturazione nell' Economia Italiana*. Turin: Einaudi.

Brusco, S. (1975b). "Relazione al Convegno FLM di Bergamo sull' Organizzazione del Lavoro e Decentramento." *Inchiesta*, 17, pp. 3-26.

Brusco, S. and C. Sabel (1981). "Artisanal Production and Economic Growth." In Wilkinson, F. (Ed.), *The Dynamics of Labor Market Segmentation*, New York: Academic Press.

Calzabini, P. and P. Vinay (1975). "Riconversione Produttiva e Lotte Operaie: il Settore degli Strumenti Musicali." *Inchiesta*, 20, pp. 54-66.

Comito, V. (1982). *La FIAT tra Crisi e Ristrutturazione*. Rome: Editori Riuniti.

Deaglio E. (Ed., 1975). *La FIAT com' é. La Ristrutturazione difronte all' Autonomia Operaia*. Milan: Feltrinelli.

Del Monte, A. and M. Raffa (Eds., 1977). *Tecnologia e Decentramento Produttivo*. Turin: Rosemberg e Sellier.

FLM di Bergamo (Ed., 1975). *Sindacato e Piccola Impresa, Strategia del Capitale e Azione Sindacale sul Decentramento Produttivo*. Bari: de Donato.

Forcellini, P. (1978). *Rapporto sull' Industria Italiana*. Rome: Editori Riuniti.

Garofoli, G. (1978). "Ristrutturazione Industriale e Territoriale: Alcune Note Introduttive." *Archivio di Studi Urbani e Regionali*, 4, pp. 7-20.

Libertini, L. (1975). "La Questione FIAT: tra la Grande Impresa Motrice e la Piccola e Media Industria." In C. Catena (Ed.) *La Piccola e la Media Industria nella Crisi dell' Economia Italiana* , Vol. II, Rome: Editori Riuniti - Istituto Gramsci.

Masiero, A. (1975). "Il Nodo del Decentramento e il Ruolo della Piccola e Media Industria." *Classe*, 11.

Revelli, M. (1982). "Defeat at FIAT." *Capital and Class*, 16, pp. 95-108.

Trentin, B. (1978). "La Politica della FIAT Oggi." In Istituto Gramsci, *FIAT e Stato*. Turin: Istituto Gramsci.

Small and Medium Industry

Bianchini, G. et Al. (1974). "Il Decentramento nelle Strategie della Grande Impresa." *Economia e Politica Industriale*, 7-8, pp. 69-75.

Capecchi, V. (1975). *Ristrutturazione e Organizzazione del Lavoro nell Fabbriche Metalmeccaniche Bolognesi*. Rome: SEUSI.

Capecchi, V. et al. (1978). *La Piccola Impresa nell' Economia Italiana. Politica del Lavoro e Proposte per il Mezzogiorno nell' Iniziativa del Sindacato*. Bari: de Donato.

Caselli, L. (1974a). "Decentramento Produttivo e Sviluppo Dualistico." *Economia e Politica Industriale*, 6, pp. 28-43.

Caselli, L. (1974b). "Ambivalenza del Decentramento Produttivo." *Economia e Politica Industriale*, 7-8, pp. 79-84.

Catena, C. (1973). "Il Dibattito sulla Piccola e Media Industria." *Politica ed Economia*, 6, pp. 64-68.

Cozzi, G. (1974). "Autonomia e Funzionalitá Industriale per le Piccole Imprese?" *Economia e Politica Industriale*, 7-8, pp. 29-36.

Ferrero, F. (1979). "La Piccola e Media Impresa nel 'Sistema delle Imprese'." In Ferrero, F. and S. Scamuzzi (Eds.) Op. Cit.

Federazione Lavoratori Metalmeccanici di Bologna (1978). *La Piccola Impresa nell' Economia Italiana*. Bari: De Donato.

Forte, F. (1974). "L' Impresa: Grande, Piccola, Pubblica, Privata."In Cavazza, F. and S.R. Grimbaud (Eds.) *Il Caso Italiano*. Milan: Garzanti.

Frey, L. (1973). "Dal Lavoro a Domicilio al Decentramento dell' Attività Produttiva." *Quaderni di Rassegna Sindacale*, 44-45, pp. 34-56.

Frey, L. (1974a). "La Flessibilitá del Lavoro nell Industria Italiana." *L' Industria*, 5-6, pp. 5-16.

Frey, L. (1974b). "La Problematica del Decentramento Produttivo." *Economia e Politica Industriale*, 6, pp. 5-27.

Frey, L. (Ed., 1975). *Lavoro a Domicilio e Decentramento dell' Attività Produttiva nei Settori Tessile e dell' Abigliamento*. Milan: F. Angeli.

Livraghi, L. (1977). "Le Ricerche sul Decentramento Produttivo." *Quaderni di*

Rassegna Sindacale, 64-65, pp. 234-238.

Paci, M. (1975). "Crisi, Ristrutturazione e Piccola Impresa." *Inchiesta*, 20, pp. 3-8.

Peggio, E. (1975)."La Piccola e Media Industria nella Crisi dell' Economia Italiana." In C. Catena (Ed.), Op. Cit.

Pennacchi, L. (1980). "Decentramento Produttivo o Divisione del Lavoro?" *Politica ed Economia*, 2, pp. 33-40.

Rullani, E. (1974). "Un' Inversione di Prospettiva nello Studio del Decentramento Produttivo." *Economia e Politica Industriale*, 7-8, pp. 44-51.

Silvestrelli, R. (1979). "Principali Fattori del Decentramento Produttivo nel Settore del Mobile." In Varaldo, R. (Ed.) Op. Cit.

Syntheses

Antonelli, C. and C.Balcei. (1980). *Piccola Impresa Come Sistema*. Rome: Buffetti.

Bagnasco, A. (1978). "Il Decentramento Produttivo e la Complessità Regressiva del Capitalismo Italiano." *Economia e Politica Industriale*, 16, pp. 3-24.

Bagnasco, A. and M. Messori (1976). "Problematiche dello Sviluppo e Questione della Piccola Impresa." *Inchiesta*, 22, pp. 64-80.

Balloni, V. (1980). "Riflessioni sulle Politiche Industriali per la Crescita della Piccola Impresa." *L' Industria*, 1, pp. 107-128.

Ferrero, F. and S. Scamuzzi (Eds., 1979) *L' Industria in Italia*. Rome: Editori Riuniti.

Tousijin, W. (1978). "La Piccola Impresa in Italia: Divisione Internazionale del Lavoro e Rapporti Tra Classi Sociali." *L' Impresa*, 4-5, pp. 347-354.

Varaldo, R. (Ed., 1979). *Ristrutturazioni Industriali e Rapporti tra Imprese*. Milan: F.Angeli.

Territorial Problematic: *The Fabbrica Diffusa*

General Works

Accornero, A. (1978). "Fabbrica Diffusa e Nuova Classe Operaia." *Inchiesta*, 34, pp. 12-17.

Arcangeli, F., C. Borzaga and S. Goglio (1980). "Patterns of Peripheral Development in Italian Regions, 1964-77." *Papers of the Regional Science Association*, vol. XLIV, pp. 19-44.

Ascoli, U. (1979). "Economia Periferica e Società Periferica". *Inchiesta*, 37, pp. 71-74.

Bagnasco, A. (1977). *Tre Italie. La Problematica Territoriale dello Sviluppo Italiano*. Bologna: Il Mulino.

Bagnasco, A. (1981)."Labour Market, Class Structure and Regional Formations in Italy." *International Journal of Urban and Regional Research*, V, 1, pp. 40-44.

Bagnasco,, A. (1988). *La Costruzione Sociale del Mercato*. Bologna: Il Mulino.

Becattini G. (1979). "Dal 'Settore' Industriale al 'Distretto' Industriale." *Rivista di Economia e Politica Industriale*, 1, pp. 7-22.

Becattini, G. (Ed., 1987). *Mercato e Forze Locali: Il Distretto Industriale*. Bologna: Il Mulino.

Bellandi, G. (1982) "Il Distretto Industriale in Alfred Marshall." *L' Industria*, 3. Reproduced in Becattini G. (Ed., 1987). Op. Cit.

Brusco, S. (1989). *Piccole Imprese e Distretti Industriali*. Turin: Rosenberg e Sellier.

Calzabini, P. (1978). *Economia Periferica e Classi Sociali*. Naples: Liguori.

Del Boca, D. and M. Turvani (1979). *Famiglia e Mercato del Lavoro*. Bologna: Il Mulino.

Fuá, G. and C. Zacchia (Eds., 1983) *Industrializzazione Senza Fratture*. Bologna, Il Mulino.

Garofoli, G. (1981). "Lo Sviluppo delle 'Aree Periferiche' nell' Industria Italiana degli Anni 70." *L' Industria*, 3, pp. 391-404.

Innocenti, R. (Ed., 1985). *Piccola Cittá e Piccola Impresa*. Milan: F. Angeli.

Martellato, D. (1979). "Aspetti Ciclici e Regionali dello Sviluppo Italiano dal 1951 al 1976." Franco G. (Ed.) *Sviluppo e Crisi dell' Economia Italiana*. Milan: Etas Libri.

Michelsons, A. (1985). "La Problematica dell' Industrializzazione Diffusa nelle Scienze Sociali Italiane." In Innocenti R. (Ed.) Op. Cit.

Piore, M.J. and C.F. Sabel (1983) "Italian Small Business Development: Lessons For U.S. Industrial Policy." In Zysman J. and L. Tyson (Eds.) *American Industry in International Competition*. Ithaca: Cornell University Press.

Sabel, C. and J. Zeitlin (1982). "Alternative Storiche alla Produzione di Massa." *Stato e Mercato*, 5, pp. 213-258.

Sabel, C. and J. Zeitlin (1985). "Historical Alternatives to Mass Production: Politics, Markets, and Technology in Nineteenth-Century Industrialization." *Past and Present*, 108, pp. 133-176.

Siniscalco, D. (1978). "Produzione e Occupazione nei Settori dell' Industria Italiana." *Rivista di Economia e Politica Industriale*, 2.

Unione Regionale Camere di Commercio Lazio, Marche, Toscana, Umbria, Centro Studi (1970). *La Terza Italia*. Florence: URGGT.

Case Studies

Becattini, G. (1975). *Lo Sviluppo Economico della Toscana*. Florence: Guaraldi Editore.

Becattini, G. (1978). "The Development of Light Industry in Tuscany: an Interpretation." *Economic Notes*, 2-3, pp. 107-123.

Becattini, G., M.Bellandi and A.Falorni (1983). "L' Industrializzazione Diffusa in Toscana: Aspetti Economici." In Fuá G. and C.Zacchia (Eds.) Op. Cit.

Bianchi, G. and A. Falorni (1980). "L' Industria Intermedia in Toscana: un' Esperienza di Studio a Scala Regionale sull' Evoluzione dell' Apparato Produttivo." IRPET, *Nuovi Contributi allo Studio dello Sviluppo Economico della Toscana*. Paper Presented at the Italian Conference of Regional Science. Rome.

Brusco, S. (1982). "The Emilian Model: Productive Decentralization and Social Integration." *Cambridge Journal of Economics*, 6, pp. 167-184.

Brusco, S. (1983). "Flessibilitá e Soliditá del Sistema: l' Esperienza Emiliana." In Fuá, G. and C.Zacchia (Eds.) Op. Cit.

Cacciari, N. (1975). "Struttura e Crisi del Modello Sociale Veneto." *Classe*, 11, pp. 3-19.

Cencini, C., G. Dematteis and B. Menegatti (Eds., 1984) *L' Italia Emergente*. Milan: F. Angeli.

CENSIS (1988). *L' Italia dei Tre Censimenti*. Milan: Edizioni Comunitá.

FLM di Bologna (1978a). *Occupazione, Sviluppo Economico, Territorio*. Rome: SEUSI.

Garofoli, G. (1983b). *Industrializzazione Diffusa in Lombardia, Sviluppo Territoriale e Sistemi Produttivi Locali*. Milan: F. Angeli.

Garofoli, G. (Ed., 1978). *Ristrutturazione Industriale e Territorio*. Milan: F. Angeli.

Paci, M. (1978). "Dispersione dell' Industria, Famiglia Contadina, Mercato del Lavoro." In Anselmi S. (Ed.) *Economia e Societá: le Marche tra XV e XX Secolo*. Bologna: il Mulino.

Paci, M. (1979). "Riflessione sui Fattori Sociali dello Sviluppo della Piccola Impresa nelle Marche." *Economia Marche*, 6, pp. 71-88.

Piro, F. (1976). "Utopia e Realtá del Modello Emiliano." *Quaderni del Territorio*, 2, pp. 143-176.

CONTRIBUTORS

Marco Cenzatti studied architecture and urban planning at the University of Florence and worked as an architect for several years in Italy. His interest in industrial restructuring began in those years in an attempt to understand the reasons for the social and economic turmoil Italy was undergoing in the seventies. In his following studies, at the Architectural Association in London (where he obtained an Honors Diploma in Housing) and at the Graduate School of Architecture and Urban Planning at UCLA (where he is completing his doctoral dissertation) his focus on restructuring has progressively broadened from changes in industrial structures to include urbanization processes and the theoretical restructuring that underlies the emergence of postmodernism. His publications include work on urban issues and on planning theory.

Jacqueline Maria Hagan is an Assistant Professor of Sociology at the University of Houston. Since her arrival in Houston, she has explored the settlement patterns of Central Americans in the city. She is presently working on a forthcoming book in which she examines the effects of the Immigration Reform and Control Act of 1986 on the development of a Central-American community in Houston.

Allen David Heskin is a Professor in the Urban Planning Program in UCLA. More importantly, he was just elected to the Board of Directors of Marathon Cooperative by his fellow cooperators after years of defeat in this political quest. The article presented in this volume is derived from *The Struggle for Community*, Westview Press, 1991.

Roger Keil has recently finished his doctoral dissertation in Political Science, University of Frankfurt, on the politics of internationalization and world-city formation in Los Angeles, California. He was a Visiting Scholar at the Graduate School of Architecture and Urban Planning at UCLA and recently worked as a research consultant in the GreenBelt-Project Office in Frankfurt. He has published on urban, community, labor and environmental politics, world-city formation, and spatial restructuring in the U.S.A. and Germany, including "The Urban Future Revisited: Politics and Restructuring in L.A. after Fordism," *Strategies* (1990) and "Planning for a Fragrant Future: Air Pollution Control, Restructuring, and Popular Alternatives in Los Angeles (with Robin Bloch), *Capitalism/Nature/Socialism* (1991). He lives in Toronto, Canada.

Peter Lieser teaches planning at Technical University, Darmstadt. He has been the managing director of the GreenBelt-Project Office, Frankfurt am Main. He did his academic work in urban planning and sociology in Germany and California, doing a study on telecommunications in the San Francisco area. His publications cover a wide range of planning issues ranging from world-city formation to regional development. Most recently, he wrote on GreenBelt-planning in Frankfurt in Tom Koenigs (ed.) *Vision Offener Grünräume* (1991) and on the development of Frankfurt's riverfront at Stadtbauwelt III (1991). He lives in Frankfurt am Main.

Nestor P. Rodriquez is an Associate Professor in the Department of Sociology at the University of Houston. Since 1985 he has studied Latino immigration in Houston and the subsequent evolving relations between new Latino immigrants and established residents. His recent research includes a survey of undocumented Central American children detained by the INS in Texas (conducted with Ximena Urrutia-Rojas), an ethnography of Latino political mobilization in Houston, and a study of undocumented immigrant student involvement in higher education in the Houston area.

Edward W. Soja is Professor and Associate Dean in the Graduate School of Architecture and Urban Planning at UCLA. He is the author of *Postmodern Geographies: The Reassertion of Space in Critical Social Theory* (Verso, 1989) and numerous articles which, like the essay included here, uninhibitedly use the regional metropolis of Los Angeles as a window through which to see and understand the contemporary processes of urban and regional development throughout the world. He describes his past, present, and future field of interest as CURSED: critical urban and regional studies with an additional emphasis on epistemological deconstruction. He also does not mind being called a spatiologist.

Richard Tardanico is a sociologist in the Latin American and Caribbean Center at Florida International University in Miami where he is a deputy editor of *Hemisphere: A Magazine of Latin American and Caribbean Affairs*. His current research projects are: "Households in a Wider World: The Social Side of Structural Adjustment in a Costa Rican Barrio;" "Dynamics of Urbanization: Households and Labor Market in San José, Costa Rica" (with Mario Lungo Uclés); and "Development Patterns and Policy Options: Latin American Employment in a Restructuring World Economy" (with Rafael Manjívar Larín and Edelberto Torres-Rivas). The latter is a comparative study of labor-market restructuring in five Latin American capital cities.

Sharon Zukin and Associates. Louis Amdur, Janet Baus, Dalton Conley, Stephen Duncombe, Herman Joseph, Daniel Kessler, Jennifer Parker, and Huaishi Song are students in the Ph.D. Program in Sociology, City University of New York; Philana Cho is an auditor in the program. This article was conceived and produced in a one-semester research seminar taught by Sharon Zukin, professor of sociology and author of *Landscapes of Power: From Detroit to Disney World.*